A Course on Digital Image Processing with MATLAB®

A Course on Digital Image Processing with MATLAB®

P K Thiruvikraman

*Department of Physics, Birla Institute of Technology and Science, Pilani,
Hyderabad Campus, India*

IOP Publishing, Bristol, UK

Supplementary files to accompany this book are available at https://iopscience.iop.org/book/978-0-7503-2604-9.

ISBN   978-0-7503-2604-9 (ebook)
ISBN   978-0-7503-2602-5 (print)
ISBN   978-0-7503-2605-6 (myPrint)
ISBN   978-0-7503-2603-2 (mobi)

DOI   10.1088/978-0-7503-2604-9

Version: 20191101

IOP ebooks

British Library Cataloguing-in-Publication Data: A catalogue record for this book is available from the British Library.

Published by IOP Publishing, wholly owned by The Institute of Physics, London

IOP Publishing, Temple Circus, Temple Way, Bristol, BS1 6HG, UK

US Office: IOP Publishing, Inc., 190 North Independence Mall West, Suite 601, Philadelphia, PA 19106, USA

To my teachers for inspiring me and to my family for supporting me.

Contents

Preface

We live in the Information Age and one of the forms of exchanging information is through images. Digital image processing deals with the manipulation of digital images to enhance them and to extract information from them.

Digital image processing has applications in almost all areas of science and engineering. Remote sensing and medical imaging are two areas where the techniques of image processing find wide application. While commercial packages are readily available to implement the techniques used in image processing, it is necessary for practitioners of this field to have a thorough understanding of the basic principles of image processing.

The aim of this book is to concentrate on the fundamental principles and techniques of image processing. A conscious attempt has been made to give an in-depth presentation of selected topics, rather than a comprehensive survey of the entire field. Implementation of the various image processing algorithms is an important step in learning the subject. The author has come to realise that using a package like MATLAB® (which has an image processing toolbox) quickens the learning process. While programming in a language like C has certain advantages, it is a time consuming process. The beginner is likely to be mired in syntax errors and the complexities of the programming language. This leaves the student less time to understand the algorithm being used. Two separate chapters have been devoted to the MATLAB® programming environment and the image processing toolbox. Implementation of image processing algorithms using MATLAB® is also emphasised in other chapters wherever it is considered appropriate.

Students are encouraged to run the programs discussed in this book and also to write their own code. Your appreciation of image processing will be enhanced if you write your own programs.

This book can be easily covered in a single semester. It is hoped that this book will be useful for beginners and those who want to brush up the basics of this subject. Every chapter is accompanied by a collection of exercises and programming assignments. Working through these exercises will help the student to sharpen his/her understanding of the subject. Hints and answers to these exercises are provided at the back to help the student whenever he gets stuck in a particular problem. However, he/she has to use these as a last resort!

The author welcomes comments and suggestions about this book. Readers can send their comments and suggestions to thiru@hyderabad.bits-pilani.ac.in.

Acknowledgments

I am grateful to many of my colleagues and students without whose help this book would not have been possible. I thank Birla Institute of Technology & Science, Pilani, for making it possible for me to teach this course and for providing me with the facilities to write this book. I thank IOP Publishing for giving me the opportunity to write this book. Special thanks to the production team at IOP publishing who have significantly enhanced the readability of this book. They were quick to point out any sloppiness on my part. I am grateful to Professor R R Mishra for introducing me to image processing and for many helpful discussions. I am also grateful to many of my other colleagues for helpful discussions and to many of my students whose interest in the subject inspired me to write this book. I thank Professor Aravinda Raghavan for some helpful suggestions. I gratefully acknowledge Mr Vibhutesh Singh and Dr Li Yang Ku for granting me permission to use MATLAB® programs written by them in this book. Mr Vibhutesh Singh permitted me to use his program on extracting frames from a video. This program appears in section 11.2 (Video processing). Dr Li Yang Ku permitted me to use his program for reading all images in a folder and storing the pixel values in an array (section 10.2). The program was taken from his blog https://computervisionblog.wordpress.com/2011/04/13/matlab-read-all-images-from-a-folder-everything-starts-here/. Lastly, I thank my family and friends for their constant support and encouragement.

Author biography

P K Thiruvikraman

 P K Thiruvikraman is currently a professor of physics at the Birla Institute of Technology and Science, Pilani, Hyderabad Campus. He has nearly two decades of experience in teaching courses from many areas of physics apart from digital image processing. The author has a PhD in physics from Mangalore University and a Master's degree in physics from the Indian Institute of Technology, Madras. During his teaching career he has come to realize that most subjects that are typically offered by different departments are intimately interrelated. He tries to convey this to students in his lectures by quoting examples from different areas of science and technology. An avid reader of both fiction and non-fiction, and a sports and movie enthusiast, he also tries to use these to enliven his classes.

IOP Publishing

A Course on Digital Image Processing with MATLAB®

P K Thiruvikraman

Chapter 1

Introduction

Have you seen such an image before? Chances are, you have seen many newspaper advertisements that carry such pictures (known as QR codes).

What is the use of such an image?

The answer to this question lies within this chapter.

1.1 The scope and importance of digital image processing

A human being has five senses, but receives most information through the eyes. Hence, images are very important for us. In our daily lives we capture millions of images through our eyes and process them in our brain. The automatic processing of images has become an important tool in recent times as computerization and automation have invaded many fields. The field of digital image processing is not immune to this universal trend. Most of our images are at present in the digital format, and modifying them to suit our requirements can be done in a very convenient and effective manner using computers.

Digital image processing has applications in almost all fields of science and engineering as practitioners in these fields have to, at some point, handle images.

The applications of digital image processing can be seen and felt in fields as diverse as remote sensing, astronomy, material science, and medical diagnosis. Even ordinary citizens now encounter on a routine basis automatic fingerprint recognition, iris recognition, and biometric systems. Surveillance systems are being automated to a great extent and driverless cars and pilotless planes may soon be a reality.

While the applications of image processing are very obvious, where does somebody who wants to learn the basics of this subject start? What are the recurring threads that connect the myriad applications of this field?

This book is an attempt to answer such questions.

We start by looking at some of the important themes of this field:

1. Image enhancement

It is a common experience for many of us to take a photograph in a hurry and repent at leisure about its abysmal quality. This usually happens because of insufficient lighting or the scene being lit from the wrong direction. For example, we might have taken a photograph at night without using the flash, or we might have photographed somebody when the Sun was behind them.

In certain cases, like in wildlife photography, it may even be desirable to photograph at night without using an artificial source of light. Is it possible to process such images and enhance their contrast?

2. Image restoration

We usually find that objects that are moving at high speeds with respect to the photographer appear to be blurred. This is true of photographs of sporting events and also of aerial or satellite photographs. Can we 'restore' the photographs and remove the blur? Blurring can also occur due to other reasons, such as atmospheric turbulence (which is relevant for aerial/satellite photographs) or improper focusing.

3. Image compression

Most image files (especially those with a *.bmp extension) occupy a large space on the hard disk and may take a long time to transmit over the internet. Can we 'compress', i.e., reduce the size of these files without compromising the information they convey? Are there any theoretical limits to the amount of compression we can achieve?

4. Image recognition and classification

We would like computers and robots to imitate the ease with which we human beings recognize and classify millions of images. This is not only a challenge to our intellect, but also a dire need in the present age, where millions of images are being generated continuously and it may not always be possible to have a human being look at all the images and pick out those of interest. Furthermore, image recognition is used extensively in unmanned vehicles. The development of Google's selfdriving car is an example of the current interest in automatic image recognition.

Before we embark on our journey to understand these themes, we will define and understand the terms used to describe digital images.

1.2 Images

The information contained in an analog image (image captured by a nondigital camera) can be represented by a plot of the intensity versus the spatial coordinates of the image. This abstraction helps us to easily manipulate such images. Since intensity is the energy falling on a unit area of the surface of the photographic film (or photo-detector) per unit time, the intensity mentioned above is actually the intensity falling at a particular point integrated over the time for which the image was acquired.

Let us consider a simple image: a circular spot of light in which the brightness reduces as we move away from the center of the spot. Let us consider the intensity variation as we move along a diameter of the circular spot (figure 1.1).

Note that in an analog image (for example an image captured on a photographic film) both x and $f(x)$ can vary continuously. If we want to store this information on a computer having a finite storage space, we have to discretize both x and $f(x)$.

The conversion from analog to digital is done in the following manner. The intensity is recorded at specific values of x (or x, y in the case of two-dimensional (2-D) images). This process is called *sampling* (see figure 1.2).

Since the values of the intensities have to be stored in binary format, they will vary from 0 to a maximum value $L - 1$ (which depends on the number of bits used to

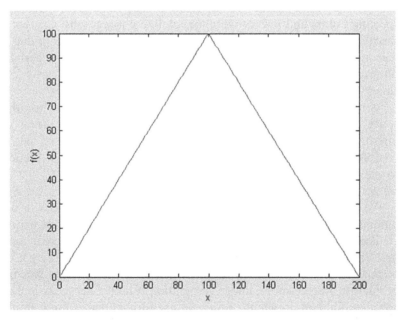

Figure 1.1. Variation of intensity with distance along the diameter of a circular spot. The origin is on the circumference of the circle.

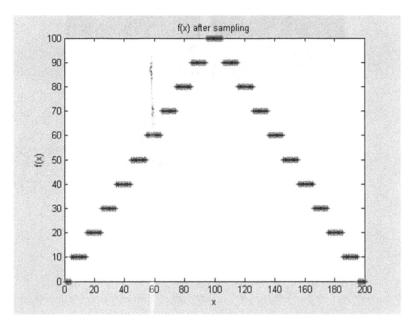

Figure 1.2. Sampled and quantized version of the image in figure 1.1.

store the values of $f(x)$). If k bits are used to store the values of $f(x)$, then $L = 2^k$. The process by which the values of $f(x)$ are discretized is known as *quantization*.

In our further treatment, we will deal only with digital images, but we will refer to the continuous function $f(x, y)$ in order to prove certain results.

1.3 Digital images

The spatial variation of intensity in a digital image can occur only in discrete steps. Therefore, for a 2-D image, a square of a certain area can be identified within which the intensity is almost constant. This smallest element of the image is known as a *pixel* (short for picture element). If for a given area there is a greater number of pixels, then the resolution is higher and the discrete nature of the image is not so apparent.

We will now clarify the convention normally used for digital images. The origin is usually chosen to be at the top-left corner of the image and the *x*- and *y*-axes are along the vertical and horizontal directions as shown below (figure 1.3). This convention, although different from the usual way of defining Cartesian coordinates, is used in image processing because it matches with the convention used for referring to elements of a matrix; since images will finally be represented in terms of matrices, this convention is particularly convenient for digital image processing.

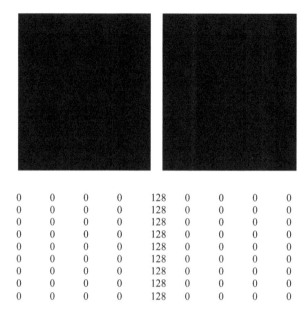

0	0	0	0	128	0	0	0	0
0	0	0	0	128	0	0	0	0
0	0	0	0	128	0	0	0	0
0	0	0	0	128	0	0	0	0
0	0	0	0	128	0	0	0	0
0	0	0	0	128	0	0	0	0
0	0	0	0	128	0	0	0	0
0	0	0	0	128	0	0	0	0
0	0	0	0	128	0	0	0	0

Figure 1.3. A simple 2-D image and the gray levels of each pixel, shown as a 2-D array.

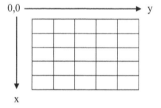

In this book we will deal mostly with grayscale images. The same techniques can be easily extended to apply to color images. In the case of grayscale images, a single number (the intensity) is associated with each pixel (this number is called the gray value). Hence, we can visualize (see figure 1.3) a 2-D image as a 2-D array (matrix) of numbers. If the grayscale values are stored in binary format and if we use k bits to store each pixel of an M × N image, then the total number of bits used to store the entire image will be M × N × k. The aim of image compression (which will be dealt with in chapter 4) is to reduce the total number of bits used to store the image.

1.4 Processes involved in image processing and recognition

Before we dive into the details of image processing and its applications, let us pause for a minute and get an overall picture of the processes involved. Since image analysis and object recognition are of critical importance in today's world and drive most of the applications we see around us, we provide below a block diagram of the steps involved in image recognition.

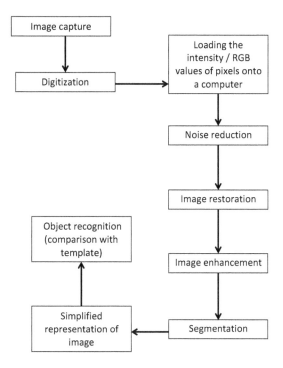

An image is typically captured by a camera with appropriate lenses. For ease of processing, such an image, which is continuous, has to be digitized and digital values (numbers) acquired and stored within a computer for further processing.

The next step, i.e., image enhancement, involves enhancing the 'quality' of the image for the benefit of a human viewer. The process of enhancement is often subjective and involves enhancing the contrast and/or brightness of the acquired image. Image enhancement is usually required to aid the human observer and to enhance the esthetic appeal of an image.

Many images may suffer from noise or blurring due to various reasons, and it is usual practice to 'restore' the image before taking up further processing. Nowadays, digital cameras have almost replaced (analog) cameras with photographic films. Digital cameras contain many electronic circuits that are susceptible to external electromagnetic disturbances. These disturbances can give rise to a 'noisy' image. Noise is also intrinsic to all electronic circuits. Hence, noise reduction techniques are essential in the case of many images.

Once the preprocessing of images (restoration and noise reduction) has been completed, the job of recognition of objects of interest within an image can be taken up. However, image segmentation is usually required, i.e., to separate an image into its constituent parts, so that the process of recognizing an object becomes easier.

The importance of segmenting an image is easily appreciated if we consider an application like character recognition. Recognizing characters of a script (either handwritten or printed) is rendered much easier if we can separate individual characters and store them as separate images. After segmenting an image into individual characters, recognition only involves a comparison of the character under consideration with characters stored in a database. Of course, this is easier said than done, as the character in the database may differ from the character in the image in size, orientation, and other attributes. The algorithms that are used in recognition must therefore be robust and insensitive to changes in size and orientation of the characters.

Character (and in general, object) recognition, is made easier if instead of comparing the raw image of the character with an image in the database, we extract a simple representation of the character and compare it with its counterpart in the database. What is meant by a 'simplified' representation of a character? You will readily agree that the recognition of a character is rendered very difficult by variations in the thickness of the strokes used in writing the character. This is especially true for handwritten characters.

Consider for example a program that is trying to recognize the letter 'L'. The process of recognition is complicated by the thickness of the two arms of the 'L'. What we would like to do is reduce the thickness of both arms so that we have only lines that are 1 pixel thick.

This is shown in figure 1.4.

Figure 1.4(b) contains a simplified representation (known as a skeleton) of the letter in figure 1.4(a). Notice that the arms of the letter 'L' now have a thickness of 1 pixel. This considerably helps us in the process of character recognition. You will learn more about skeletons in chapter 5.

In certain other cases, the representation of an image may not even be an image, but may consist of (for example) a string of numbers that bears a certain relationship to the original image.

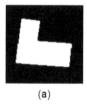

(a)

Figure 1.4(a). Binary image of the letter L.

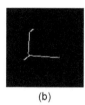

(b)

Figure 1.4(b). 'Skeleton' of the letter 'L' in figure 1.4(a). A skeleton is a simplified representation of an object.

The different types of representations that are normally used in image recognition will be discussed in chapter 5.

It is possible that in certain image processing systems some of these steps are skipped. For example, if noise is not present (or is very minimal) in the acquired images, then noise reduction may not be required. Image enhancement is usually required to enhance the visual appeal of an image and to aid a human observer; it may not be required in systems that are completely automated.

Furthermore, the details of image restoration will depend on the conditions under which the images are captured. For example, images captured from airborne aircraft or satellites will suffer from blurring due to motion and will require restoration algorithms that are different from those used for blurring due to atmospheric turbulence.

1.5 Applications of image processing

We now list some of the applications of image processing that we see around us:

  (i) Character recognition: This has many applications and we would like to mention one that is very relevant to the present times. Recently, many old documents and books have been scanned and made available in digital form. The process of scanning a page of text creates an image file. It will be very convenient if individual characters can be recognized within a page of text. This will help us to convert the image file into a text file, which can then be edited.

 (ii) Object recognition: Robotics has developed tremendously in recent times and the automatic processing of images and recognition of objects is essential to further progress.

(iii) Unmanned vehicles: These are closely related to the developments in robotics. Unmanned vehicles are being used in many places (from the surface of Mars to the depths of the Indian/Pacific Ocean). Unmanned vehicles are being used extensively by the military (many countries use pilotless drones). Unmanned civilian vehicles may also soon be a reality if one goes by the progress of Google's driverless car project.

 (iv) Remote sensing: Remote sensing satellites have been launched by many countries, and India is in the forefront of this field. Remote sensing can be used for a variety of military and civilian applications. It can be used for detecting and monitoring movement of vehicles and also for calculating areas under cultivation or covered by forests. Very-high-resolution photographs and maps are available for even common people courtesy of Google Earth, Wikimapia, and ISRO's Bhuvan[1].

  (v) Medical image processing: Processing of medical images has helped enormously in the diagnosis and treatment of many diseases. Image processing and analysis is being used extensively to detect cancerous

---

[1] Bhuvan is the Indian Space Research Organization (ISRO)'s gateway to Earth Observation. Visit http://bhuvan.nrsc.gov.in/bhuvan_links.php for more details.

tumors and diseases of the eye. Computerized tomography (CT) has revolutionized medicine and helped us to generate three-dimensional images that are very helpful to doctors.

We now give an example of how image processing and analysis can help in the detection of cancer.

Normal cell   **Cancerous cell**

From the figure shown above, which is a magnified version of the original image, it is very clear that the shape of a cancerous cell is very different from that of a normal cell. The shape of a normal cell is very nearly circular while the cancerous cell is more elliptical. A human observer can immediately notice the difference between the two cells, but is it possible to develop computer programs that will automatically extract the shape information of each image and hence 'automatically' identify the presence of a cancerous cell? Yes, provided we are able to extract the information about the shape of the cell from its image. Information about the shape and color of an object is very useful in identifying its presence in an image.

What we have given above is only one possible application of image processing in the interpretation of medical images. The possibilities are actually endless in this field.

(vi) Image processing in the field of entertainment and electronic/ print media: You may be aware of the extent to which images are manipulated or entirely fabricated to create the 'special effects' seen in movies. While many of the special effects involve the creation of artificial images using computer graphics, sometimes existing images are also 'processed' or manipulated to create the desired effect.

We give below one example of how image processing can be used to create special effects.

In figure 1.5, we see that a water bottle is apparently 'hanging' in the air without any support. How was this achieved? You might have seen many similar special effects in movies. Figure 1.5 is actually a combination of two images that were shot one after the other.

The two separate images that were used to create figure 1.5 are shown in figures 1.6 and 1.7.

Figure 1.5 was obtained from figures 1.6 and 1.7 by replacing the pixels corresponding to the support for the water bottle by pixels in the background so that the board that was supporting the water bottle apparently disappears. The success of such a digital manipulation depends on the lighting being invariant in figures 1.6 and 1.7. As seen from figure 1.5, the manipulation in the image is obvious. Why do you think the manipulation in figure 1.5 was not a complete success? Can

Figure 1.5. Image of a water bottle hanging in the air.

Figure 1.6. Image showing how the water bottle was supported.

you do anything to salvage the situation? Maybe you will be in a better position to answer this question after a detailed study of the filtering techniques described in chapters 2 and 3. Appropriate filters can smooth the sharp edges that point to the manipulation inherent in figure 1.5.

The technique used to obtain figure 1.5 is widely used in movies. Background replacement is routinely used in movies where you see people defying gravity and 'flying' through the air.

Figure 1.7. Background image (identical to the image in figure 1.6, except that the water bottle has been removed).

Another special effect used in many movies is that of a man gradually changing into a tiger or some other animal. This effect, known as morphing, is accomplished simply by taking a linear combination (weighted average) of two images (one of the man and the other of a tiger). By progressively changing the weights assigned to each image, it can be made to appear that the man changes into a tiger.

We conclude this brief introduction by giving an example of how image processing is being used by ordinary people in their everyday activities. Smartphones, which are now widespread, allow us to capture and process images with effortless ease. One of the ways in which you can use a smartphone is to point it at an advertisement containing a QR code. Upon 'reading' the QR code, the smartphone will automatically open a website relevant to the advertisement or perform a relevant function over the internet. The QR code (shown at the beginning of this chapter) is a 2-D version of the bar code, which is commonly used in supermarkets. The QR code is a binary image (each pixel has a value that is either 0 or 1) that contains information.

Exercises

1. How many bits are required to store a 1024 × 1024, 12 bit image?
2. Is the conversion of a continuous image to a digital image reversible? If it is not perfectly reversible, is it possible to create an image from the digital image that looks like the original continuous image? How would you do this?
3. What do you think is the role of the black squares at three of the corners of the image of the QR code? Such black squares are also seen in optical mark recognition or optical mark reading (OMR) answer sheets which are used in many examinations.

Chapter 2

Image enhancement in the spatial domain

In many applications, it is desirable to enhance the 'quality' of an image. Stated more precisely, we would like to improve the contrast of an image and/or reduce the noise content in it. Image enhancement can be done both in the spatial as well as in the Fourier domains. In this chapter, we will consider image enhancement in the spatial domain.

2.1 Enhancement of contrast

Before we attempt to enhance the contrast of an image, we should have a good definition of contrast. The dynamic range (i.e., the actual range) of the gray levels present in an image can be considered to be a crude measure of the contrast in an image. While discussing histogram processing, we will see that the standard deviation of the gray levels provides a quantitative measure of the contrast.

The figure below (figure 2.1) shows an example of an image having low contrast. One of the main objectives of image processing is to improve the contrast of such images. The contrast in such images could be poor due to inadequate lighting. This is especially true of wildlife photography, where bright lights would disturb the animals and hence the images are usually captured using natural light alone.

The spatial domain techniques that are used to improve (stretch) contrast are
1. Gray level transformations;
2. Histogram processing;
3. Spatial domain filtering.

2.2 Gray level transformations

Gray level transformations map the gray levels of an input image (r) to those of the desired output image ($s = T(r)$). An example of such a transformation is shown below.

Figure 2.1. Example of an image having low contrast. Photograph credit: Professor Anshuman Dalvi.

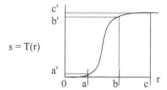

A simple gray level transformation for contrast stretching is shown above.

In the gray level transformation mentioned earlier, it is seen that the range 0 to *a* and *b* to *c* are 'compressed', while the range *a* to *b* is expanded to occupy almost the entire range of gray levels. If most of the pixels in the input image have gray levels in the range *a* to *b*, the dynamic range of the output image will be high, i.e., the contrast is increased by this transformation.

2.2.1 Thresholding

In the above transformation, if the range *a* to b is shrunk to a single point, the transformation is called thresholding (see figure given below).

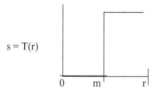

In thresholding, if the input is above a certain value *m* (threshold), the output is set to a fixed value (usually the maximum possible value $L - 1$). If the input is below *m*, the output is set to 0.

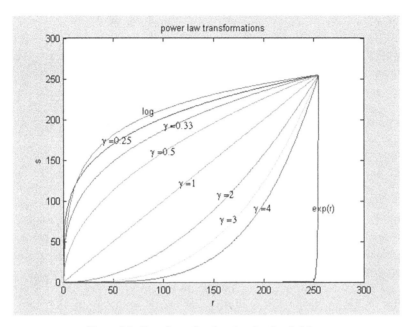

Figure 2.2. Transformation function for thresholding.

2.2.2 Power law, log, and exp transformations

Power law transformations can be used to increase the contrast. They are also used for certain other reasons, which will be stated shortly. Power law transformations are of the form $s = cr^\gamma$. The value of c is determined from the fact that both s and r fall in the range 0 to $L - 1$. Power law transformations are shown below for various values of γ.

We will now consider transformations with $\gamma > 1$ and $\gamma < 1$. Let us first discuss the effect of applying a power law transformation with $\gamma > 1$. For example, let us look at $\gamma = 4$. This transformation maps the input interval 0–200 to the output interval 0–100. Therefore, this input range is squeezed while the range 200–255 is expanded to occupy the range 100–255. Imagine that this transformation is applied on an image in which all the pixels have a gray value in the range 200–255. Since this is the range getting stretched, the contrast of this image would improve. If we choose a transformation with $\gamma = 1/4$, the range 0–50 is mapped to the interval 0–175. Such a transformation would improve the contrast of an image in which most of the pixels are lying in the range 0–50. Hence, we choose $\gamma > 1$ to improve the contrast of bright images and $\gamma < 1$ to improve the contrast of dark images.

There are also other applications of power law transformations. Many devices used for image capture, printing, and display respond according to a power law.

For example, cathode ray tubes have an intensity-to-voltage response that is a power function, i.e., $I = \text{const } x \ V^\Omega$, where Ω varies from 1.8 to 2.5.

Such display systems with $\Omega > 1$ would produce images that are darker than the actual object. Therefore, the transformation $s = c\, r^{1/\Omega}$ is used to pre-process the input before giving it as input to the monitor.

The log transformation is defined as

$$s = c \log(1 + r),$$

where according to our usual convention, s and r are the output and input gray levels, respectively.

The log transformation compresses the higher gray level range while expanding the lower gray level range. Hence, this transformation can be used to accentuate objects that are part of a dark background and are obscured by a bright light. It is also used to view Fourier transforms. In Fourier transforms, some of the Fourier coefficients (usually the low-frequency ones) may be very large, hence making the other coefficients invisible in comparison. The log transformation is applied to the Fourier transform before displaying it in order to improve the visibility of the Fourier coefficients having a small magnitude.

Figure 2.3 shows a building in which some parts appear totally dark because of inadequate lighting. Application of the log transformation to this image yields figure 2.4, in which all parts of the building are visible.

Notice how it is possible to clearly see the branches of the tree (top-left portion of the image) and also the balcony of the house.

In some cases, application of gray level transformations may actually lead to a decrease in the contrast! Hence, we see that it is very difficult to provide an objective criterion for what constitutes 'enhancement' of an image. Enhancement lies in the eyes of the beholder!

Figure 2.3. A low-contrast dark image.

Figure 2.4. The low contrast image in figure 2.3 enhanced by application of the log transformation.

2.2.3 Piecewise linear transformations

Piecewise linear transformations have an advantage over power law, log, and exponential transformations in that they can be arbitrarily complex. The flip side is that they require more inputs from the user. The simplest type of piecewise linear transformation is shown below.

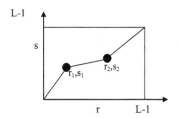

The transformation is completely specified by the points (r_1, s_1) and (r_2, s_2). As is clearly seen from the above figure, the transformation has three linear regions. This transformation would expand the range of the gray levels from 0 to r_1 if $s_1 > r_1$; otherwise, it would contract this range. Similarly, assuming that $(L - 1 - s_2) > (L - 1 - r_2)$, it would expand the range from r_2 to $L - 1$. This would be useful for enhancing images with both very bright and very dark regions. Such a transformation would enhance both regions, while a power law or a log transformation would enhance only one of them. Let us try such a transformation on figure 2.5, which has both very bright and very dark regions. This would brighten the dark portions of the image while preserving the contrast.

Figure 2.5 shows a low-contrast image while figure 2.6 shows the result of the application of a piecewise linear transformation on this image. Note that while

Figure 2.5. Original image.

Figure 2.6. Result of applying a piecewise linear transformation on figure 2.5.

figure 2.6 has not brightened the dark regions of the image as much as the log transformation, it does not have the washed-out appearance that the log-transformed images suffer from. There is also a perceptible improvement in contrast. Better results can probably be obtained by a more careful choice of the parameters involved in the transformation.

2.2.4 Gray level slicing

Gray level slicing is usually used to highlight a certain range of gray levels. Applications include enhancing features such as masses of water in satellite imagery and enhancing flaws in x-ray images. There are two common approaches to gray level slicing. One approach is to display a high value for all gray levels in the range of interest and a low value for all other gray levels (figure 2.7). The other approach is to enhance the gray levels in the range of interest while preserving all other ranges (figure 2.8).

2.3 Bit plane slicing

Bit plane decomposition of an image has very important applications, especially in image compression. If we are able to select the most significant bit (MSB) of the binary representation of the gray level of all the pixels in an image, the result would be a binary image. Similarly, we can select the mth bit of all pixels in a k-bit image and display it as a binary image. As expected, the MSB plane would bear the closest resemblance to the original image, while the least significant bit plane will be a random collection of 1s and 0s. In figure 2.9, we present the image of a fractal; the different bit planes of this image are given in figure 2.10.

The MSB plane is extracted by applying a threshold function on the original image. The transformation functions for the other bit planes can be worked out, but an easy way of extracting the mth bit plane is to do a bitwise AND operation of the gray level of each pixel with 2^m and multiplying the result by an appropriate scale factor.

If the first few bit planes (say four–seven) are sent, they convey most of the information about the image. Hence, these bit planes can be sent initially and if more precision is desired then the remaining bit planes of lesser significance can be sent.

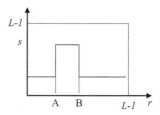

Figure 2.7. Gray level slicing highlighting the range [A, B] while reducing all other ranges.

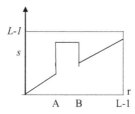

Figure 2.8. Transformation that highlights the range [A, B] but preserves all other ranges.

Figure 2.9. Image of a fractal.

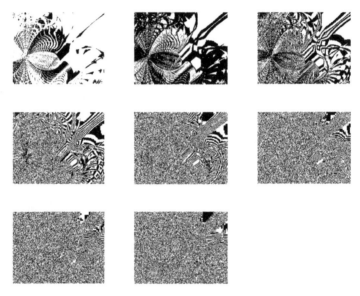

Figure 2.10. The eight bit planes of the image in figure 2.9. The MSB plane is at the top-left corner.

2.4 Histogram processing

Histogram processing is another powerful technique for enhancing the quality of an image in the spatial domain. Before we start discussing the various techniques under histogram processing, let us look at some basic definitions and concepts with regard to the histogram of an image.

Let r represent the gray levels of an image. Then, $n(r)$, which is the number of pixels with the gray level r, is called the histogram of an image.

We can visualize the process of generating the histogram of an image in the following manner. We scan the entire image pixel by pixel and 'drop' each pixel into the rth bin (r ranges from 0 to $2^k - 1$ for a k-bit image). At the end of the scan, we count the number of pixels in each bin and make a plot of $n(r)$ along the y-axis and r along the x-axis.

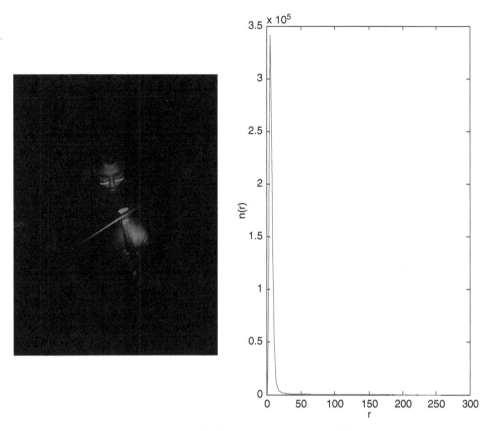

Figure 2.11. A low-contrast dark image and its histogram. Note that most of the pixels have their gray level in the range 0 to 50.

From figures 2.11–2.13, it should be clear that an image with good contrast has a broad histogram, i.e., the range of gray levels present in the image (also known as the dynamic range) is quite broad. A slightly more quantitative measure of the contrast of an image is obtained from the standard deviation (or variance) of the gray levels of an image. The standard deviation is given by

$$\sigma = \sqrt{\sum_{r=0}^{L-1} (r - \bar{r})^2 \frac{n(r)}{N}}, \tag{2.1}$$

where N is the total number of pixels in the image, and $\bar{r}$ is the mean value of r. However, an image with the highest possible standard deviation may not be desired in many circumstances. For instance, a binary image, which has only pixels that are completely bright or those that are completely dark, has the maximum possible standard deviation, but an image with a uniform histogram, which may have a smaller σ value, is considered to be more desirable since it will have all shades of gray.

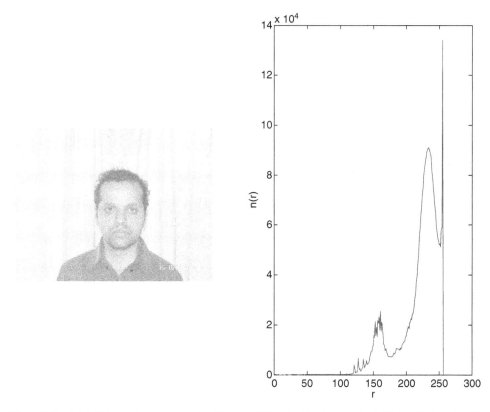

Figure 2.12. A bright image (average gray level is around 220) that has low contrast. Notice that most of the pixels have a gray level around 255.

2.4.1 Histogram equalization

From the above discussion, we conclude that a uniform histogram is the ideal histogram. Hence, in histogram processing, we look for a gray level transformation (mapping) that will produce a uniform histogram.

In order to determine the mapping that produces a uniform histogram, let us first look at images with a continuous variation in their gray level. The results of the analysis given below will be generalized to the case of discrete images.

Let us assume that the gray levels (r) of the input image vary continuously from 0 to 1. For a continuous variable, we will deal with the probability density of r instead of talking about the histogram for r. A histogram is usually used only for discrete variables.

Let $p(r)$ be the probability density of r, i.e., the probability that a pixel chosen at random has a gray value in the range r to $r + dr$ is given by $p(r) \, dr$. Similarly, let s represent the gray levels of the output image. s also varies from 0 to 1, and $p(s)$ is the probability density for s. It is a common misconception to assume that $p(r)$ should lie between 0 and 1. Since $p(r)dr$ and not $p(r)$ itself is the probability, there is no restriction

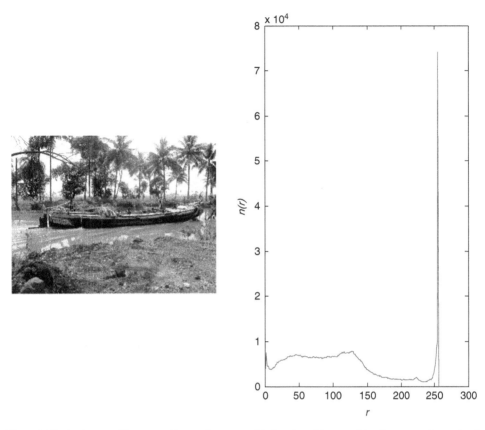

Figure 2.13. An image with reasonably good contrast. Notice the wide spread in the range of gray levels present in the image.

on the possible values of $p(r)$. $p(r)$ itself can be arbitrarily large. Since it is multiplied by an arbitrarily small quantity dr, the product can lie in the range of 0 to 1.

Since we desire a uniform probability distribution for s, $p(s) = 1$ for all values of s. We also use the following result from elementary probability theory:

$$p(r)dr = p(s)ds. \tag{2.2}$$

Using the fact that $p(s) = 1$, for all values of s, we integrate the above equation on both sides to determine the value of s corresponding to a given value of r:

$$s = \int_0^r p(r)dr. \tag{2.3}$$

We can easily justify equation (2.2), in the following manner. Multiplying both sides by N (the total number of pixels in the image) yields the number of pixels in the range r to $r + dr$ for the left-hand side (LHS) and the number of pixels in the range s to $s + ds$ for the right-hand side (RHS). Since we are considering a one-to-one mapping, all the pixels that lie in the range r to $r + dr$ will be mapped to the range

s to $s + ds$. Hence, the number of pixels in the range dr about r will be equal to the number of pixels in the range ds about s, i.e., we are considering a number-preserving transformation. We note from equation (2.3) that s is given by the cumulative distribution function of r.

We can now easily discretize equation (2.3) to yield

$$s_k = \sum_{j=0}^{k} \frac{n(r_j)}{N}, \tag{2.4}$$

where the integral has been replaced by a summation and the probability of obtaining a certain gray level r_j is given by $n(r_j)/N$.

We have thus obtained the required mapping. In practice, we would have to round-off s_k to the nearest integer and multiply it by $L - 1$ since we would want the output gray levels to lie in the range of 0 to $L - 1$.

We present a small numerical example of histogram equalization applied to a 3-bit image to illustrate this method (table 2.1).

We can note a few important points regarding histogram equalization from this example. If only a certain number of gray levels (say, m) are present in the original image out of the L possible levels, only the same number of gray levels will be present in the output image. This is because we are applying a one-to-one mapping to our original gray levels. Hence the number of gray levels present in the image cannot increase. In fact, in many cases, there may be fewer than m gray levels present in the output image. This is because many values of s_k may be rounded-off to the same integer. This implies that, in practice, we can never achieve a uniform histogram for a digital image if initially some of the gray levels are absent. For the above-mentioned example, there is an increase in contrast due to histogram equalization. In some cases, especially for the case of predominantly dark images, there could be a decrease in contrast. The following example illustrates this.

In this example (table 2.2), all the pixels, which had a gray level of 0, are shifted to a gray level of 3. The dynamic range (i.e., the actual range of gray levels present in the image) is reduced. Hence, the contrast is reduced. This can be confirmed by

Table 2.1. Histogram equalization applied on a 3-bit image.

r	$n(r)$	Cum. sum	Rounded
0	2	0.02	0
1	10	0.12	1
2	52	0.64	4
3	30	0.94	7
4	6	1	7
5	0	1	7
6	0	1	7
7	0	1	7

making a comparison of the standard deviation before and after histogram equalization. The input image of table 2.2 has a mean gray level of 3.8 and a standard deviation of 3.16 while the output image has a mean gray level of 4.7 and a standard deviation of 1.67.

2.4.2 Histogram specification

Histogram specification is a technique that tries to avoid the inadequacies of the histogram equalization technique. Here, we specify a 'desired' or 'target' histogram and determine the mapping of the gray levels that will produce the target histogram. Since we can obtain the equalized histogram starting from any histogram, we use the gray levels corresponding to the equalized histogram as an intermediate step to go from r to z (which are the gray levels corresponding to the specified histogram) (table 2.3).

Let the target histogram for the histogram given in table 2.1 be given by $n(z)$, where $n(z)$ is the histogram specified in table 2.3:

We can 'match' the two histograms. That is, from equation (2.2), it follows that

Table 2.2. Implementation of the first summation in histogram specification as per equation (2.5).

r	$n(r)$	Cum. sum	Rounded (s)
0	40	0.4	3
1	0	0.4	3
2	0	0.4	3
3	0	0.4	3
4	0	0.4	3
5	10	0.5	4
6	20	0.7	5
7	30	1.0	7

Table 2.3. Implementation of the second summation in histogram specification as per equation (2.5).

z	$n(z)$	Cum. sum
0	0	0
1	5	0.05
2	10	0.15
3	15	0.30
4	25	0.55
5	30	0.85
6	10	0.95
7	5	1

Table 2.4. Mapping obtained using histogram specification for the image in table 2.1.

r	z
0	1
1	2
2	5
3	6
4	7
5	7
6	7
7	7

$$s_k = \sum_{j=0}^{k} \frac{n(r_j)}{N} = \sum_{j=0}^{k'} \frac{n(z_j)}{N} = s_{k'}. \tag{2.5}$$

Since strict equality may not be achieved between s_k and $s_{k'}$, we can apply the condition that the value of z corresponding to a given value of r has to satisfy the condition

$$s_{k'} = \sum_{j=0}^{k'} \frac{n(z_j)}{N} \geqslant \sum_{j=0}^{k} \frac{n(r_j)}{N} = s_k. \tag{2.6}$$

This equation is implemented iteratively, i.e., for each value of k, we look for the lowest value of k' that satisfies the above inequality.

We see that this approach will lead to the mapping shown in table 2.4 from r to z.

There is a neat geometric interpretation for histogram specification. Let $p(r)$ be the probability density of the input image, and $p(z)$ be the required (specified) probability distribution. $p(r)$ and $p(z)$ are the continuous analogs of $n(r)$ and $n(z)$, respectively. The cumulative probability distribution $s_{k'}$ is nothing but the area under the $p(z)$ versus z-curve. Hence the technique of histogram matching involves matching the area under the two curves (see figures below).

The area under the curve $p(r)$ versus r in the range $r = 0$ to r_k is equal to s_k. We look for a certain value of z equal to z_k such that that the area under the $p(z)$ versus z curve in the limit $z = 0$ to $z = z_k$ is equal to s_k. In the case of r and z being continuous variables, we can ask for the two areas to be exactly equal. However, in the discrete case, where r and z can take only integer values, exact equality of the two areas may not be possible; therefore, we start with $z = 0$ and increment z each time until the area under the curve $p(z)$ versus z becomes greater than s_k. This is the value of z that we have been looking for! Usually the specified histogram should be somewhat similar to the original histogram (with marginal changes that will improve the contrast).

2.5 Filtering in the spatial domain

2.5.1 Averaging

We now consider another kind of spatial domain operation, where the gray level of a pixel is replaced by a value that is dependent on the gray levels of the neighboring pixels. The simplest filtering operation in the spatial domain is simple averaging.

For averaging, a 'mask' of size $m \times n$ is chosen, and the mask is imagined to be placed on top of the image, with the center of the mask coinciding with the pixel under consideration. The pixel value is replaced by the average value of all the pixels inside the mask. The replacement is done after the calculation is done for all the pixels in the image, i.e., the original value (and not the averaged value) of the ith pixel is used in the calculation for the $(i + 1)$th pixel. The procedure is also known (for reasons to be explained later) as convolving a mask with the given image. Averaging is also known as a low-pass spatial domain filter. This statement will be clear once we have discussed Fourier domain filtering.

We present below (figures 2.14–2.17) a test image and the result of averaging it with masks of various sizes.

From the above figures, we observe that averaging, in general, leads to blurring of the images: the edges are no longer sharp. Also, since we have a white background surrounding the black rectangles, the gray level of the pixels within the rectangles will increase after averaging. Hence, if we use a large enough mask, the smallest rectangles will be virtually indistinguishable from the background (see exercise 9 at the end of this chapter).

Averaging filters are generally used to reduce noise in an image. In general, the effect of noise is localized to a few pixels. Therefore, if we apply an averaging filter on an image, the 'noisy' pixels, which have gray levels slightly different from the background, will merge with the background.

Why does noise affect only a few pixels?

This is because most digital image capture systems (like a CCD camera) have many sensors located on a rectangular/square grid. Light falling on each of the sensors is converted into a signal. The output of each sensor can then be written to a

Figure 2.14. Test image to illustrate the effect of averaging.

Figure 2.15. Image shown in figure 2.14, filtered by a simple averaging mask of size 3 × 3.

Figure 2.16. Image in figure 2.14 filtered using a simple averaging mask of size 9 × 9.

Figure 2.17. Test image (figure 2.14) filtered using a mask of size 35 × 35.

storage system (usually by multiplexing). A sudden transient electrical disturbance will then cause only a few pixels to be affected.

Even if the noise affects many pixels, it is assumed to be random (with zero mean). Therefore, averaging will reduce the noise.

Averaging is just one example of linear filtering. The most general expression for linear filtering of an image $f(x, y)$ of size $M \times N$, using a mask of size $m \times n$ is

$$g(x, y) = \sum_{s=-a}^{a} \sum_{t=-a}^{b} w(s, t)f(x + s, y + t) = \sum_{i=t}^{mn} w_i z_i. \qquad (2.7)$$

Here, $w(s, t)$ is the weight assigned to the pixel at the location (s, t). This operation is also known as 'convolution' of a mask with an image. The meaning of this statement will be clearer when we discuss the Fourier domain.

While simple averaging is easy to understand and implement, an important consideration here is the number of computations involved in this operation. We see that if we have a mask of size $n \times n$, then we require $n^2 - 1$ fresh additions and one multiplication each time we move the mask. Obviously, we would look for an algorithm that reduces the number of computations. We can see from the figure given below that if we do the additions along the columns and preserve the sum for each column, then we can reduce the number of computations.

$f(x-1,y-1)$	$f(x-1,y)$	$f(x-1,y+1)$	$f(x-1,y+2)$
$f(x,y-1)$	$f(x,y)$	$f(x,y+1)$	$f(x,y+2)$
$f(x+1,y-1)$	$f(x+1,y)$	$f(x+1,y+1)$	$f(x+1,y+2)$

$\quad\quad C_1 \quad\quad\quad\quad C_2 \quad\quad C_3 \quad\quad\quad C_4$

When we calculate the average value corresponding to the pixel (x, y), we first determine the sum of the pixel values for the three columns C_1, C_2, and C_3. Let us denote this by S_0:

$$S_0 = C_1 + C_2 + C_3. \qquad (2.8)$$

We notice that the sums C_2 and C_3 will be required for the pixel at $(x, y + 1)$. Therefore, if S_1 is the sum required in the calculation of the average for $(x, y + 1)$, then

$$S_1 = S_0 + C_4 - C_1. \qquad (2.9)$$

We see that we require two fresh additions ($n - 1$ for a mask of size $n \times n$) to calculate C_4, and two more additions (the subtraction can be considered equivalent to addition for computational purposes) appear in equation (2.9). Hence, by using this algorithm, we require only $n + 1$ additions. This is definitely less than the $n^2 - 1$

Figure 2.18. The weighted averaging mask has weights distributed according to their distance from the center of the mask.

additions required in a brute force calculation. The computational advantage is given as follows:

Computational advantage $= (n^2 - 1)/(n + 1) = n - 1$.

This computational advantage can be quite significant for large values of n.

In simple averaging, we assign the same weight $(1/n^2)$ to all the pixels, i.e., to calculate the average we add the gray levels of all n^2 pixels that lie within the mask and then divide by n^2. While this would reduce the noise, it would also blur the edges to a large extent.

A superior technique that does not blur the edges to the same extent while reducing noise is weighted averaging. Figure 2.18 shows one of the widely used masks for weighted averaging.

It makes sense to assign higher weights to nearby pixels since they can be expected to have a greater effect than pixels that are farther away.

2.5.2 Median filter

Both averaging and weighted averaging are examples of linear filters. We will now discuss the median filter, which is an example of a nonlinear filter. The median filter is an example of a class of filters known as order-statistics filters. This is because the mean, median, and mode are quantities that come up when we discuss the statistical properties of an array (or set) of numbers.

By definition, the median of an array of N values, where N is odd, is the middle element of the array once all the elements have been arranged in ascending (or descending) order. We will see in chapter 6 that the median filter is especially well suited for the removal of what is known as salt and pepper noise. Another advantage of the median filter is that, unlike the averaging filter, it does not lead to blurring of edges.

We will now prove that the median filter does not lead to blurring of edges by considering a simple binary image. We assume that one half of the image consists of foreground pixels (gray level = 255) and the other half consists of background pixels (gray level = 0). The pixels along the edge will retain their original value after application of the filter as shown below.

If an averaging filter had been applied on figure 2.19(a), then we would have obtained a blurred edge. When applying a median filter on figure 2.19(a), we pad the image by duplicating the rows/columns along the borders. In general, duplicating the border will give better results than padding the image with a row/column of zeros.

The median filter is usually implemented in the following manner:

First, we consider a mask of size $n \times n$ (where n is odd). We sort the pixel intensities within the mask in ascending (or descending) order and place these values in a one-dimensional (1-D) array. The median of the values in the array is the element that occupies the middle position in the array. For example, if we take the

255	255	255	0	0
255	255	255	0	0
255	255	255	0	0
255	255	255	0	0
255	255	255	0	0

Figure 2.19(a). Simple image with a sharp edge.

255	255	255	0	0
255	255	255	0	0
255	255	255	0	0
255	255	255	0	0
255	255	255	0	0

Figure 2.19(b). Result obtained after applying the median filter.

mask size as 3×3, then then there are nine pixel values within the mask and we pick the 5th element in the sorted list to replace the value of the pixel at the center of the mask. Note that this operation (of computing the median) has to be repeated for each and every pixel within the image. Hence, the total number of computations can be expected to be very large. The best sorting algorithms require $n \log n$ operations to sort a list having n numbers. Slightly less efficient algorithms will require n^2 operations to sort a list. If there are N^2 pixels in an image, then the total number of computations required to apply the median filter on that image will be of the order of $N^2 \times n^2$, which can be prohibitively large.

A small MATLAB® program for applying the median filter on an image is given below.

Let us consider a grayscale image and assume that the intensity values of the pixels are stored in an array A.

We first write the pixel values within the mask to a 1-D array and then sort it.

```
For i=2:no_of_rows-1
For j=2:no_of_columns-1
```

The two *for* loops given above are for scanning the entire image (over all rows and columns.

```
K=1;
For m=-1:1
For n=-1:1
A1(K)=A(i+m,j+n);
K=K+1;
End
End
```

From the above program it is seen that the intensities of the pixels that lie within the mask are transferred to a 1-D array *A1*.

We now have to sort the values within *A1*.

```
For l=1:5
For p=l+1:9
If A1(l)>A1(p)
Temp=A1(l);
A1(l)=A1(p);
A1(p)=temp;
End
End
End
```

Here, we are comparing each element of an array with every other element and then swapping them if they are not in order. Note that we can stop the ordering process once we reach the 5th element in the array *A1*. We need not put the entire list in order. We are only required place the first five elements in the correct order. The remaining elements (element numbers 6 to 9) can be disordered as they do not affect the value of the median. In this way we reduce the number of computations required to calculate the median.

We now mention an alternative approach to compute the median of a list of numbers.

The alternative approach does not involve sorting the values stored in the 1-D array A1. Instead, we create a histogram of the pixel values within the mask (in other words, we create a histogram of the values stored in A1). We start from the number of pixels corresponding to the lowest pixel value and maintain a cumulative sum of the histogram values. When the cumulative sum crosses 5 we know that we have obtained the desired number (i.e., the median value).

A short MATLAB® program illustrating this approach is given below.

```
For m=1:9,
Hist(al(m)+1)=hist(al(m)+1)+1;
End
Sum=0;
i=1;
While sum<5,
Sum=sum+hist(i);
i=i+1;
End
Median=i-2;
```

```
For m=1:9,
Hist(a1(m))=0;
End
```

The histogram approach seems to have some computational advantage when compared to the approach that involves sorting all the values. However, the reader is urged to confirm for themselves that the histogram approach is computationally advantageous (see exercise 12 at the end of this chapter). Note that the histogram has to be re-initialized to zeros each time we move the mask. This adds to the computational overload of this method.

We now terminate our discussion on the relative computational advantages of the various algorithms for applying the median filter, and focus on some of the shortcomings of the median filter.

One of the problems associated with the median filter is that it removes small features like thin lines and points. Furthermore, it shifts edges that are not straight.

Consider a thin, one-pixel-wide line in an image as shown in the figure given below.

0	255	0	0	0
0	255	0	0	0
0	255	0	0	0
0	255	0	0	0
0	255	0	0	0

Upon application of the median filter, the line will be completely erased since at any given point, only three out of the nine pixels within the mask will have a gray level of 255. Isolated points and other fine features will also be erased due to the application of the median filter. This problem can be tackled by modifying the mask for the median filter. Instead of considering a square mask of size 3 × 3, we consider a modified mask (which also has nine pixels, as shown below).

0	0	1	0	0
0	0	1	0	0
1	1	1	1	1
0	0	1	0	0
0	0	1	0	0

Note that the mask given above corresponds to nine pixels as earlier, but unlike in the case of using a 3 × 3 median filter, vertical and horizontal lines will be preserved when applying this modified mask. Of course, such a mask will not preserve one-pixel-thick lines oriented at other angles.

Another problem with the median filter is that even though it does not lead to blurring of edges, it can lead to shifting of edges. While the simple vertical edge discussed earlier (figure 2.19(a)) is not affected in any way by the application of the median filter, curved edges are shifted from the original positions as shown below.

Consider a curved edge in a binary image, as shown below.

255	0	0	0	0
255	255	0	0	0
255	255	255	0	0
255	255	0	0	0
255	0	0	0	0

After we apply a 3 × 3 median filter, the above image will be modified as below.

255	0	0	0	0
255	255	0	0	0
255	255	0	0	0
255	255	0	0	0
255	0	0	0	0

Although this may seem like a minor effect, in certain applications this subtle modification in the shape and location of the edge can have important repercussions.

2.6 Sharpening in the spatial domain

In the previous section, we have seen that averaging an image leads to blurring of the edges in the image. Since averaging involves an addition or summation (equivalent to integration), it is natural to expect that differentiating an image will sharpen an image. Of course, as a corollary, we expect that taking the derivative of an image will increase the noise in it.

Although it is possible to numerically calculate the nth derivative of an image, we will confine ourselves to a discussion of the first and second derivatives of an image.

Let us first consider a 1-D image $f(x)$ and its derivatives. The first derivative of $f(x)$ is usually defined to be

$$\frac{\Delta f}{\Delta x} = \frac{f(x + \Delta x) - f(x)}{\Delta x}. \tag{2.10}$$

Equation (2.10) gives the change in $f(x)$ due to a small change (Δx) in x. Since, in the case of digital images, Δx cannot be smaller than one pixel $(\Delta x = 1)$ in the expression given above, the first derivative of $f(x)$ at $x + 1$ is given by

$$\frac{df}{dx} = f(x + 1) - f(x). \tag{2.11}$$

The first derivative of $f(x)$ at x can be written as

$$\frac{df}{dx} = f(x) - f(x - 1). \tag{2.12}$$

Taking the difference between these two expressions would tell us the rate at which the first derivative changes with x, i.e., it would give us the second derivative:

$$\frac{d^2f}{dx^2} = f(x + 1) + f(x - 1) - 2f(x). \tag{2.13}$$

For 2-D images, we can define, in a similar manner, the second derivative with respect to y:

$$\frac{\partial^2f}{\partial y^2} = f(x, y + 1) + f(x, y - 1) - 2f(x, y). \tag{2.14}$$

Adding together the two second derivatives gives us a quantity known as the Laplacian:

$$\begin{aligned}
\nabla^2 f &= \frac{\partial^2 f}{\partial x^2} + \frac{\partial^2 f}{\partial y^2} \\
&= f(x + 1, y) + f(x - 1, y) + f(x, y + 1) + f(x, y - 1) \\
&\quad - 4f(x, y).
\end{aligned} \tag{2.15}$$

The above expression for the Laplacian can be represented by a mask of the following form.

0	1	0
1	−4	1
0	1	0

The Laplacian mask is widely used for edge detection. If it is required to preserve the background, then the original image is added to the Laplacian of the image. This is known as high-boost filtering.

A few pixels could have negative values after the application of this procedure. For displaying the transformed image, the following transformation (scaling) is applied to the image:

$$g(x, y) = \frac{(f(x, y) - f_{min})}{(f_{max} - f_{min})} * 255.$$

Here, $f(x, y)$ is the output obtained after application of the Laplacian, and f_{max} and f_{min} are the maximum and minimum pixel values obtained after this operation. Here, it is assumed that we want $g(x, y)$ to be in the range 0–255.

Exercises:

1. A histogram of an image with the distribution function $(p(r) = A \sin(\pi r))$ is shown in the below figure.

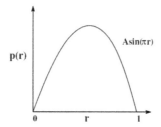

a) Find A.
b) Find the transformation function needed to equalize the shown histogram.
c) Plot the transformation function obtained in b).

2. A 1-D image is defined as

$$f(x) = x \quad \text{for } x = 0 \text{ to } 255.$$

a) Draw the histogram for this image. If the most significant bit of each pixel is set to zero, draw the resulting histogram.
b) Calculate the average gray level of the image $f(x)$.
c) Let all the odd-numbered pixels in $f(x)$ be set to zero while the even-numbered pixels are left unchanged. Write down expressions, $n(s)$, for the histogram of the modified image.
d) Calculate the average gray level of the modified image.

3. Let the gray level r of an image vary continuously in the range of 0 to 1. Let s represent the gray levels of the negative of this image and $\bar{r}$ and $\bar{s}$ represent the average gray level of the image and its negative, respectively.
a) Derive the relation between $\bar{r}$ and $\bar{s}$.
b) If σ_r and σ_s represent the variances of r and s, respectively, derive the relationship between them.

4. The histogram for a particular image is given below.

r	n(r)
0	5
1	10
2	50
3	2
4	3
5	10
6	15
7	5

a) Calculate the average gray level of this image. Calculate the standard deviation of this histogram.
b) Derive the mapping of the gray levels that would give an equal or uniform histogram.
c) Calculate the mean (average) and the standard deviation of the output histogram. Compare the brightness and contrast of the output image with respect to the input image.

5. Does the histogram of an image uniquely specify the image? Why? Consider a binary image having $n \times n$ pixels. If the number of bright pixels is equal to the number of dark pixels, then how many different images correspond to this histogram?

6. Assume that the following gray level slicing transformation is carried out on the image $f(x)$ in exercise 2.

$$s = r \quad \text{for } 128 > 128\ r \geqslant 0$$
$$s = 255 \text{ for } 192 > r \geqslant 128$$
$$s = r \quad \text{for } 255 \geqslant r \geqslant 192$$

a) Draw the histogram of the image after the application of this gray level slicing.
b) How many pixels are there with a gray level of 255?
c) What is the average gray level of the output image?

7. Let r represent the gray levels (in the range of 0 to 1) of a continuous image. The probability density for r is given by

$$p(r) = 6r(1 - r) \quad \text{for } 0 \leqslant r \leqslant 1$$
$$= 0 \qquad\qquad \text{otherwise.}$$

a) Determine the mean and standard deviation of r.

    b) A gray level transformation of the form $s = cr^{0.5}$ is applied to the image. What should be the value of c if the output gray level s is also to range from 0 to 1?

    c) Derive the probability density $p(s)$.

    d) Determine the mean and standard deviation for s, and then compare the brightness and contrast of the input and output images.

8. The following algorithm[1] has been suggested to automate the process of image enhancement using power law transformations ($s = cr^{\gamma}$): it is known that dark images are enhanced by choosing $\gamma < 1$ and bright images are enhanced by choosing $\gamma > 1$. To further generalize this process, we determine the highest peak (r_{max}) in the histogram (assuming that there is only one such peak) and then determine the value of γ for which the slope of the transformation function (ds/dr) at r_{max} is a maximum. To implement this algorithm, determine the following:

    a) The value of c if both s and r vary from 0 to $L - 1$.

    b) The value of γ for which $\left[\dfrac{ds}{dr} \right]_{r=r_{max}}$ is a maximum. The result should be given in terms of c and r_{max}.

9. An image consists of a black square (gray level = 0) 5 × 5 pixels at the center of a white background (gray level 255) as shown below.

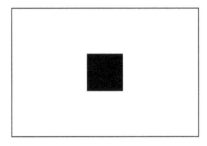

If the human eye cannot distinguish a change in intensity of up to 5 gray levels (i.e., a pixel with a gray level of 250 appears identical to a pixel with a gray level of 255), what is the size of the smallest square averaging mask that when applied on this image will make the black square indistinguishable from the background for a human observer?

10. Describe a computationally advantageous algorithm for the mask shown in figure 2.18. Hint: Modify the algorithm described in section 2.5 for simple averaging.

---

[1] A detailed discussion of this algorithm can be found in the article, 'Automated image enhancement using power law transformations' by S P Vimal and P K Thiruvikraman, *Sadhana* vol 37, part 6, December 2012, pp 739–45.

11. Carefully look at the two images given below.

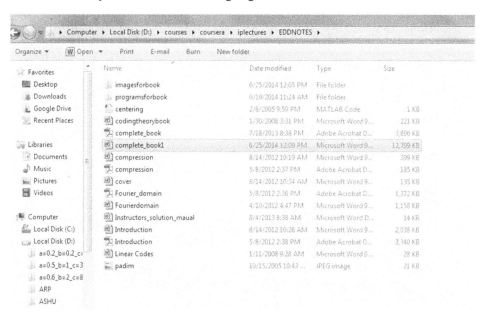

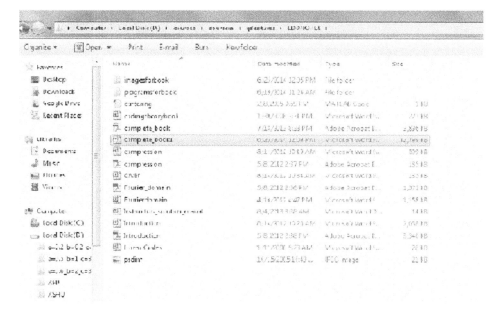

The first one is a screenshot of the desktop of a computer (obtained by pressing 'prt sc' or 'print screen' key on the keyboard). The second one was obtained by copying the first image into MS Paint and then resizing it, i.e., the image was pasted into MS Paint and then was reduced to ¼ of its original size by clicking and dragging. It was then brought back to its original size by using the mouse. Notice that the letters in the second image are not clear. Can you explain what has happened? Hint: Think about how an image can be 'resized', i.e., what happens when the size of an image is increased? Where do the extra pixels come from? See programming assignments 4 and 5 of this chapter.

12. Compare the computational efficiency of the sorting and histogram algorithms for implementing the median filter (section 2.5.2). Make an explicit calculation of the total number of assignment operations involved in each of the two methods.

Programming assignments

1. Write a program (in MATLAB®) that will implement histogram equalization for a given image.

   Note: Do not use in-built MATLAB® functions.

2. Develop a program that will implement simple averaging on an input image. The program should take the size of the mask as user input. The program can be written such that the filter is not applied to the pixels near the edges, i.e., padding is not required.

3. Given below is a MATLAB® program for determining the variance of blocks of size 64 × 64 in an image and calculating the maximum variance. Such a process is used in image registration.

```
1 a=imread('cameraman.bmp','bmp');
2 a=double(a);
3  blr=size(a,1)/64;
4  blc=size(a,2)/64;
5  k=1;
6  for i=1:blr
7      for j=1:blc
8          r=1;
9          for m=1:64
10             for n=1:64
11                 b(r)=a(i,j);
12                 r=r+1;
13             end
14         end
15         varb(k)=var(b,1);
16         k=k+1;
17     end
18 end
20 max(varb)
```

a) There is a logical error due to which the program will not give the desired output. Identify the line number that has the error and give the correction that has to be applied so that the program gives the desired output.

   b) How many number of times will line number 11 be executed when the program runs?

4. Develop a MATLAB® program that will reduce the given image to 1/4 of its initial size. The program should do this by selecting alternate rows (1st, 3rd, 5th, ... etc.) and columns and storing them as a new array. Store the output as a separate image file. The program should also calculate the average gray level of the output image.

5. Develop a MATLAB® program that will increase the number of rows and columns by a factor of two (so the final image will be four times the original size). The program should do this by introducing rows and columns between the existing rows and columns. An obvious choice for the gray levels of these new pixels is to take average value of adjacent pixels. For example, if A(1,1) and A(1,2) are the intensities of the first two pixels in the first row, then generate a new pixel (let us call it B(1,2)) whose intensity is the average of these two values. Similarly, take the average of A(2,1) and A(2,2) to generate B(2,1). Then, use the average value of B(1,2) and B(2,1) to generate B(2,2).

6. Study the following MATLAB® program:

```
1 n=3;
2 a=imread('filename.jpg','jpg');
3 s1=size(a,1);
4 s2=size(a,2);
5 for k=(n+1)/2:s1-(n-1)/2,
6     for l=(n+1)/2:s2-(n-1)/2,
7         sum=0;
8         for i=k-(n-1)/2:k+(n-1)/2,
9             for j=l-(n-1)/2:l+(n-1)/2,
10                sum=sum+a(k,l);
11            end
12        end
13        b(k,l)=sum/n;
14    end
15 end
16 b=uint8(b);
17 imwrite(b,'output.jpg','jpg');
```

   a) Which operation is this program attempting to implement?

   b) There are three errors in the above program due to which the desired output will not be obtained. Point out these errors (indicating the line numbers that have an error) and indicate the corrections that are required so that we can get the desired output.

IOP Publishing

A Course on Digital Image Processing with MATLAB®

P K Thiruvikraman

Chapter 3

Filtering in the Fourier domain

3.1 From the Fourier series to the Fourier transform

We have looked at various filtering operations in the spatial domain. While the spatial domain filters are in many cases easy to specify, formulate, and implement, they are, in general, computationally expensive. Convolving an image with a mask involves, in general, computations of the order of n^2. Computationally advantageous algorithms can be designed only for specific cases (for example in averaging).

We will now look at filtering in the Fourier domain. Filtering in the Fourier domain makes use of an idea by the French mathematician Jean Baptiste Joseph Fourier. His idea was that any periodic function $f(x)$ could be represented as a series of sine and cosine terms:

$$f(x) = \frac{a_o}{2} + \sum_{n=1}^{\infty} a_n \cos nx + \sum_{n=1}^{\infty} b_n \sin nx. \tag{3.1}$$

The a_ns and b_ns corresponding to a particular function $f(x)$ are called the Fourier coefficients of $f(x)$. The crucial idea here is that all the information about the function is contained in the Fourier coefficients. One can either specify the value of $f(x)$ for different values of x, which would specify the function in the spatial domain, or specify the Fourier coefficients.

The Fourier series, even though conceptually very beautiful and path-breaking, has limited applicability since it is valid only for functions that are periodic. For nonperiodic functions we have to use Fourier transforms.

The Fourier transform can be derived from the Fourier series in the following manner.

We note[1] that

---

[1] $i = \sqrt{-1}$. Later on in the text we will use j instead of i, since that notation is more widely used in engineering.

$$\sin nx = \frac{e^{inx} - e^{-inx}}{2i} \quad \text{and}$$

$$\cos nx = \frac{e^{inx} + e^{-inx}}{2}. \tag{3.2}$$

Substituting these expressions for sin nx and cos nx in the Fourier series, we obtain a series of the form

$$f(x) = \sum_{n=-\infty}^{\infty} c_n e^{inx}. \tag{3.3}$$

If we assume that $f(x)$ has a period of 2π, then we can determine a particular c_n (let us call it C_m) in the following manner. Multiply both sides of the equation by e^{-imx} and integrate in the range of $-\pi$ to $+\pi$:

$$\int_{-\pi}^{+\pi} f(x)e^{-imx}dx = \sum_{n=-\infty}^{\infty} c_n \int_{-\pi}^{+\pi} e^{i(n-m)x}dx. \tag{3.4}$$

Here we have interchanged the order of integration and summation. Integration of the RHS leads to

$$\int_{-\pi}^{+\pi} f(x)e^{-imx}dx = \sum_{n=-\infty}^{\infty} c_n \frac{(e^{i(n-m)\pi} - e^{-i(n-m)\pi})}{i(n-m)} \tag{3.5}$$

$$\int_{-\pi}^{+\pi} f(x)e^{-imx}dx = \sum_{n=-\infty}^{\infty} c_n \frac{2i \sin(n-m)\pi}{i(n-m)}. \tag{3.6}$$

Now, since n and m are integers, the RHS will be zero, unless $n = m$, in which case the denominator is also zero. For $n = m$, the RHS reduces to $2\pi c_m$. This is so since

$$\frac{\sin(n-m)\pi}{(n-m)\pi} = 1 \text{ for } n = m \tag{3.7}$$

$$\therefore c_m = \frac{1}{2\pi} \int_{-\pi}^{+\pi} f(x)e^{-imx}dx. \tag{3.8}$$

In the general case involving functions that might be nonperiodic or periodic, the above equation gets modified to

$$\therefore F(u) = \frac{1}{2\pi} \int_{-\infty}^{+\infty} f(x)e^{-iux}dx. \tag{3.9}$$

Here, $F(u)$ is known as the Fourier transform of $f(x)$. In the above equation, u is a continuous variable that can take values in the range of $-\infty$ to $+\infty$. The above definition for the Fourier transform can be justified based on the fact that a nonperiodic function can be viewed as a function whose period is ∞. For building the Fourier representation of nonperiodic functions, one would require all possible frequencies and hence u would become a continuous variable.

For convenience, we scale the spatial domain by a factor 2π so that the Fourier transform can be redefined as

$$F(u) = \int_{-\infty}^{+\infty} f(x)e^{-2\pi iux}dx. \tag{3.10}$$

Then the inverse Fourier transform is defined as

$$f(x) = \int_{-\infty}^{+\infty} F(u)e^{2\pi iux}du. \tag{3.11}$$

There is a certain amount of freedom in the way the forward and inverse Fourier transforms are defined. For example, one could switch the negative and positive signs in the exponents occurring in the forward and the inverse Fourier transforms.

For digital images, we would be using the discrete version of the Fourier transform, but it is worthwhile spending some time on the continuous Fourier transform in order to grasp its full meaning and importance.

3.2 Meaning of the Fourier transform

Example 3.1
Compute the Fourier transform of $f(x)$ where

$$f(x) = \sin(2\pi u_o x). \text{ for } -L \leqslant x \leqslant L \\ = 0 \ |x| > L. \tag{3.12}$$

From the definition of the continuous Fourier transform given above, we have[2]

$$F(u) = \int_{-L}^{L} \sin(2\pi u_0 x)\exp(-2\pi jux)dx. \tag{3.13}$$

To evaluate the integral, it may be convenient to write the sine function in terms of the complex exponential functions.

$$\sin(2\pi u_o x) = \frac{\exp(2\pi ju_o x) - \exp(-2\pi ju_o x)}{2j} \tag{3.14}$$

By substituting (3.14) into (3.13), we get

$$F(u) = \int_{-L}^{L} \left[\frac{\exp(2\pi ju_o x) - \exp(-2\pi ju_o x)}{2j} \right] \exp(-2\pi jux)dx \tag{3.15}$$

$$= \frac{1}{2j} \left[\int_{-L}^{+L} \exp(2\pi j(u_o - u)x)dx - \int_{-L}^{+L} \exp(-2\pi j(u_o + u)x)dx \right]. \tag{3.16}$$

---

[2] Here, $j = \sqrt{-1}$. From this section onward, we will use j in place of i in the complex exponential.

This can be easily integrated to give

$$\frac{1}{2j}\left[\frac{\exp(2\pi j(u_o - u)x)}{2\pi j(u_o - u)}\Bigg|_{-L}^{+L} + \frac{\exp(-2\pi j(u_o + u)x)}{2\pi j(u_o + u)}\Bigg|_{-L}^{+L}\right]. \qquad (3.17)$$

By substituting the limits of integration, we obtain

$$\frac{1}{2j}\left[\frac{Sin(2\pi(u_o - u)L)}{\pi(u_o - u)} - \frac{Sin(2\pi(u_o + u)L)}{\pi(u_o + u)}\right]. \qquad (3.18)$$

Hence, the Fourier transform of the given function, which is a finite sine wave, is a pair of sinc functions that peak at u_o and $-u_o$, respectively (see figure 3.1). In figure 3.1, we have taken $u_0 = 5$ and $L = 1$, and the modulus of the Fourier transform has been plotted.

Both functions in the brackets in (3.18) are of the form sin x/x. Hence, they are called sinc functions.

The function sin x/x, has a maximum value at $x = 0$, where its value is 1, and decays rapidly on either side to become 0 at $x = \pi$ (see figure 3.2).

Similarly, the two terms in (3.18) have maxima at $u = u_o$ and $u = -u_o$, respectively.

For the time being, we will ignore the second term in (3.18) since it corresponds to a negative frequency $-u_o$.

The first term has a peak at $u = u_o$ and a minimum at

$$u = u_o \pm \frac{1}{2L}. \qquad (3.19)$$

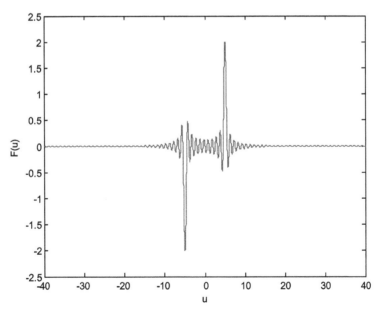

Figure 3.1. Fourier transform of a finite sine wave.

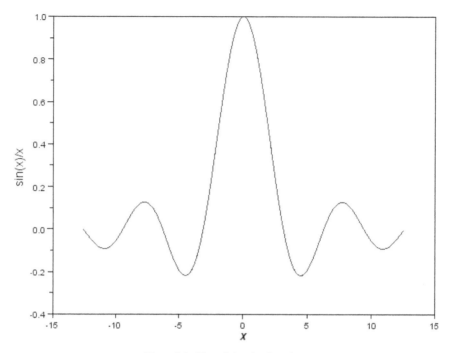

Figure 3.2. Plot of the sinc function.

It is seen from figure 3.2 that the sinc function is an oscillatory (but decaying) function. It is also seen from (3.19) that the width of the central peak is inversely proportional to L. If L tends to infinity, $F(u)$ will have a very sharp, infinitely high peak at u_o.

Let us try to analyze the nature of $F(u)$.

$f(x)$ has a single frequency, and its representation in the Fourier domain, $F(u)$, has a single peak at the corresponding frequency. Hence, it may be seen that the Fourier transform helps us to decompose the function $f(x)$ into its constituent frequencies.

Another point to be noted in this case is that $F(u)$ is purely imaginary. From the definition of $F(u)$, it is to be expected that $F(u)$ will, in general, be complex.

When will it be complex and when will it be real? We analyze this in our next example.

Example 3.2

Show that for real functions $f(x)$,

(i) the Fourier transform is always real, if $f(x)$ is an even function; and
(ii) purely imaginary, if $f(x)$ is an odd function.

(i) From the definition of the Fourier transform,

$$
\begin{aligned}
F(u) &= \int_{-\infty}^{+\infty} f(x)e^{-2\pi iux}dx \\
&= \int_{-\infty}^{+\infty} f(x)\cos(2\pi ux)dx - j\int_{-\infty}^{+\infty} f(x)\sin(2\pi ux)dx.
\end{aligned}
\tag{3.20}
$$

Since, the sine function is an odd function, the second integral will vanish if $f(x)$ is even (the product of the two functions will be odd in that case).

(ii) If $f(x)$ is odd, then the second integral will be nonzero, but the first integral will vanish since it involves the product of $f(x)$, which is an odd function with an even function (the cosine function).

We now understand why $F(u)$ was purely imaginary in example 3.1.

We will now compute the Fourier transform of some more functions in order to understand the nature of the Fourier transform in a better manner.

3.3 The impulse function

The next function we choose to study is an even simpler function. It is the impulse function. In physics, this function is known as the Dirac delta function.

The impulse function is defined to be zero at all points except at one point. Hence, the impulse function is not a function in the usual sense of the term, but can be thought of as the limit of more gently varying functions. For example, we produced the impulse function from the sinc function in example 3.1 by shrinking the width of the peak.

In terms of image processing, the impulse function can be used to represent a bright spot against a dark background. Hence it is one of the simplest possible images. Because of its simplicity, the impulse function is widely used in image processing to study the working of various filters and image restoration algorithms.

When we reduce the width of a function, like the sinc function, to produce the impulse function, we keep the area under the curve a constant. In fact, we can choose the area under the impulse curve to be unity (for simplicity).

Therefore, the impulse function, represented by $\delta(x)$, can be defined by

$$\delta(x) = \infty \text{ for } x = 0$$
$$= \text{ for } x \neq 0 \quad \text{and} \quad \int_{-\infty}^{\infty} \delta(x)dx = 1. \tag{3.21}$$

Using, the above property of the impulse function, we can also deduce another interesting property, i.e., the sifting property:

$$\int_{-\infty}^{\infty} f(x)\delta(x)dx = f(0). \tag{3.22}$$

The sifting property immediately follows from the fact that the impulse function is nonzero only at the origin. Hence, the integral has a contribution from only one point.

An impulse function $\delta(x - a)$, which is located at the point $x = a$, can be similarly represented by

$$\int_{-\infty}^{\infty} f(x)\delta(x - a)dx = f(a). \tag{3.23}$$

From the above equation, the sifting property of the impulse function is quite apparent.

It should be interesting (and easy!) to compute the Fourier transform of the impulse function:

$$\Im[\delta(x)] = \int_{-\infty}^{\infty} \delta(x)\exp\left(-2\pi jux\right)dx = \exp\left(-2\pi ju0\right) = 1. \tag{3.24}$$

The Fourier transform of the impulse function is a constant function, which is nonzero everywhere.

It can be shown that the converse is also true. The Fourier transform of a constant function is the impulse function.

This leads us to the next important property of the Fourier transform: the reciprocal nature of a function and its representation in the Fourier domain. The Fourier transform of an infinitely narrow function (the impulse function) is the infinitely broad (constant) function.

The reciprocal nature was also obvious in example 3.1. Increasing the range of the function, L, in the spatial domain, decreased the width in the Fourier domain.

We will now study the effect of shifting a function in the spatial domain. Let the Fourier transform of a function $f(x)$ be $F(u)$. How is $F(u)$ related to the Fourier transform of $f(x-a)$? This is shown in equation (3.25).

$$\Im[f(x-a)] = \int_{-\infty}^{\infty} f(x-a)\exp(-2\pi jux)dx \tag{3.25}$$

We now do a coordinate transformation, $x' = x - a$, to obtain

$$= \int_{-\infty}^{\infty} f(x')\exp(-2\pi ju(x'+a)dx \tag{3.26}$$

$$= \int_{-\infty}^{\infty} f(x')\exp(-2\pi jux')\exp(-2\pi jua)dx' \tag{3.27}$$

$$= \exp(-2\pi jua)F(u). \tag{3.28}$$

Hence, if a function is shifted in the spatial domain, there is a phase shift in the Fourier domain. It is left as an exercise to the reader to prove that a shift in the Fourier domain leads to a phase shift in the spatial domain.

Even though we would be requiring the 2-D Fourier transform[3], because our images are 2-D in nature we are at present discussing the properties of the 1-D Fourier transform since it is easier to derive results concerning Fourier transforms in one dimension. All the results carry over to two dimensions with obvious modifications.

---

[3] A physical realization of the 2-D Fourier transform of an aperture can be obtained by looking at the Fraunhofer diffraction pattern of the aperture. See *Optical Physics* by A Lipson, S G Lipson and H Lipson, 4th edn, Cambridge University Press.

Another important result we will now derive is the Fourier transform of a chain of impulses. We require this since the process of digitizing involves sampling the continuous image at periodic intervals. Each sampling event can be viewed as an impulse (in time).

3.4 Fourier transform of a train of impulses

Let the train of impulses be represented by $s(x)$, where $s(x)$ is given by

$$s(x) = \sum_{n=-\infty}^{\infty} \delta(x - na) \tag{3.29}$$

$$\Im[s(x)] = \int_{-\infty}^{\infty} \sum_{n=-\infty}^{\infty} \delta(x - na)\exp(-2\pi jux)dx \tag{3.30}$$

$$= \sum_{n=-\infty}^{\infty} \exp(-2\pi juna). \tag{3.31}$$

How do we sum this series? It is obviously a geometric series of common ratio $exp(-2\pi jua)$. However, instead of summing it as a geometric series, the summation can be done in a very interesting and instructive manner by representing the terms in the series on a phasor (or Argand) diagram.

From the phasor representation, it will be clear that if $u = 0$, all the phasors will point in the same direction: they will point along the real axis. Since there are infinitely many terms in the series, it will sum to infinity.

The result is similar if $u = 1/a$ or multiples of this value. Then the argument of the complex exponential will be an integer times 2π, which is equivalent to the argument being zero. Again the sum will be infinity.

For all other values of u, the sum is either zero or is finite (a nonzero but small quantity). This is because the phasors will point in different directions and will almost cancel each other out.

Hence, the Fourier transform of a train of impulses of period a will be a train of impulses of period $1/a$.

We can also prove the above result in a more rigorous manner, as follows. Equation (3.31) can be written as

$$= \left(\sum_{n=0}^{\infty} 2\cos(2\pi una)\right) - 1. \tag{3.32}$$

The terms for positive and negative values of n in (3.31) can be paired to give the cosine series in (3.32). The sine terms in equation (3.31) for the positive and negative values of n will cancel out, giving us equation (3.31).

This is so because $\sin(-2\pi una) = -\sin(2\pi una)$.

The cosine function can be written as the real part of a complex exponential. Hence, (3.32) can be written as

$$= \left(\mathrm{Re} \sum_{n=0}^{\infty} 2 \exp(2\pi juna) \right) - 1. \tag{3.33}$$

The above manipulations were done because even though (3.31) is a geometric series, it is difficult to sum it directly because of the positive and negative values of n. Equation (3.33) can be readily summed to give

$$= 2 \, \mathrm{Re} \left\{ \frac{1 - \exp(2\pi juNa)}{1 - \exp(2\pi jua)} \right\} - 1. \tag{3.34}$$

Note that we have to take the limit $N \to \infty$ in equation (3.34).

We now proceed to rewrite (3.34) so that the real part can be extracted easily:

$$= 2 \, \mathrm{Re} \left\{ \frac{\exp(\pi juNa)}{\exp(\pi jua)} \frac{[\exp(-\pi juNa) - \exp(\pi juNa)]}{[\exp(-\pi jua) - \exp(\pi jua)]} \right\} - 1 \tag{3.35}$$

$$= 2 \left\{ \cos[\pi u(N - 1)a] \frac{\sin(\pi uNa)}{\sin(\pi ua)} \right\} - 1. \tag{3.36}$$

In the limit $N \to \infty$, $N - 1 \sim N$, and hence (3.36) can be written as

$$= 2 \left\{ \frac{\sin(2\pi uNa)}{\sin(\pi ua)} \right\} - 1. \tag{3.37}$$

It can be shown (by using L'Hospital's rule) that the term in brackets has a maximum value of $4N$ when $u \to 0$. This maximum value occurs when u is an integral multiple of $1/a$. For all other values of u, the function is very small as shown in figure 3.3.

The above result is useful in understanding the effect of sampling an analog image to create a digital image.

When we acquire an image, we are essentially sampling the image function $f(x)$ at spatially periodic intervals. This is equivalent to multiplying $f(x)$ with a train of impulses. If two functions are multiplied in the Fourier domain, what is the corresponding operation in the Fourier domain? An important theorem known as the 'convolution theorem' provides the answer to this question.

3.5 The convolution theorem

In sampling, we multiply two functions in the spatial domain. However, we will now consider the 'convolution' of two functions in the spatial domain, and show that it is equivalent to multiplying the corresponding Fourier transforms. The converse of the theorem also holds, i.e., multiplying two functions in the spatial domain is equivalent to convolving their Fourier transforms.

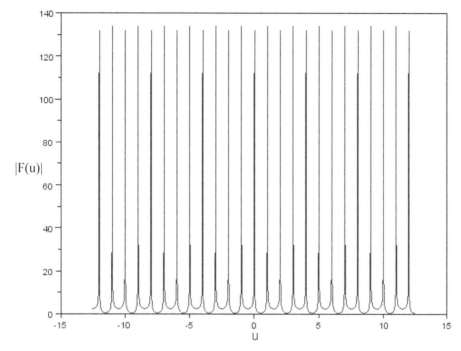

Figure 3.3. Magnitude of the Fourier transform of an impulse train.

The convolution of two 1-D functions $f(x)$ and $h(x)$ is defined as

$$g(x) = f(x) \otimes h(x) = \int_{-\infty}^{\infty} f(\tau)h(x - \tau)d\tau. \tag{3.38}$$

Note that the operation of convolution involves two operations:
  (i) We invert one of the functions, say, $h(\tau)$ and shift it by an amount x.
  (ii) Next we multiply it with $f(\tau)$ and integrate the product over all space.

In general, the convolution of two arbitrary functions may be difficult to visualize. However, for our present purposes, it is enough to look at the convolution of an arbitrary function with the impulse function:

$$g(x) = \delta(x - a) \otimes h(x) = \int_{-\infty}^{\infty} \delta(\tau - a)(x - \tau)d\tau. \tag{3.39}$$

Using the property of the impulse function, the above integral is equal to $h(x - a)$ since the impulse function is nonzero at only $\tau = a$.

Hence, we reach the important conclusion that convolving a function with an impulse function reproduces the function at the location of the impulse function. This result has obvious applications. If we want to reproduce the same function at many different locations, we simply convolve the given function with many impulse functions located at each of those locations. This result is also very important for sampling images and signals, as we will see shortly.

Let us get back to our primary task, which is to look at the Fourier transform of $g(x)$ in the Fourier domain. By definition, the Fourier transform of $g(x)$ is given by

$$G(u) = \int_{-\infty}^{\infty} \int_{-\infty}^{\infty} f(\tau)h(x - \tau)e^{-2\pi jux}d\tau dx.$$

Making the change of variables shown below, we see that $G(u)$ can be written as a product of $F(u)$ and $H(u)$.

$$x' = x - \tau$$

$$
\begin{aligned}
G(u) &= \int_{-\infty}^{\infty} \int_{-\infty}^{\infty} f(\tau)h(x')e^{-2\pi jux'}e^{-2\pi ju\tau}d\tau dx \\
&= \int_{-\infty}^{\infty} f(\tau)e^{-2\pi ju\tau}d\tau \int_{-\infty}^{\infty} h(x')e^{-2\pi jux'}dx = F(u)H(u).
\end{aligned}
\tag{3.40}
$$

Hence, convolving two functions in the spatial domain is equivalent to multiplying their Fourier transforms. Conversely, multiplying two functions in the spatial domain, as in sampling, is equivalent to convolving their Fourier transforms.

We will be using the concept of convolution in many situations. In particular, it will be shown that convolving two functions in the spatial domain is computationally expensive while the corresponding operation in the Fourier domain, i.e., multiplication, is relatively easier to accomplish.

It is interesting to note that it is possible to have a physical realization of the convolution operation[4].

Let us now look at the implications of the convolution theorem for the operation of sampling a function at periodic intervals.

The operation of sampling, as mentioned above, essentially involves the multiplication of the function being sampled with a train of impulses. In the Fourier domain, this will involve convolving the Fourier transform of the function with a train of impulses (of inverse spacing).

We have already noted that convolution of a function with a delta function reproduces the function at the location of the delta function. Therefore, the result of convolving the Fourier transform of the sampled function with a train of impulses will reproduce the function at the location of each of the impulses:

$$
\begin{aligned}
G(u) &= \sum_{n=0}^{\infty} \delta(u - na') \otimes H(u) = \int_{-\infty}^{\infty} \sum_{n} \delta(\tau - na')H(u - \tau)d\tau \\
&= \sum_{n=0}^{\infty} H(u - na').
\end{aligned}
\tag{3.41}
$$

---

[4] It is possible to have a physical realization for convolution. Take a mirror of some arbitrary shape, a square or a rectangle, and use it reflect sunlight onto a wall. It will be seen that the reflection on a nearby wall will have the shape of the mirror, while the reflection on a faraway wall will have the shape of the Sun (circle). What is seen on the wall is the convolution of the Sun and the mirror. In the first case, the Sun acts as a delta function, while in the second, since the wall is far away from the mirror, the mirror acts as a delta (impulse function).

In the Fourier domain we would have many copies of $H(u)$ spaced at periodic intervals of $a' = 1/a$ (using equation (3.37)). We might be able to extract one copy of $H(u)$ by doing a low-pass filtering. This is possible if $H(u)$ is a band-limited function.

A band-limited function is one that has a certain maximum frequency, as shown below.

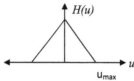

$H(u)$ is the Fourier transform of the continuous (analog function) $h(x)$.

But due to the sampling of the function, we will actually be dealing with the function $H^*(u)$, which is shown below.

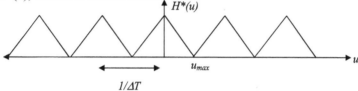

The function shown above corresponds to the situation where $u_{max} = 1/(2\Delta T)$, where ΔT is the time interval between two samples of the function $h(x)$. We can now extract $H(u)$ by applying a low-pass filter with a cut-off frequency u_{max}. If we sample at a frequency less than this, the triangles, which correspond to $H(u)$, will overlap and extracting $H(u)$ from $H^*(u)$ will not be possible.

Therefore, we arrive at the following important result:

$$\frac{1}{\Delta T} > 2u_{max}. \tag{3.42}$$

This critical frequency is known as the Nyquist rate, and equation (3.42) is known as the sampling theorem.

It should be kept in mind that band-limited signals are difficult to realize because signals/images are of finite duration/extent. Hence, high frequencies will always be present.

3.6 The discrete Fourier transform (DFT)

So far, we have discussed only the continuous Fourier transform. However, since our images are digital and have a finite number of pixels, we need to define the discrete version of the Fourier transform.

The DFT is defined by

$$F(u) = \frac{1}{M} \sum_{x=0}^{M-1} f(x)\exp\left(-\frac{2\pi jux}{M}\right) \tag{3.43}$$

for $u = 0, 1, 2, \ldots M - 1$.

At this stage, you may be wondering whether we are going around in circles. We started with the Fourier series (3.1), wherein the frequencies were discrete (integral multiples of a fundamental frequency). Later we allowed the frequency u to vary continuously, and arrived at the continuous Fourier transform (3.10), and now we are once again making the frequencies discrete!

However, note that the Fourier series is applicable only for periodic functions and hence is not in general useful for digital images, which are rarely expected to be periodic.

The DFT, unlike the Fourier series, is applicable for all functions, whether periodic or not.

The inverse DFT is defined by

$$f(x) = \sum_{u=0}^{M-1} F(u)\exp\left(\frac{2\pi jux}{M}\right)$$

(3.44)

for $x = 0, 1, 2, \ldots M - 1$.

Just as in case of the continuous Fourier transform, there is a certain amount of freedom in the above definition. For example, the signs of the exponent and/or the $1/M$ factor can be switched between the Fourier transform and its inverse.

We will now prove that (3.43) is consistent with (3.44). We substitute for $F(u)$ from (3.43) into (3.44):

$$f(x) = \frac{1}{M} \sum_{u=0}^{M-1}\sum_{x=0}^{M-1} f(x)\exp\left(\frac{-2\pi jux}{M}\right)\exp\left(\frac{2\pi jux'}{M}\right).$$

(3.45)

Note that, when we are summing over u, x is to be kept constant (hence it is denoted by x').

Interchanging the order of summations, we have

$$f(x) = \frac{1}{M} \sum_{x=0}^{M-1} f(x) \sum_{u=0}^{M-1} \exp\left(\frac{2\pi ju(x' - x)}{M}\right).$$

(3.46)

The summation over u is obviously a geometric series; however, it can also be viewed as the addition of many phasors.

It can be seen that, if $x = x'$, the summand is 1; otherwise, the summand is zero.

The summand being 1 when $x = x'$, is obvious, so let us look at the other case. In figure 3.4, we have plotted the case $M = 6$.

In drawing the above phasor diagram, we have taken $x - x' = 1$. Hence, the angle between successive phasors is $2\pi/6$. Therefore, they form a regular hexagon and sum to zero. If $x - x'$ is not 1, but some other integer, then the angle between the phasors would be different from $2\pi/6$; nonetheless, they would add up to zero.

When the summand is 1, the summation is equal to M, which cancels the M in the denominator of (3.46), thus showing that the RHS of (3.46) is equal to the LHS of (3.46).

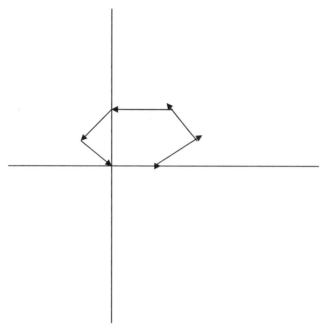

Figure 3.4. Phasor diagram for evaluating (3.46) with $M = 6$ and $(x - x') = 1$.

Those who are fond of algebra (and are not totally convinced about the above proof) may note that the geometric series in (3.46) can be summed as follows:

$$\sum_{u=0}^{M-1} \exp\left(\frac{2\pi ju(x - x')}{M}\right) = \frac{1 - \exp(2\pi u(x' - x))}{1 - \exp\left[\frac{2\pi ju(x' - x)}{M}\right]} = 0. \tag{3.47}$$

Equation (3.47) is true if $x \neq x'$.

If $x = x'$, then the summation is equal to M as already mentioned.

Having proved that the definition of the inverse DFT is consistent with the definition of the DFT, we now proceed to prove certain important properties of the DFT.

We note in passing that the definition of the DFT can be easily modified for the case of two dimensions:

$$F(u, v) = \frac{1}{MN} \sum_{x=0}^{M-1} \sum_{y=0}^{N-1} f(x, y) \exp\left(-\frac{2\pi jux}{M}\right) \exp\left(-\frac{2\pi jvy}{N}\right). \tag{3.48}$$

3.7 Additional properties of the DFT

The DFT satisfies the properties of the continuous Fourier transform. In addition, it satisfies some additional properties (which are not there for the continuous Fourier transform).

One such property is the periodic nature of the DFT. It can be easily shown that $F(u) = F(u+M)$.

Proof:

$$F(u + M) = \frac{1}{M}\sum_{x=0}^{M-1} f(x)\exp\left(-\frac{2\pi j(u + M)x}{M}\right)$$

$$= \frac{1}{M}\sum_{x=0}^{M-1} f(x)\exp\left(\frac{-2\pi jux}{M}\right)\exp(-2\pi jux) \qquad (3.49)$$

$$= \frac{1}{M}\sum_{x=0}^{M-1} f(x)\exp\left(\frac{-2\pi jux}{M}\right) = F(u)$$

The periodic nature of the DFT helps us in formulating an algorithm known as the fast Fourier transform (FFT), which reduces the number of computations required for the DFT. However, it can also be a nuisance.

Due to the periodic nature of the DFT, the spectrum of an image can appear scrambled. A low-frequency component can masquerade as a high-frequency component.

Note that

$F(N - 1) = F(-1)$.

$u = -1$ is actually a low frequency, but because of the periodic property of the DFT, it appears at $N - 1$, which would be the highest possible frequency in an N point transform.

The Fourier transform of a 2-D rectangular function (in its scrambled form) is shown in figure 3.5.

We can unscramble the DFT by shifting the zero-frequency component to the center $(M/2 - 1, N/2 - 1)$.

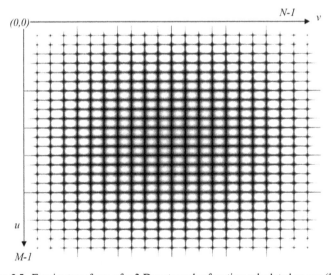

Figure 3.5. Fourier transform of a 2-D rectangular function calculated as per (3.48).

The centered Fourier transform for the image in figure 3.6 is shown in figure 3.7. We now discuss how the centering of the Fourier transform can be achieved.

In (3.28), we saw that shifting a function in the spatial domain leads to a phase shift in the Fourier domain. Conversely, we can conclude that shifting the spectrum in the Fourier domain can be accomplished by doing a phase shift in real space.

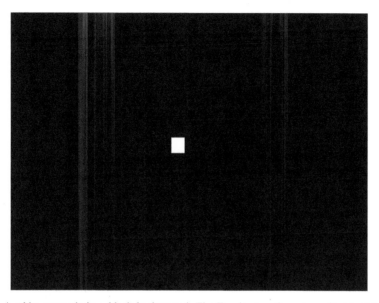

Figure 3.6. A white rectangle in a black background. The Fourier transform (magnitude) of this image is shown in figure 3.5.

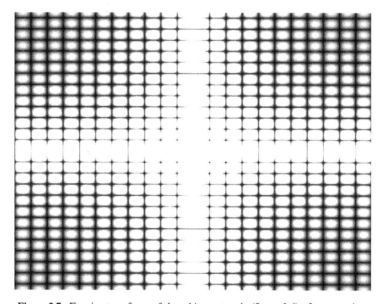

Figure 3.7. Fourier transform of the white rectangle (figure 3.6) after centering.

It can be easily shown that multiplying $f(x, y)$ by $(-1)^{x+y}$ leads to 'centering' of the Fourier spectrum.

To prove this, multiply $f(x, y)$ by $(-1)^{x+y}$ before taking the Fourier transform:

$$
\begin{aligned}
F(u, v) &= \frac{1}{MN} \sum_{y=0}^{N-1} \sum_{x=0}^{M-1} (-1)^{(x+y)} f(x, y) \exp\left(-\frac{2\pi j u x}{M} - \frac{2\pi j v y}{N}\right) \\
&= \frac{1}{MN} \sum_{y=0}^{N-1} \sum_{x=0}^{M-1} \exp(\pi j x + \pi j y) f(x, y) \exp\left(-\frac{2\pi j u x}{M} - \frac{2\pi j v y}{N}\right) \\
&= \frac{1}{MN} \sum_{y=0}^{N-1} \sum_{x=0}^{M-1} f(x, y) \exp\left(-\frac{2\pi j (u - M/2) x}{M} - \frac{2\pi j (v - N/2) y}{N}\right) \\
&= F\left(u - \frac{M}{2}, v\frac{N}{2}\right).
\end{aligned}
\tag{3.50}
$$

This implies that the zero-frequency component has been shifted to $(u - M/2, v - N/2)$, or, in other words, the transform has been 'centered'.

Significance of Fourier components:

The meaning of the Fourier transform was already discussed in section 3.2, but the DFT has some additional features that are of interest. To begin with, let us look at the zero-frequency component, i.e., $F(0, 0)$.

From (3.48),

$$
F(u, v) = \frac{1}{MN} \sum_{x=0}^{M-1} \sum_{y=0}^{N-1} f(x, y) \exp\left(\frac{-2\pi j u x}{M}\right) \exp\left(\frac{-2\pi j v y}{N}\right)
$$

$$
F(0, 0) = \frac{1}{MN} \sum_{x=0}^{M-1} \sum_{y=0}^{N-1} f(x, y) = \text{Average of } f(x, y).
\tag{3.51}
$$

It can also be easily seen that the zero-frequency component is greater in magnitude than any other Fourier component. We see from the phasor diagram in section 3.6 that, for the zero-frequency component, all the phasors would line up along the real axis and add in phase. Hence the resultant of these would have the highest magnitude.

For any nonzero-frequency, the phasors will be pointing in different directions and hence the resultant would be less than the zero-frequency component. The fact that the zero-frequency component has the largest value has important consequences for image compression, which will be covered in detail in chapter 4.

The following example helps us analyze the nature of the DFT.

Example 3.3 Compute the DFT of the 5×5, 3-bit image shown in figure 3.8.

This image corresponds to a bright horizontal line of gray level 5 in a dark background.

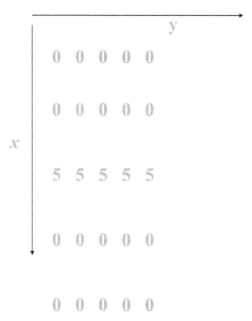

Figure 3.8. The 5 ×5, 3-bit image discussed in example 3.3.

Let us evaluate the DFT of this figure. From the definition of the DFT (equation (3.48)), we have

$$= \frac{1}{25} \sum_{y=0}^{4} 5 \exp\left(\frac{-2\pi j v y}{5}\right) \exp\left(\frac{-4\pi j u}{5}\right). \tag{3.52}$$

From figure 3.8, it is seen that $f(x,y) = 5$ for $x = 2$, and zero for all other values of x. Equation (3.52) has been obtained using this information.

An important conclusion that can be drawn from this example is that a sharp change in the intensity of an image, in a certain direction (along the x-axis in this case), gives rise to high-frequency components in that direction. Hence, we see high-frequency components along the u direction, but not along the v direction. Therefore, an edge present in an image in a particular direction is expected to give rise to high frequencies in the direction perpendicular to the edge. This fact may be used for highlighting or detecting edges.

Also note that we have displayed only the magnitude of the DFT in figure 3.9. Each of the Fourier components has a phase factor $exp(-4\pi ju/5)$, which contains the information about the location of the line ($x = 2$). If the line had occurred in a different location (for a different value of x), then the phase factor would have been different.

3.8 Filtering in the Fourier domain

We discussed filtering in the spatial domain in chapter 2. We can also apply filters to the Fourier transform of an image. This is known as filtering in the Fourier domain.

If $v = 0$, then the summation $= 5$; else it is 0. Therefore, the FT of the image is as shown below:

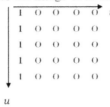

$$
\begin{array}{|ccccc}
\hline
1 & 0 & 0 & 0 & 0 \quad v \\
1 & 0 & 0 & 0 & 0 \\
1 & 0 & 0 & 0 & 0 \\
1 & 0 & 0 & 0 & 0 \\
1 & 0 & 0 & 0 & 0 \\
\end{array}
$$

u

Figure 3.9. Magnitude of the DFT of the image given in figure 3.8.

The first step in any filtering operation in the Fourier domain involves the computation of the Fourier transform of the image. The various steps involved in filtering in the Fourier domain are listed below.

1. Multiply the input image by $(-1)^{(x + y)}$ to center the transform
2. Compute $F(u, v)$
3. Multiply $F(u, v)$ by a filter function $H(u, v)$ (componentwise) to obtain $G(u, v)$
4. Compute the inverse DFT of $G(u, v)$
5. Multiply the result by $(-1)^{(x + y)}$ to undo the effect of step 1
6. Obtain the real part of the result in step 5 to get the output image $g(x, y)$

The final step is required because, whatever the filtering operation, the function corresponding to the output image is expected to be real. However, due to some rounding-off errors in the various computations, some spurious imaginary part may be there in $g(x, y)$. The imaginary part of $g(x, y)$ is simply neglected since it is of spurious origin.

Instead of using the above procedure, it is also possible to center the Fourier transform by shifting the transform in the Fourier domain. Essentially, we have to swap quadrant 1 with 3 while quadrant 2 is swapped with 4 (see figure below).

$$
\begin{array}{cc}
0,0 & N-1 \\
\begin{array}{|c|c|}
\hline
2 & 1 \\
\hline
3 & 4 \\
\hline
\end{array} & \\
M-1 & \\
\end{array}
$$

Some of the filters that are commonly used in image processing are listed below:

1. Low-pass filters
2. High-pass filters
3. Notch filters

Within each type of filter, we may have some variations. These will be discussed in the subsequent sections.

3.9 Low-pass filters

As the name suggests, we retain (or 'pass') the low-frequency Fourier components in an image while suppressing the high-frequency components.

The simplest low-pass filter is the ideal low-pass filter. The filter function for the ideal low-pass filter is shown below.

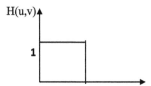

Here, D is the distance of a particular Fourier component (u, v) from the center of the Fourier transform. Accordingly, D is given by

$$D = \sqrt{(u - M/2)^2 + (v - N/2)^2}. \tag{3.53}$$

Even though it is called an 'ideal' low-pass filter, due to the fact that it has a sharp cut-off, it is not ideal in some aspects, and suffers from 'ringing'.

Overall, the effect of the low-pass filter is similar to that of averaging because it leads to some amount of blurring, as seen from figure 3.14.

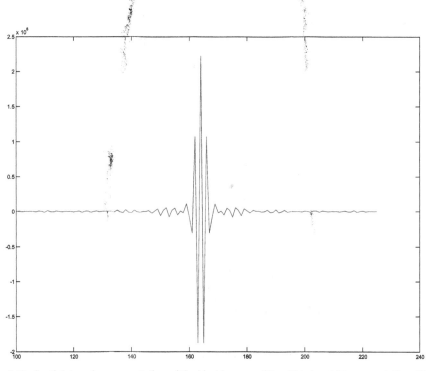

Figure 3.10. Spatial domain representation of the ideal low-pass filter. This is a 1-D representation. The 2-D representation of the function is given in figure 3.12.

While blurring of an image is to be expected, when a low-pass filter is applied on an image, an undesirable side effect is the phenomenon of ringing.

What is the origin of ringing?

Well, we are multiplying the Fourier transform of the image with the filter function. If we multiply two functions in the Fourier domain, it is equivalent to convolving their spatial domain representations.

To understand ringing, consider an image that has just a bright spot in a dark background. Such an image can be represented by an impulse function. The impulse function is to be convolved with the spatial domain representation of the ideal low-pass filter function (ILPF).

The spatial domain representation of the ideal low-pass filter is shown in figure 3.10.

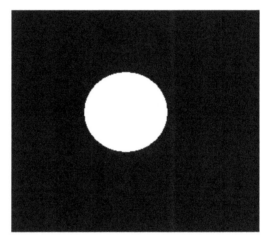

Figure 3.11. The ILPF seen as an image in the Fourier domain.

Figure 3.12. The 2-D spatial domain representation of the ILPF. A log transform has been applied to improve the visibility of the secondary rings.

This was obtained by applying the inverse Fourier transform on the filter function $H(u,v)$.

Notice that in the spatial domain, the ideal low-pass filter has a representation that peaks at the origin and has a functional form that is both oscillatory and decaying in nature. The two 'secondary' peaks on either side of the central peak give rise to the ringing effect.

The 2-D spatial domain representation of the ILPF is shown in figure 3.12.

Convolving, the impulse function(s) with any function (like the one in figure 3.12) will simply reproduce the function at the location of the impulses (refer to section 3.5).

Hence, 'rings' are produced around every object on which the ILPF has been applied. A sample image (figure 3.13) and its low-pass filtered version are shown below (figure 3.14).

Figure 3.13. A test image for application of the ILPF.

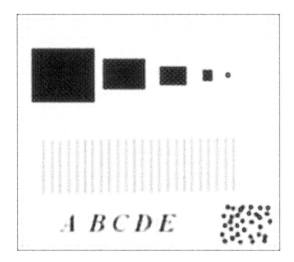

Figure 3.14. The output figure when an ILPF is applied on the image in figure 3.13. Notice the ringing effect.

3.10 Other low-pass filters

How do we design filters that perform a function similar to the ideal low-pass filter discussed in the previous section, but avoid the ringing effect?

The careful reader would have traced ringing to the fact that the spatial domain representation of the ILPF had a nonmonotonic functional form—the spatial domain representation had a maximum at the center, went through zero at a certain radius, and peaked again ('secondary' peaks) at a certain distance from the center.

Therefore, filter functions whose spatial domain representations have a monotonic variation (they decrease monotonically from the center to become zero only at infinity) will not give rise to ringing.

Two such filter functions are the Gaussian filter and the Butterworth filter of the first order. We will prove analytically, in the example problem that follows, that the spatial domain representation of the Gaussian filter has a monotonic character. The Gaussian filter is defined by

$$H(u, v) - \exp\left(\frac{-D^2(u, v)}{2\sigma^2}\right). \tag{3.54}$$

Here, D is the 'distance' from the center of the Fourier domain, calculated using the usual distance formula:

$$D = \left[\left(u - \frac{M}{2}\right)^2 + \left(v - \frac{N}{2}\right)^2\right]. \tag{3.55}$$

Example 3.4 Determine the spatial domain representation of the Gaussian filter, defined by (3.54).

$$\int_{-\infty}^{\infty} \int_{-\infty}^{\infty} H(u, v)\exp\left(2\pi j(ux + vy)\right)dudv$$

$$= \int_{-\infty}^{\infty} \int_{-\infty}^{\infty} \exp(-(u'^2 + v'^2)/2\sigma^2)\exp(2\pi j(ux + vy))dudv$$

Using $u' = u - M/2$ and $v' = v - N/2$,

$$= \exp\left(\pi j(Mx + Ny)\right) \int_{-\infty}^{\infty} \int_{-\infty}^{\infty} \exp(-(u'^2 + v'^2)/2\sigma^2)\exp(2\pi j(u'x + v'y))du'dv'. \tag{3.56}$$

We can rewrite the integral as

$$= \int_{0}^{\infty} \int_{0}^{2\pi} \exp(-\rho^2)\exp(-(2\pi^2\sigma^2x^2 + 2\pi^2\sigma^2y^2))\rho d\rho d\phi.$$

Converting this integral into polar coordinates yields

$$= \int_0^\infty \int_0^{2\pi} \exp(-\rho^2)\exp(-(2\pi^2\sigma^2 x^2 + 2\pi^2\sigma^2 y^2))\rho d\rho d\phi. \quad (3.57)$$

If we substitute $\rho^2 = t$, we get

$$\begin{aligned}
&= \int_0^\infty \int_0^{2\pi} \exp(-t)\exp(-(2\pi^2\sigma^2 x^2 + 2\pi^2\sigma^2 y^2))\frac{dt}{2}d\phi \\
&= \pi \exp(-(2\pi^2\sigma^2 x^2 + 2\pi^2\sigma^2 y^2)).
\end{aligned} \quad (3.58)$$

Hence, we have shown that the spatial domain representation of a Gaussian filter is also a Gaussian. Note from (3.58) that the width of the Gaussian in the spatial domain has an inverse relation to its width in the Fourier domain. Of course, this is to be expected based on the discussion in section 3.3.

Another important class of filters is the Butterworth filters, which are defined by

$$H(u, v) = \frac{1}{1 + [D(u, v)/D_0]^{2n}}. \quad (3.59)$$

Here, $D(u, v)$ is the distance from the center of the transform, D_0 is the distance of the cut-off frequency from the center, and n is the order of the Butterworth filter. Sharper cutoffs are obtained with higher values of n but at the cost of an increase in the ringing effect.

It can be shown that Butterworth filters of the first order do not suffer from ringing. Ringing is present for all higher-order filters.

The functional forms of the Butterworth filters are shown in figure 3.15.

3.11 High-pass filters

While low-pass filters lead to blurring of edges (as seen in sections 3.9 and 3.10), application of high-pass filters leads to an opposite effect: sharpening of edges. Hence, high-pass filters may be used as a first step in edge detection.

A high-pass filter can be easily generated from the expression for the low-pass filter, by using the expression

$$H_{hp}(u, v) = 1 - H_{lp}(u, v). \quad (3.60)$$

Since the two filter functions are linearly related, the preceding discussion (sections 3.9 and 3.10) on ringing holds for high-pass filters as well.

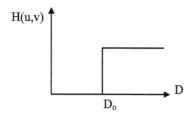

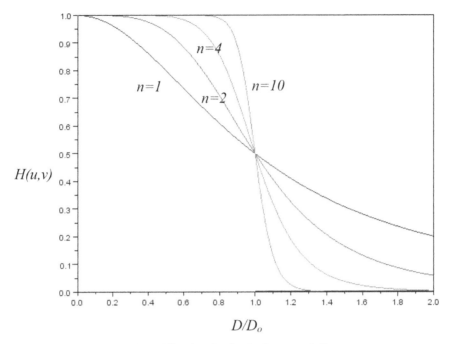

Figure 3.15. Filter function for the Butterworth filters.

The ideal high-pass filter is shown in the above figure. The ideal high-pass filter, by definition, removes all frequencies within a distance D_o from the zero-frequency. Hence, the output images will be darker than the input images in addition to being sharper.

Using (3.60) and (3.59), we obtain the following expression for the Butterworth high-pass filters:

$$H(u, v) = \frac{1}{1 + [D_o/D(u, v)]^{2n}}. \tag{3.61}$$

3.12 The FFT

While many filters can be specified very elegantly in the Fourier domain (as opposed to the spatial domain), the main advantage of doing filtering in the Fourier domain is that there exists a very efficient and fast algorithm for computing the DFT. This algorithm, known as the FFT, was developed in 1965 by Cooley and Tuckey[5].

To appreciate the development of the FFT algorithm, let us take a look at the number of computations involved in evaluating the 1-D DFT.

The DFT, is defined by (3.43):

---

[5] It was shown recently that a similar algorithm was known to the great mathematician Carl Friedrich Gauss (1777–1855).

$$F(u) = \frac{1}{M} \sum_{x=0}^{M-1} f(x) \exp\left(-\frac{2\pi j u x}{M}\right)$$

for $u = 0, 1, 2, \ldots M-1$.

We note that computation of a single frequency component of $F(u)$ involves M multiplications of $f(x)$ and the complex exponential and $M-1$ additions (adding the M terms in the summation involves $M-1$ + signs).

These computations (additions and multiplications) have to be repeated for each of the M Fourier components. Hence, on the whole, we have to do M^2 multiplications and $M(M-1) \sim M^2$ additions.

As we will see, the FFT reduces the number of additions and multiplications to a much smaller number.

In order to easily follow the algorithm, we need a more compact notation for the DFT. Therefore, we rewrite the DFT as follows:

$$F(u) = \frac{1}{M} \sum_{x=0}^{M-1} f(x) W_M{}^{ux} \tag{3.62}$$

where $W_M = \exp(-2\pi j / M)$.

We will assume that M is a power of 2. It is possible to formulate the FFT algorithm for any number (even for a prime number M); however, the algorithm is simpler to understand for an even value of M (which is also a power of 2).

We assume that $M = 2^n$.

Therefore, $M = 2K$; K is some positive integer. Rewriting the summation once again, we have

$$F(u) = \frac{1}{2K} \sum_{x=0} f(x) W_{2K}{}^{ux} \tag{3.63}$$

$$W_{2K} = \exp(-2\pi j / 2K).$$

We now break up the summation into two parts and sum the odd and even values of x separately:

$$F(u) = \frac{1}{2}\left[\frac{1}{K} \sum_{x=0}^{K-1} f(2x) W_{2K}{}^{u(2x)} + \frac{1}{K} \sum_{x=0}^{K-1} f(2x+1) W_{2K}{}^{u(2x+1)} \right] \tag{3.64}$$

$$= \frac{1}{2}\left[\frac{1}{K} \sum_{x=0}^{K-1} f(2x) W_K{}^{ux} + \frac{1}{K} \sum_{x=0}^{K-1} f(2x+1) W_K{}^{ux} W_{2K}{}^{u} \right]. \tag{3.65}$$

We name these two summations as

$$F_{\text{even}}(u) = \frac{1}{K} \sum_{x=0}^{K-1} f(2x) W_K{}^{ux} \tag{3.66}$$

$$F_{\text{odd}}(u) = \frac{1}{K}\sum_{x=0}^{K-1} f(2x+1)W_K^{ux}. \tag{3.67}$$

Therefore, (3.65) can be written as

$$F(u) = \frac{1}{2}\Big[F_{\text{even}}(u) + F_{\text{odd}}(u)W_{2K}^{u}\Big]. \tag{3.68}$$

So far, we have just redefined some quantities that occur in the DFT and have written it in a more elegant manner. However, the computational efficiency of the FFT will become obvious when we compute $F(u+K)$:

$$F(u+k) = \frac{1}{2}\Big[F_{\text{even}}(u) - F_{\text{odd}}(u)W_{2K}^{u}\Big]. \tag{3.69}$$

It can be easily seen that $F(u+K)$ simplifies to:
(3.69) is obtained by substituting $u + K$ in place of u in (3.68) and noting that

$$W_{2K}^{K} = \exp(-2\pi jK/2K) = -1. \tag{3.70}$$

Therefore, if we divide the original summation into even and odd terms, we have to evaluate only one half of $F(u)$; the other half follows with no extra multiplications!

In fact, we need not stop here. We can go on dividing each summation into even and odd terms and this can be continued until we reach a two-point transform! This process is called the successive doubling method or decimation.

Let us now calculate the number of operations involved in this new method and hence the computational advantage.

Let $m(n)$ and $a(n)$ represent the number of multiplications and additions, respectively, for a transform with $M = 2^n$ data points. For a two-point transform, $M = 2$ and $n = 1$.

For a two-point transform, the summation runs from 0 to $k - 1(= 0)$ and we have to compute $F(0)$ and $F(1)$.

Evaluation of $F_{\text{even}}(0)$ and $F_{\text{odd}}(0)$ requires no multiplications since $W^{ux} = 1$. One addition and one multiplication are required to evaluate

$$F(0) = F_{\text{even}} + F_{\text{odd}}W_{2K}^{u}. \tag{3.71}$$

$F(1)$ follows with one more addition.
Therefore,

$$m(1) = 1 \quad \text{and} \quad a(1) = 2.$$

A four-point transform can be split into two two-point transforms, and two more multiplications are required when we multiply F_{odd} by W_{2K}^{u}.
Therefore,

$$m(2) = 2m(1) + 2 \quad \text{and}$$
$$a(2) = 2a(1) + 4.$$

Each time we combine F_{even} and F_{odd} we need to do an extra addition.
Similarly,

$$m(3) = 2m(2) + 4 \quad \text{and}$$
$$a(3) = 2a(2) + 8.$$

We can generalize these results as follows:

$$m(n) = 2m(n-1) + 2^{n-1}$$
$$a(n) = 2a(n-1) + 2^n.$$

Therefore,

$$m(n) = 2[m(n-2) + 2^{n-2}] + 2^{n-1}.$$

We have to recursively substitute for $m(n-2)$ in terms of $m(n-3)$ and so on. Each time we substitute for $m(k)$ in terms of $m(k-1)$, we have to multiply by 2 and add 2^{n-1}.
Therefore,

$$
\begin{aligned}
m(n) &= 2.\,2.\,2....2m(n-(n-1)) + 2^{n-1} + ...2^{n-1} \\
&= 2^{n-1}m(1) + (n-1)2^{n-1} \\
&= 2^{n-1}(1 + (n-1)) = (n/2)2^n = \left(\frac{M}{2}\right)\log_2 M
\end{aligned}
$$

(3.72)

$$
\begin{aligned}
a(n) &= 2[2a(n-2) + 2^{n-1}] + 2^n \\
&= 2^{n-1}a(1) + (n-1)2^n \\
&= 2^n(1 + n - 1) = n2^n = M\log_2 M.
\end{aligned}
$$

(3.73)

The computational advantage of the FFT over a direct implementation of the 1-D DFT can be defined as

$$C(M) = \frac{M^2}{M\log_2 M} = \frac{M}{\log_2 M} = \frac{2^n}{n}.$$

(3.74)

As seen from (3.74), the computational advantage of the FFT over the DFT increases with increasing n.
For example, when $n = 15$ (32 768 pixels),
$C(M) = 2200$.
Therefore, we can expect for this case that the FFT is computed 2200 times faster than the DFT (figure 3.16).

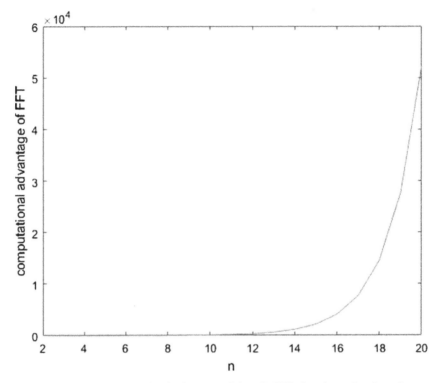

Figure 3.16. The computational advantage of the 1-D FFT plotted as a function of n.

We will now see how to implement the FFT algorithm so that we can exploit its computational advantage to the maximum extent.

We will present a numerical example for a small value of n. This should give an indication about the implementation of the algorithm. The reader can refer to any standard text that deals with the implementation of the FFT[6].

For simplicity, we will consider an eight-point transform. For an eight-point transform,

$$F(u) = \frac{1}{8} \sum_{x=0}^{7} f(x)\exp\left(-\frac{2\pi j u x}{8}\right)$$

(3.75)

for $u = 0, 1, 2, \ldots 7$.

By splitting into even and odd terms, we have

$$F(u) = \frac{1}{2}\left[\frac{1}{4}\sum_{x=0}^{3} f(2x)W_4^{ux} + \frac{1}{4}\sum_{x=0}^{3} f(2x+1)W_4^{ux}W_8^{u}\right].$$

(3.76)

---

[6] A good reference on the implementation: Teukolsky *et al* 2007 *Numerical Recipes in C* 3rd edn (New York: Cambridge University Press).

Carrying this further, the process of decimation yields the following expression for $F(u)$:

$$= \frac{1}{2} \left[\begin{array}{l} \frac{1}{2} \left[\frac{1}{2} \sum_{x=0}^{1} f(4x) W_2^{ux} + \frac{1}{2} \sum_{x=0}^{3} f(4x+2) W_2^{ux} W_8^{2u} \right] \\ + \frac{1}{2} \left[\frac{1}{2} \sum_{x=0}^{1} f(4x+1) W_2^{ux} + \frac{1}{2} \sum_{x=0}^{1} f(4x+3) W_2^{ux} W_8^{2u} \right] W_8^{u} \end{array} \right].$$

Finally, upon substituting the values of x, we have

$$F(u) = \frac{1}{2} \left[\begin{array}{l} \frac{1}{2} \left[\frac{1}{2}[f(0) + f(4) W_8^{4u}] + \frac{1}{2}[f(2) + f(6) W_8^{4u}] W_8^{2u} \right] \\ + \frac{1}{2} \left[\frac{1}{2}[f(1) + f(5) W_8^{4u}] + \frac{1}{2}[f(3) + f(7) W_8^{4u}] W_8^{2u} \right] W_8^{u} \end{array} \right].$$

The above expression is sometimes represented by the 'butterfly' diagram shown below.

In figure 3.17, not all the W factors have been shown so as avoid cluttering the diagram. The w factors can be easily worked out based on equation (3.76). The diagram indicates how the algorithm may be implemented. The gray level values $f(x)$ are stored in the first column of a 2-D array, which is shown in the leftmost column of the image. The results of the computation are stored in the next column. Each stage of the combination of F_{even} and F_{odd} is stored in a new column of the array until the final result, i.e., the FFT, is obtained after n stages.

As seen from the diagram, the FFT is obtained in the bit-reversed fashion. Hence, the actual FFT is obtained by applying bit reversal on the last column.

3.13 Comparison of the FFT with convolution

Even though the FFT is faster than the DFT, the question that will definitely arise in the mind of the discerning reader is the following.

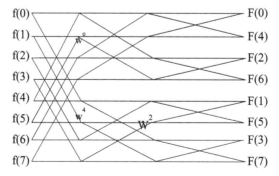

Figure 3.17. 'Butterfly' diagram illustrating the FFT algorithm.

'Why should I transform to the Fourier domain? Can't I do the corresponding operation (convolution) in the spatial domain?'

We will now show that transforming to the Fourier domain is computationally less expensive when compared to convolution in the spatial domain.

We have already seen that, in general, convolution in one dimension involves N^2 multiplications (with the weights in the mask) and N^2 additions (section 2.5).

Let us now look at the corresponding operation in the Fourier domain (multiplication with the mask in the Fourier domain) instead of convolution.

The number of computations for each stage are as below:

1. Transforming both mask and image to the Fourier domain involves $2Nlog_2N$ additions and $Nlog_2N$ multiplications.
2. After transforming to the Fourier domain, we have to multiply the representation of the mask in the Fourier domain with the Fourier representation of the image. This involves N multiplications (componentwise multiplication in the Fourier domain).
3. Then we need $Nlog_2N$ additions and $(N/2)log_2N$ multiplications to transform the product back to the spatial domain.

Therefore, in total, we have $3Nlog_2N$ additions and $(3N/2)log_2N + N$ multiplications.

For $N = 1024$ (for example)

Convolution in the spatial domain involves $N^2 = 1048\,576$ additions and an equal number of multiplications; meanwhile, doing the corresponding operation in the Fourier domain involves $30\,720$ additions and $16\,384$ multiplications.

Thus, in spite of going back and forth between the spatial and the Fourier domains, multiplication in the Fourier domain makes sense (if we use FFT) while convolution in the spatial domain does not.

In section 2.5, we discussed efficient algorithms for certain masks. However, the algorithms are specific to those masks. These algorithms are unlike the FFT, which is a standard algorithm with universal applicability.

So we have to thank Fourier for his idea that continues to help us even after two centuries!

Exercises

1. a) Determine the Fourier transform of the following function and give a rough plot of your result.

$$f(x) = \exp(-|x|/x_o): \quad \text{where } x_o > 0$$

b) Suppose that $f(x)$ is used as a filter function (replace x by u and x_o by u_o). Compare this filter with a Butterworth filter of the first order, i.e., which filter attenuates a given frequency to a greater extent?

2. a) Calculate the DFT of the 1-D function given below:

$$f(x) = 1 \quad \text{for } x = 0 \text{ to } M/2 - 1$$
$$f(x) = 0 \quad \text{for } x = M/2 \text{ to } M - 1.$$

b) Calculate the magnitude of the DFT calculated above.
c) What is the value of $F(0)$?

3. A 2-D image $f(x, y)$ having $M \times N$ pixels is rotated by 180° about its center to obtain $g(x, y)$. Write down an expression for $g(x, y)$ in terms of $f(x, y)$. If $F(u, v)$ is the Fourier transform of $f(x, y)$, what will be the DFT of $g(x, y)$? The result should be related to $F(u, v)$. Note that x and y are the coordinates of a pixel with respect to the top-left corner of the image (usual convention).

4. Derive the continuous Fourier transform of the following function:

$$f(x) = \cos(2\pi u_0 x) \quad \text{for } -L \leqslant x \leqslant L$$
$$= 0 \quad \quad \quad \text{for } |x| > L.$$

5. a) Determine the continuous Fourier transform of the function shown below

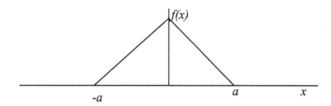

b) Now use the above result and the convolution theorem to determine the continuous Fourier transform of the function shown below.

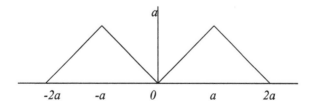

6.

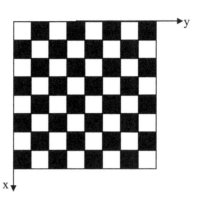

a) An image of a chessboard is shown above. Write down an expression $f(x, y)$ that describes the variation in the gray levels of the image (the origin is at the pixel in the top-left corner, according to normal conventions, and each square corresponds to one pixel). Take the black squares to have a gray level of 0 and the white squares to have a gray level of 1.

b) Calculate the DFT of this image using the expression you have given for $f(x,y)$. Which of the Fourier components are nonzero and what are their magnitudes?

Hint: Look for the smallest repeating unit of the image. The chessboard can be viewed as the convolution of the repeating pattern and a set of appropriately placed impulse functions.

7. A 1-D binary image has N pixels, where N is an even number.
   a) Calculate the DFT of the image if the pixels values $f(x)$ are given by

   $$f(x) = 1 \text{ for all even values of x(i.e., } x = 0, 2, 4, \ldots N - 2)$$
   $$f(x) = 0 \text{ for all odd values of x(i.e., } x = 1, 3, 5, \ldots N - 1).$$

   b) For which values of u is $F(u)$ nonzero? What is the value of $F(u)$ corresponding to these values of u?

8.   a) Let $f(x)$ represent the gray levels of an 8-bit 1-D image that has N pixels. Let $g(x)$ represent the negative of $f(x)$. If $F(u)$ and $G(u)$ are the DFTs of $f(x)$ and $g(x)$, respectively, then derive the relation connecting $F(u)$ and $G(u)$.
   b) What is $G(0)$ equal to?

9. The action of a filter $h(x)$, on any 1-D image, is such that it leaves the even-numbered pixels (pixels are numbered from 1 to N) unchanged, while setting the odd-numbered pixels to zero.
   a) Write down an expression for $h(x)$.
   b) Obtain the representation of this filter in the Fourier domain by using the DFT.
   c) Would you classify this filter as a low-pass or a high-pass filter? Why?

10. Two different digital images have identical histograms. Will they have the same Fourier spectrum? Will any of the Fourier components necessarily have to be equal? Explain.

11.

0	0	6	6	0	0
0	0	6	6	0	0
0	0	6	6	0	0
0	0	6	6	0	0
0	0	6	6	0	0

The figure given above shows a 5×6 digital image. Compute the DFT of the image.

The origin is at the top-left corner of the image. The x coordinate of each pixel runs from 0 to 4 and the y coordinate runs from 0 to 5. Display the magnitude of the Fourier transform as an image, and give the phase of each Fourier component.

Programming assignments:

1. Write a program that will create the image of a chessboard and check your results for exercise 6 above. Use the inbuilt function that calculates the FFT of the image or write your own program for computing the DFT.
2. Write a program that will apply an ideal low-pass filter on the DFT of an input image. The program should compute the inverse DFT after applying the filter.
3. Write a program that will apply an ideal high-pass filter on the DFT of an input image. The program should compute the inverse DFT after applying the filter.
4. Write a program that will apply a Butterworth high-pass filter on the DFT of an input image. The program should compute the inverse DFT after applying the filter. Check the results for filters of various orders (see equation (3.61)).

IOP Publishing

A Course on Digital Image Processing with MATLAB®

P K Thiruvikraman

Chapter 4

Image compression

4.1 Basics of image compression

In this digital age, all of us are used to handling digital images. When these digital images are stored on your computer, you might have noticed that they have different file extensions, like .jpg, .bmp, .tif, and .pdf. What do these different extensions mean? Have you noticed that the same image has different file sizes when stored in different formats?

Look at the following image[1] (figure 4.1), which was created in MS Paint.

This image has $585 \times 342 = 200\,070$ pixels and occupies a space of 600 kilobytes on my hard disk. The same image can be saved as a .jpg file, but the size is just 23.4 kilobytes (figure 4.2)!

Are you able to notice any difference between the two images? Then why is there such a huge difference in the size of the files?

The answer is that the .bmp file just stores the raw data, i.e., the gray levels of each pixel, or, in the case of a color image, store three numbers (corresponding to the levels of the three primary colors) for every pixel. Hence, the size of the file can be easily calculated from the number of pixels in the image. However, in the case of a .jpg file, the data is stored in a compressed format and hence the size of the file is much less than what one would expect from the number of pixels in the image. When you try to open the file, a program running in your computer 'decompresses' the file and displays it on your monitor.

The different file extensions mentioned earlier, i.e., .jpg, .tif, .pdf, etc. all correspond to compressed formats and use various compression schemes, which we will be discussing shortly.

Many of these compression schemes use multiple algorithms for achieving compression.

---

[1] This image was created by my son, when he was six years old. I sincerely thank him for his contribution.

Figure 4.1. A 585 × 342 image created in MS Paint and stored as a .bmp file.

Figure 4.2. The image in figure 4.1, stored in .jpg format.

Compression algorithms can be broadly classified into 'lossless' and 'lossy'. To begin with, we will be mostly discussing lossless algorithms, postponing the discussion of lossy compression algorithms to a later stage.

Compression is essentially achieved by reducing the amount of redundancy in a message (or an image). Redundancies can be classified into the following categories:

 (i) Coding redundancy;
 (ii) Interpixel redundancy;
 (iii) Psycho-visual redundancy.

We will first look at coding redundancy. This naturally brings us into the realm of coding theory.

4.2 Basics of coding theory

In order to properly understand the various schemes used for data compression, one needs to first understand the foundations of information theory, which were laid out by Shannon's seminal paper[2].

Before we study Shannon's theorem, let us first try to clarify a few terms that are used in information theory.

As was said earlier, *data* is distinct from *information*. While *data* refers to the actual symbols that appear in a message or file, *information* refers to the abstract 'idea' that the message is supposed to convey. Hence, while data may change with a change in language (or the code that is used), the amount and nature of information is not supposed to change (for the case of lossless compression).

The length of a message may vary depending on the language (i.e., code) used; the information, which is to be conveyed, does not. Hence, while it is easy to quantify the total amount of data in a message (or a file stored on a computer), it is difficult to quantify information, which is a subtler beast.

From the foregoing discussion, it is apparent that to compress the total amount of information to be conveyed or stored, one has to look for a suitable language (i.e., code). The word 'language', has, until now, been used interchangeably with the word 'code' so that the word 'code' is understood in a proper sense. In normal everyday English, a 'coded' message implies secrecy, while in coding theory it simply means a rule or algorithm that is used for compression, error correction/detection, or cryptography. Only in the case of cryptography is there any secrecy involved.

Since we need to understand 'codes' before we can talk of compression, let us start with a few everyday examples of codes without regard to their ability to 'compress' a message.

4.3 Uniquely decodable codes (UDCs), instantaneously decodable codes (IDCs), and all that

Mathematically, a *code* is a rule (i.e., algorithm) that assigns a codeword to every *source symbol*. The source symbols could be (for example) the characters of the English language while the codewords are written using *code alphabets* that could be characters or numbers. In this digital age, one is tempted to immediately think of 1 and 0 as the code alphabets. A code that uses 1 and 0 as the only code alphabets is known as a *binary code*. A code that uses 0, 1, and 2 as code alphabets would be a ternary code, while a code using 0, 1, 2, and 3 would be a quaternary code. In general, if the alphabets are 0, 1, 2....$q - 1$, it is known as a q-ary code.

Therefore, a code is a mapping or transformation from a set of source symbols to a set of codewords. The process of applying the rule is called encoding, and the output of this process would be an encoded message. The reverse process of getting the original message from the encoded message is called decoding.

---

[2] This paper, which was published in 1948, is available at http://math.harvard.edu/~ctm/home/text/others/shannon/entropy/entropy.pdf.

Codes can be broadly classified into *block codes* (where all codewords have the same length) and *variable length codes* (where codewords may be of different lengths).

The recipient of an encoded message would obviously like the received message to be uniquely decodable. While block codes are always uniquely decodable if the mapping between source symbols and codewords is one-to-one, variable length codes can suffer from ambiguous decoding! We give below an example of a variable length code that is not uniquely decodable.

Suppose a part of the message to be conveyed is BD. This would be encoded by the sender as 101, and the recipient would have two ways of interpreting the received message. They might interpret 101 as BD or as C. While there are ways of overcoming this ambiguity (by conveying to the recipient the number of characters in the message or by introducing a character that signifies the end of a codeword), such schemes are not considered since it means that the code is not self-contained. Furthermore, in most of the codes we consider, we do not use an end-of-codeword character since it spoils the efficiency of compression of the code.

Codes that can be unambiguously or uniquely decoded are known as UDCs.

It is interesting to note that we do use codes in daily life (especially for the purpose of compression). These are nothing but abbreviations. In using abbreviations, the rule is usually to use the first letter (or sometimes first part) of a word as the codeword. Some common abbreviations are UNO (United Nations Organization), USA (United States of America), and TV (television). The advantage of the first-letter rule used in abbreviations is that a *look-up table* is not necessary (unlike in the case of the code in table 4.1). However, a moment's thought will confirm that abbreviations are an example of a code that is not a UDC: WWF might be decoded as World Wildlife Fund or as World Wrestling Federation! Similarly, NBA may stand for the National Basketball Association, National Board of Accreditation, or Narmada Bachao Andolan.

In coding theory, simple rules (like in abbreviations) for encoding are the exception rather than the rule. Hence, for most codes, it is necessary for the sender to send the look-up table along with the encoded message so that the recipient of the message can decode it. Of course, the look-up table is not sent if it is a cryptic (secret) code.

While we would like all our codes to be UDCs, we would also like them to be instantaneously decodable, i.e., each codeword should be recognized and decoded as soon as it is received. In order to clarify the meaning of an IDC, we give (in table 4.2) an example of a variable length code that is not an IDC.

Table 4.1. Example of a variable length code that is not an IDC

Source symbol	Codeword
A	0
B	10
C	101
D	1

If at some stage of receiving a message we come across a 0, we would not be sure if it is to be decoded as B, or whether it will turn out to be the first part of a C or D! Hence, we cannot decode a symbol as soon as we receive it. However, in the above example, we can decode the entire message if we wait until we receive the entire message. If we receive a string of 0s, we can count the number of 0s preceding a 1; if we see that the number of 0s between two 1s is a multiple of 3 (say 27), then we can decode that part of the message as corresponding to 9 Ds. We can similarly decode the received message correctly if the number of 0s is of the form $3n + 1$ or $3n + 2$ (which covers all possibilities).

Therefore, the code given in table 4.2 is an example of a code that is an UDC but not an IDC. In fact, we can conclude on the basis of the codes given above (and a little reflection) that IDCs form a subset of UDCs. In the language of Venn diagrams:

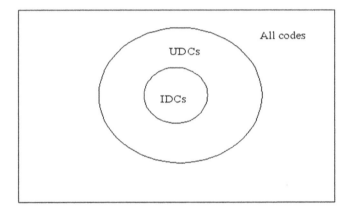

That is, all IDCs are UDCs, but all UDCs are not IDCs.

We notice that the code given in table 4.2 fails to be an IDC because it fails to satisfy the no-prefix condition, i.e., the codeword for B is 0, which is also the first part (prefix) of the codeword for C and D. Similarly, the codeword for C forms a prefix of the codeword for D. Therefore, the no-prefix condition has to be satisfied for a given code to be an IDC. This condition can be used to check whether a given code is an IDC. No such simple condition exists for testing whether a given code is an UDC.

While the no-prefix condition acts as a sure-fire test to check whether a given code is an IDC, we would like to have something that guides us in the construction of instantaneous codes.

Table 4.2. Example of a code which is a UDC, but not an IDC

Source symbol	Codeword
A	1
B	00
C	000
D	0000

We now present an inequality known as *Kraft's inequality*, which tells us whether it is possible to construct a code to a given set of specifications (which are in terms of the lengths of the codewords).

4.4 Kraft's inequality

Let l_1, l_2, l_3, ... l_n be the lengths of n different codewords that are part of a code. Let $l_1 < l_2 < l_3 ....l_n$.

We can arbitrarily choose the first codeword of length l_1. We choose one of the possible 2^{l_1} codewords. However, when we choose the second codeword of length l_2, we have to avoid words that have a length l_1 as a prefix. Therefore, we are left with only $2^{l_2-l_1}$ possibilities for choosing the second word (out of the total number of 2^{l_2} possible words of length l_2). Now since we should be left with at least one word of length l_2, we impose the condition that

$$2^{l_2} \geqslant 2^{l_2-l_1} + 1. \tag{4.1}$$

It should be noted that while Kraft's inequality tells us whether it is possible to construct an instantaneous code for a given length of codewords, it cannot be used to test whether a given code is an IDC. Only the no-prefix condition can be used for this purpose. It is seen that the code in table 4.2 satisfies Kraft's inequality but violates the no-prefix condition. Hence, it is not an IDC. The fact that the code in table 4.2 satisfies Kraft's inequality tells us that there is an IDC with the same length of codewords. We give in table 4.3 a code that has the same length as the code in table 4.2, but which is also an IDC.

It is seen that the code in table 4.3 satisfies the Kraft's inequality as well as the no-prefix condition. Therefore, we can say that all IDCs satisfy Kraft's inequality, but all codes that satisfy Kraft's inequality are not IDCs.

The efficiency of the code in table 4.3 can be easily improved. Consider the code given in table 4.4.

This code is considered to be more efficient than that given in table 4.3 since the codeword for D has a smaller number of code alphabets. The efficiency of a code is also an important criterion in addition to its being an IDC. We deal with the efficiency of codes in the next section. In particular, we give the algorithm for the construction of an optimum instantaneous (Huffman) code.

Table 4.3. Example of a code which is an IDC. The codewords have the same length as the corresponding words of the code given in table 4.2

Source symbol	Codeword
A	1
B	00
C	010
D	0110

Table 4.4. A more efficient version of the code given in table 4.3.

Source symbol	Codeword
A	1
B	00
C	010
D	011

4.5 Efficiency of instantaneous codes

Many algorithms that are designed to construct instantaneous codes assume that we have knowledge of the probability (frequency) of occurrence of the various source symbols. These source symbols are produced by an information source: imagine a person sitting in front of a computer and tirelessly punching away on the keyboard and producing this book. Such a person is an example of an information source. At the moment, we also assume for simplicity, and that the source does not have memory: the person randomly presses one key after another without remembering what they pressed previously. Hopefully this not true of the person writing this book!

If we have access to all the symbols produced by a source, then we can easily estimate the source probabilities. If n_i is the number of occurrences of the ith source symbol, then the probability of its occurrence (p_i) is simply n_i/N, where N is the total number of symbols produced by the source.

We judge the efficiency of a code by calculating the average length of the codewords. If there are a total of m source symbols in the code, then the average is easily calculated in the following manner:

$$l_{\text{ave}} = \sum_{i=1}^{m} l_i p_i, \qquad (4.2)$$

where the p_is have already been calculated using the formula given previously. A code is supposed to be more efficient than another if it has a lower value of l_{ave}. It is quite apparent that variable length codes are to be used if we are to have a low value of l_{ave}. This we achieve by assigning shorter-length codewords to more frequently occurring source symbols (which determine the value of l_{ave} to a greater extent than source symbols that are infrequent).

As an example, consider a source that produces the source symbols A, B, C, and D with the probabilities given below.

Source symbol	Probability	Codeword
A	0.4	1
B	0.3	00
C	0.2	010
D	0.1	011

If the codewords are assigned as shown above, then l_{ave} will turn out to be

$$l_{ave} = 1 \times 0.4 + 0.3 \times 2 + 0.2 \times 3 + 0.1 \times 3 = 1.9.$$

If we had used a block (binary) code, l_{ave} would have been 2. The codewords would have been 00, 01, 10, and 11, each of length 2.

We have managed to reduce l_{ave} from 2 to 1.9 by using a variable length code in place of a block code. But how do we know that there does not exist another instantaneous code with a value of l_{ave} lower than 1.9? Before we get into specific schemes for the construction of instantaneous codes, we should investigate the limits to which we can compress. Is there a lower limit to the value of l_{ave} that one can achieve?

4.6 Information theory

We have an intuitive feeling that there should be a lower limit to l_{ave}. After all, a large amount of information cannot come out of a small amount of data.

In fact, it is the 'amount' of information in a message that sets a lower limit on l_{ave}. Another useful quantity when talking about the efficiency of codes is the compression ratio C, which is defined as

$$C = \frac{\text{Number of bits in the original message}}{\text{Number of bits in the compressed message}}. \tag{4.3}$$

Since we feel that it is the amount of information that sets a lower bound on l_{ave}, we need to quantify information in order to compare it with l_{ave}.

While the amount of information associated with an event (the event in our case could be the emission of a symbol by the source) may appear to be a subjective matter, it can be seen to be related to the probability of the event.

In fact, the higher the probability of the occurrence of an event, the lower the information content of the message that says that the event has occurred. If for example, a message says that the Sun has risen in the east on a particular day, the message would be considered to be redundant (i.e., the amount of new information conveyed by it is very low).

In the language of a journalist, 'Dog bites man' is not news, but 'man bites dog' is!

Hence, the information content of an event (and the associated message) is intimately connected with the probability of occurrence of that event. In fact, the information content seems to reduce if the probability is higher, and vice versa.

We would now like to have a mathematical relation between the probability of an event ($P(E)$) and its information content ($I(E)$). In light of the statements made until now, what functional form would the relation take? Your first guess for the functional form of $I(E)$ might be

$$I(E) = \frac{1}{P(E)}.$$

Or this:

$$I(E) = 1 - P(E).$$

Both of these functional forms seem to satisfy the criterion that increasing probability implies decreasing information content. However, $I(E)$ has to satisfy one more criterion, which is that information content is additive, i.e., the information about an event can be conveyed in pieces and the sum of the information content of the pieces should be equal to the information content of the entire event. Let us give an example to convey the meaning of this statement.

Suppose we toss a coin twice. The result of these two throws may be conveyed at once or in two installments (where we convey the result of each throw separately). Let E_1 and E_2 denote the two throws. Then we know that

$$I(E) = I(E_1) + I(E_2)$$

and

$$P(E) = P(E_1)P(E_2).$$

If we have to satisfy both these conditions, i.e., the additive nature of information and the multiplicative nature of the probability of independent events, then we can define information content as

$$I(E) = -\log(P(E)). \tag{4.4}$$

This definition also satisfies the condition that the entropy decreases with increasing probability.

The base of the logarithm can be chosen according to our convenience, and the units for $I(E)$ will change accordingly. If the base of the logarithm is chosen to be 2, then $I(E)$ will be in bits; meanwhile, if the base is 10, then $I(E)$ will be in digits.

To get an intuitive appreciation for the correctness of this definition, consider a source that spews out meaningful English words. Let 'q' be the letter that is spewed out by this source at a given instant of time. From our knowledge of the English language, we know that the probability that the next letter would be 'u' is 1 (all words that contain q also have u as the next letter; for example, queen, aquarium, acquitted, etc). Let the event E be the appearance of 'qu', while the event E_1 can be the appearance of q and E_2 be the appearance of u. Now according to the laws of probability (Bayes' theorem),

$$P(E) = P(E_1)P(E_2|E_1). \tag{4.5}$$

Here, $P(E_2|E_1)$, is the conditional probability for the occurrence of E_2, given that E_1 has already occurred.

Now $P(E_2|E_1) = 1$, since u follows q with probability 1; therefore,

$$\begin{aligned}
I(E) &= -\log(P(E)) = -\log(P(E_1)P(E_2|E_1)) \\
&= -\log(P(E_1)) - \log(P(E_2|E_1)) \\
&= -\log(P(E_1)).
\end{aligned}$$

In other words, no new information is conveyed to the recipient of a message by informing them about the occurrence of u since they were already sure of its occurrence.

If a source emits many symbols, each having a different probability, then the information gained by receiving each of these symbols would vary depending on the probability of the symbol. In such a situation, one might want to calculate the average amount of information per source symbol.

The average amount of information for a source emitting n symbols is given by

$$H(S) = -\sum_{i=1}^{n} p_i \log p_i . \tag{4.6}$$

The average information per symbol, denoted by $H(S)$, is also known as the entropy of the source. The concept of entropy is borrowed from statistical physics, where the entropy of a system is a measure of the information required to completely specify the configuration of a system. The more random or disordered the configuration of a system, the greater the entropy will be since we would need to provide more information to specify it completely. Conversely, a highly ordered system can be specified completely by providing a very small amount of information. These ideas about entropy may be compared with our definition of $H(S)$ to see the close connection between the definitions of entropy as existing in statistical physics and information theory.

Example 4.1 What is the average information contained in a throw of an unbiased die?

Answer: An unbiased die has its faces numbered from 1 to 6, and each number has a probability equal to 1/6. Therefore, plugging in this value in equation (4.6) yields

$$H(S) = -\log_2(1/6) = 2.585 \text{ bits}.$$

Example 4.2 A pair of dice is rolled. What is the average information content per throw if the sum of the two numbers is conveyed?

Answer: Each throw generates a pair of numbers, e.g. (1,1),(2,1) ... (6,6).

Hence, each number is not equally probable. The total number of pairs of numbers (events) is 36. However, in many cases the sum of the two numbers may be the same. For example, the pairs (2,1) and (1,2) both lead to the sum 3. Hence, the probability of obtaining 3 as the sum is 2/36 = 1/18.

We give below the probability for obtaining all possible sums.

$$H(S) = \frac{2}{36} \log_2 36 + \frac{4}{36} \log_2 \frac{36}{2} + \frac{6}{36} \log_2 \frac{36}{3} + \frac{8}{36} \log_2 \frac{36}{4}$$
$$+ \frac{10}{36} \log_2 \frac{36}{5} + \frac{6}{36} \log_2 \frac{36}{6} = 3.7052 \text{ bits}$$

Sum	Pairs	Probability
2	(1,1)	1/36
3	(1,2),(2,1)	2/36
4	(2,2),(3,1),(1,3)	3/36
5	(2,3),(3,2),(1,4),(4,1)	4/36
6	(3,3),(5,1),(1,5),(4,2),(4,2)	5/36
7	(6,1),(6,1),(4,3),(3,4),(2,5),(5,2)	6/36
8	(6,2),(2,6),(3,5),(5,3),(4,4)	5/36
9	(6,3),(3,6),(4,5),(5,4)	4/36
10	(6,4),(4,6),(5,5)	3/36
11	(6,5),(5,6),	2/36
12	(6,6)	1/36

How much information is left to be conveyed? We are only conveying the sum of the two numbers, but not the numbers on each die. If the number on each die is also conveyed, then there are 36 events, each of which is equally probable.

$$H'(S) = \log_2 36 = 5.1699 \text{ bits}$$

It will be proved later that the entropy sets the lower bound for the l_{ave} for a code, i.e.,

$$H(S) \leq l_{ave}.$$

This is a very powerful result since it sets an upper bound for the efficiency of a code, i.e., however hard one may try, it is impossible to design a code such that the average length of the codewords constructed in the code is smaller than the value of $H(S)$.

In order to prove this result, one has to investigate $H(S)$ in detail and figure out the upper and lower bounds for this quantity.

The lowest possible value of $H(S)$ occurs when any one of the symbols has a probability of 1 (and hence all others have a probability of 0). In this case, $H(S) = \log 1 = 0$. Here we have used the fact that $0 \log (0) = 0$.

Since the minimum value of $H(S)$ occurs when only one of the symbols has a nonzero probability and the probability distribution is very uneven, the maximum value should occur when all the symbols have equal probabilities. Since there are n source symbols, the probability of each symbol would be $1/n$ in such a situation (since the sum of the probabilities of all the symbols has to be 1).

Hence, in such a situation, $H(S) = -\log \dfrac{1}{n} = \log n$.

We start our proof that $\log n$ is the maximum value of $H(S)$ with the apparently unrelated observation that $\log_e x \leq x - 1$ for all values of x. We give a graphical proof of this statement in figure 4.3.

Note that the statement $\log x \leq x - 1$ for all values of x is not valid for any arbitrary base of the logarithm.

We now compute the difference between $H(S)$ and $\log n$ in order to show that the latter is the maximum possible value of $H(S)$.

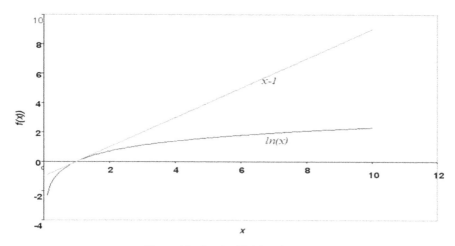

Figure 4.3. Graph of $\ln(x)$ and $x - 1$.

$$H(S) - \log n = \sum_{i=1}^{n} p_i \log_2 \frac{1}{p_i} - \sum_{i=1}^{n} p_i \log_2 n \quad \left(\because \sum_{i=1}^{n} p_i = 1 \right)$$

$$= \frac{1}{\ln 2} \sum_{i=1}^{n} p_i \left(\ln \frac{1}{p_i n} - \ln n \right)$$

Here we have changed the base of the logarithm from 2 to e.

$$= \frac{1}{\ln 2} \sum_{i=1}^{n} p_i \left(\ln \frac{1}{p_i n} \right)$$

$$\leqslant \frac{1}{\ln 2} \left(\sum_{i=1}^{n} \frac{1}{n} - \sum_{i=1}^{n} p_i \right) = 0 \text{ using the fact that } \log_e x \leqslant x - 1, \text{ and}$$

$$H(S) - \log n \leqslant 0.$$

We now prove a very important theorem.

Theorem 4.1: Every binary instantaneous code of a source S has the average length larger or equal to the entropy of S (in bits), i.e.,

$$l_{\text{ave}} \geqslant H(S).$$

We start the proof of this theorem from our definition for the average length of a code,

$$l_{\text{ave}} = \sum_{i=1}^{n} l_i p_i. \tag{4.7}$$

This can be rewritten as

$$l_{\text{ave}} = \sum_{i=1}^{n} p_i \log_2 2^{l_i}.$$

We compute the difference $H(S) - l_{\text{ave}}$:

$$H(S) - l_{\text{ave}} = \sum_{i=1}^{n} p_i \log_2 \frac{1}{p_i} - \sum_{i=1}^{n} p_i \log_2 2^{l_i}$$

$$H(S) - l_{\text{ave}} = \sum_{i=1}^{n} p_i \log_2 \left(\frac{1}{2^{l_i} p_i} \right).$$

(4.8)

Using the inequality $\log_e x \leqslant x - 1$, we have

$$H(S) - l_{\text{ave}} \leqslant \frac{1}{\ln 2} \sum_{i=1}^{n} p_i \left(\frac{1}{2^{l_i} p_i} - 1 \right) = \frac{1}{\ln 2} \sum_{i=1}^{n} \left(\frac{1}{2^{l_i}} - 1 \right) \leqslant 0$$

(4.9)

(by Kraft's inequality).

Hence, we conclude that

$$H(S) - l_{\text{ave}} \leqslant 0.$$

(4.10)

Therefore, the entropy sets the lower bound for the average length of codewords, and therefore, the amount of compression we can achieve by removing coding redundancy.

So does the result proved above set the *ultimate* lower bound on the amount of compression we can achieve?

Not quite. We can compress further by exploiting the correlations between successive symbols. Looked at another way, the definition of $H(S)$ that we have been using until now does not take into account correlations between successive source symbols.

We give an example to drive home this point. Consider a source that randomly emits the symbols '0' and '1' with equal probability. The entropy of this source would be $\log_2 2 = 1$ bit/source symbol. Consider another source that emits '0' for the first half of the data stream and '1' for the second half. The data stream for the first source would look like this:

00010110101...

It has no obvious pattern. Meanwhile, the data stream for the second source would look like this:

000000111111.

We intuitively feel that the first source contains more information (since it is more unpredictable). However, the entropy of both sources would be 1 bit per source symbol. This is because our definition of entropy looks only at the frequency of occurrence of the source symbols and does not take into account correlations between source symbols. The correlations between adjacent pixels do not affect the value of $H(S)$.

We give below two images that convey this concept in a more forceful manner. Figures 4.4 and 4.5 show two binary images. In both the cases, the frequencies of the black/white pixels are the same, and thus they will have the same value of $H(S)$. However, we intuitively feel that figure 4.4 is more 'disordered' or random than figure 4.5. This difference will be explained if we look at their higher-order entropies. The concept of higher-order entropy is discussed in the following pages.

Figure 4.4. An image in which half of the pixels are black/white, but in a random manner.

Figure 4.5. An image in which exactly half the pixels are black and the other half are white, but in an ordered manner.

These correlations would be taken into account if we look at the frequency of occurrence of pairs of source symbols (called digraphs). The corresponding entropy is called the second-order entropy, $H(S^2)$.

$H(S^2)$ is defined similar to $H(S)$:

$$H(S^2) = -\sum_{i=1}^{n^2} p_i \log p_i. \tag{4.11}$$

Here, p_i is the probability or frequency of occurrence of the ith source symbol. Since there are n source symbols, there will be n^2 pairs of source symbols. These n^2 source symbols are considered to be the second extension of the source S. In general, we can talk about the kth extension of the source (consisting of n^k symbols) and calculate the corresponding entropy $H(S^k)$.

For a memory-less source, i.e., a source where there is no correlation between successive pixels, there is a definite relation between $H(S)$ and $H(S^k)$. We prove this relation for the second extension of the source.

From the definition of $H(S^2)$, we can write

$$H(S^2) = -\sum_{l=1}^{n^2} p_l \log p_l = -\sum_{i=1}^{n}\sum_{j=1}^{n} p_j p_i \log p_i p_j. \tag{4.12}$$

For a zero-memory source, the probability of the occurrence of a pair of source symbols will be equal to the product of their probabilities (since the emission of each source symbol is an independent event).

Using the property of logarithms, this can be written as

$$H(S^2) = -\sum_{i=1}^{n}\sum_{j=1}^{n} p_j p_i \log p_l - \sum_{i=1}^{n}\sum_{j=1}^{n} p_j p_i \log p_j = 2H(S). \tag{4.13}$$

Here we have used the fact that

$$\sum_{i=1}^{n} P_i = 1.$$

Similarly, it can be proved that

$$H(S^k) = kH(S) \tag{4.14}$$

for a zero-memory source. In case the source has memory, i.e., each symbol has some relation with the previous symbol, the entropy will obviously be reduced.

Therefore, for a source with memory,

$$H(S^k) < kH(S). \tag{4.15}$$

Therefore, in general,

$$H(S^k) \leqslant kH(S). \tag{4.16}$$

The ideas of information theory have been extensively used both in the study of languages and as a tool to decode or 'break' secret codes. Shannon, the pioneer in information theory, computed the entropy of the English language.

The first-order entropy of a language can be computed based on equation (4.6). To compute the first-order entropy, we need to determine the frequency of occurrence of the source symbols, i.e., alphabet letters. While the frequencies of the letters may vary from one page of text to another, in general it has been found that the letter 'e' is the most frequent in the English language. The frequencies of the letters typically follow the distribution given in figure 4.6.

Using the distribution of frequencies given in figure 4.6, we arrive at a value of 4.14 bits/letter for the entropy of the English language. We can estimate the second-order entropy of the English language by considering the frequency of bigrams (the combination of two alphabet letters). The second-order entropy of English (defined as $H(S^2)/2$) turns out to be close to 3.56. The second-order entropy is less than the first-order entropy because out of the 26×26 possible bigrams, some (like 'in' or 'it') are more frequent than others (like 'xy' or 'xz').

Proceeding on similar lines, we can compute higher-order entropies and finally define the entropy of a language as follows:

$$H_L = \lim_{n \to \infty} \frac{H(X^n)}{n}.$$

It is interesting to note that the determination of the frequency of alphabet letters, which was mentioned above in connection with the entropy of the language, also plays a role in cracking secret codes. A complete discussion of the methods of cryptography is beyond the scope of this book, but we mention briefly the connection it has with frequency analysis.

Secret codes are created by mapping the letters in a message to some other letters using a key so that a person who does not have the key will not be able to interpret the encoded message even if they intercept it. Simple cryptographic methods use a one-to-one mapping from the letters in the message to the letters in the cipher text.

For example, 'Coming tomorrow' becomes 'frdplq wrdruurz'. Here, each of the letters in 'Coming tomorrow' has been replaced by the third letter following it in the natural order of the alphabet. Of course, straightforward frequency analysis will not yield correct results for such a short message. For longer messages, the frequencies are expected to follow the distribution given in figure 4.6. If the frequencies of occurrence of the original text are as given in figure 4.6, then the most frequent letter in the cipher text can be assumed to be 'e'. Other letters can be decoded in a similar manner.

As pointed out in the preceding paragraph, frequency analysis works only if we have a large enough sample (a large passage of text). Sometimes it may happen that even a large passage may have a distribution that is very different from that given in figure 4.6. A famous example of such an exception is the novel *Gadsby* by Ernest Vincent Wright, in which the letter 'e' does not appear even once!

If the frequencies of letters in a message do not follow the typical distribution, then more ingenuity is required to decipher such a secret message. A famous example of that occurs in the short story 'The adventure of the dancing men', where letters are replaced by small pictures (see figure 4.7).

Apart from cryptography, frequency analysis has also been used to decipher ancient scripts and languages. For example, recent studies on the script used by the

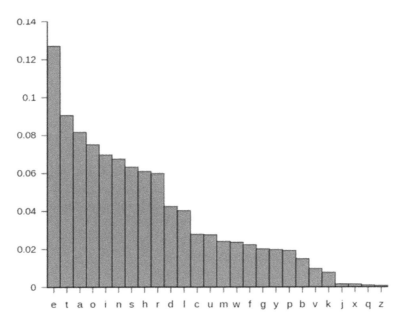

Figure 4.6. Typical frequency of occurrence of different English alphabets.

Figure 4.7. Figure taken from 'The adventure of the dancing men' by Sir Arthur Conan Doyle (source: Wikipedia).

Indus valley civilization have looked at the entropy of the symbols to show that it is close to other languages[3].

An exhaustive and entertaining history of cryptography and frequency analysis has been presented in *The Code Book* by Simon Singh.

4.7 Huffman coding: algorithm

We now discuss the procedure for obtaining the most optimum code for a given source. An optimal code known as the Huffman code has the least possible value for l_{ave} for an instantaneous code. In constructing the Huffman code, we assume that we have the information about the probability of occurrence of all the source symbols. Hence, before starting the construction of the Huffman code, one should obtain the probabilities $P(a_i)$ for all source symbols a_i.

If there are only two source symbols, then the code assignment is very simple. We allot '0' to one symbol, and '1' to the other.

---

[3] A recent paper gives more details about this: Rao R P N *et al* 2009 Entropic evidence for linguistic structure in the Indus *Science* **324** (DOI: 10.1126/science.1170391) 1165.

A source with three symbols, a_1, a_2, and a_3, of which a_1 is the most probable, can be reduced to the case of two symbols, a_1 and $a_{2,3}$, where $P(a_{2,3}) = P(a_2) + P(a_3)$. We find a Huffman code for the reduced source.

a_1	0
$a_{2,3}$	1

Then, we 'split' the codeword 1 into two words 10 and 11, thus obtaining a Huffman code for the original source.

a_1	0
a_2	10
a_3	11

For the general case of n symbols, we arrange the symbols in descending order of probabilities. We perform a 'source reduction' by combining the probabilities of the last two symbols in the list (which have the least probability). We then repeat this procedure of source reduction by combining the probabilities of the last two symbols in the list (always taking care to maintain the symbols in descending order of probabilities), until we arrive at two source symbols. Next, we assign '0' to one compound symbol and '1' to the other, and then repeatedly split the codewords until we get the original source symbols.

Therefore, for n source symbols, one would have to do $n - 2$ source reductions.

We now illustrate this procedure with an example:

The second column in the table given below displays the probabilities for a given set of source symbols. The succeeding columns show the process of source reduction.

Symbol	Probability	Probability of reduced sources			
A	0.4	0.4	0.4	0.4	0.6
B	0.3	0.3	0.3	0.3	0.4
C	0.1	0.1	0.2	0.3	
D	0.1	0.1	0.1		
E	0.05	0.1			
F	0.05				

The process of assigning the code is shown below.

0.6	0	0.4	1	0.4	1	0.4	1	0.4	1
0.4	1	0.3	00	0.3	00	0.3	00	0.3	00
		0.3	01	0.2	010	0.1	011	0.1	011
				0.1	011	0.1	0100	0.1	0100
						0.1	0101	0.05	01010
								0.05	01011

In the above table, the entries in the odd-numbered columns are the probabilities at each stage of source reduction, and the entries in the even-numbered columns are the codewords at those stages.

Notice that at each stage of source reduction, the probabilities have to be re-arranged in descending order.

Before discussing the details related to the implementation of this coding procedure, let us discuss the compression achieved in the above example.

The average length of a codeword in the above example would be

$$l_{ave} = 0.4 \times 1 + 0.3 \times 2 + 0.1 \times 3 + 0.1 \times 4 + 0.05 \times 5 + 0.05 \times 5 = 2.2 \text{ bits.}$$

If we had used fixed length coding, we would have to use 3 bits per source symbol (since there are 6 source symbols).

$$\text{Therefore compression ratio } = 3/2.2 = 1.36.$$

In this case, the entropy of the source is $H(S) = 2.1464$ bits/source symbol.

We have been able to come pretty close to the limit set by entropy, but is there any source for which the l_{ave} for a Huffman code is equal to the entropy of the source?

We get a clue if we look back at our proof for theorem 4.1. From equation (4.8), we see that if the probabilities of the source symbols are the inverse powers of 2, then $H(S)$ would become equal to l_{ave}.

For example, if the probabilities of the symbols emitted by a source are 0.5, 0.25, 0.125, and 0.125,

$$H(S) = (1/2)\log_2 2 + (1/4)\log_2(4) + (1/8)\log_2(8) + (1/8)\log_2 8$$
$$= 1 + 3/8 + 3/8$$
$$= 1.75 \text{ bits/source symbol.}$$

The Huffman codewords for such a source would be 0, 10, 110, and 111, and

$$l_{ave} = 1 \times 0.5 + 2 \times 0.25 + 3 \times 0.125 + 3 \times 0.125 = 1.75 \text{ bits.}$$

The other case when $H(S) = l_{ave}$ is when all symbols are equiprobable. In such a situation the compression ratio for a Huffman code is equal to 1. That is, no compression is achieved. In fact, in this case, l_{ave} for a Huffman code is the same as the word length for a block code.

4.8 Huffman coding: implementation

Although the algorithm for the Huffman coding is simple to understand, it requires enormous computation. We will now devote some time to discuss this important issue. The Huffman coding algorithm involves two main operations: source reduction and sorting. In fact, both these operations have to be repeated $n - 2$ times as mentioned earlier.

There are many algorithms available for sorting. The simplest algorithm to understand and implement is Bubble Sort. However, this algorithm is highly inefficient. A simple MATLAB® code for implementing sorting is given below.

```
For i = 1:n,
For j = i + 1:n,
If P(i) < P(j)
Temp = P(i);
P(i) = P(j);
P(j) = Temp;
End
End
End
```

Here, P is an array that contains the probabilities of the n source symbols.

This is a variation of the normal Bubble Sort algorithm. When $i = 1$, the inner loop will run $n - 1$ times. When $i = 2$, it will run $n - 2$ times, and so on. Therefore, the total number of comparison operations (where we compare $P(i)$ and $P(j)$) is

$$n - 1 + n - 2 + n - 3 + \ldots\ldots 1 = n(n - 1)/2 \sim n^2.$$

Now such a program has to be called repeatedly each time a source reduction is done and the probabilities have to be sorted. Since $n - 2$ source reductions will have to be done before we reduce to two symbols, the total number of comparison operations will be of the order of n^3.

However, we can reduce this number if we realize that we do not have to sort from scratch each time we do a source reduction. After one source reduction, the probabilities are already in descending order, and we have only to 'insert' the sum of the probabilities of the last two source symbols in the correct location. Hence, the sorting for Huffman coding is done more efficiently if we use the 'insertion sort'. Here we use two arrays, say, P and $P1$. We compare the sum of the probabilities of the last two elements (let us call it P_{sum}) with each element of P. If P_{sum} is less than $P(i)$, we assign $P(i)$ to $P1(i)$. For some value of i, P_{sum} will be greater than $P(i)$ and then we assign P_{sum} to $P(i)$. The remaining elements of P would have to be shifted down by one place in $P1$ (to accommodate P_{sum}). Therefore, we assign $P(i)$ to $P1(i + 1)$. A program for implementing the insertion sort is given in chapter 10.

We see that the number of comparison operations is $n - 2$. After one source reduction, it would be $n - 3$, and so on. Therefore, the total number of assignment operations is

$$n - 2 + n - 3 + n - 4 + \ldots\ldots 1 = (n - 1)(n - 2)/2 \sim n^2.$$

The number of comparison operations is now much smaller.

Even when using the insertion sort the Huffman coding scheme is computationally intensive. This is especially true of image compression where the number of source symbols can be large. For example, for an 8-bit image, there are 256 gray levels and $n^2 = 65\,536$. Hence, other schemes that do not achieve the same amount of compression as Huffman coding but require fewer computations are sometimes

Table 4.5. A source with 9 source symbols, where we can use the truncated Huffman code.

Source symbol	Probability
A	0.35
B	0.15
C	0.15
D	0.1
E	0.05
F	0.05
G	0.05
H	0.05
I	0.05

preferred. One such scheme is the truncated Huffman code, where instead of generating a Huffman code for all n source symbols, we club the least probable k symbols and treat it as a symbol with a probability equal to the probability of the k symbols. The Huffman coding algorithm is implemented on the remaining $n - k$ symbols and the compound symbol. The codeword assigned to the compound symbol is used as a prefix and the individual symbols within this group are identified by this prefix concatenated with a suitable block code. Hence, the number of computations required for assigning the codewords is considerably reduced. We now give a numerical example to illustrate the procedure for generating the truncated Huffman code.

Table 4.5 gives the probabilities for a particular source that emits nine different symbols.

We note that there are many symbols with very negligible probability (F–I). Hence, we treat these symbols together as a single compound symbol with a probability equal to the sum of the probabilities of all the symbols from F to I, i.e., 0.20.

Therefore, we now do Huffman coding for the following source consisting of six symbols.

Source symbol	Probability	Huffman codeword
A	0.35	00
FI	0.2	10
B	0.15	010
C	0.15	011
D	0.1	110
E	0.05	111

We now assign the codewords to the symbols F to I by using 10, which is the codeword for the compound symbol FI, as a prefix to the words within this group. Therefore, the final list of codewords for the original source symbols are as below.

Source symbol	Truncated Huffman codeword
A	00
B	010
C	011
D	110
E	111
F	1000
G	1001
H	1010
I	1011

The average length of the codewords for the above example is 2.85 bits per source symbol. Compare this with the entropy of 2.764.

It is left as an exercise to the reader to show that even the full Huffman coding scheme gives almost the same set of codewords and an identical compression ratio. In this particular example, we were lucky enough to get the same compression ratio for a smaller amount of computation (smaller number of source reductions), but in general the compression ratio is less for the truncated Huffman code in comparison to the normal Huffman code. However, in certain cases, the marginal decrease in compression ratio may be worth the considerable reduction in the number of computations. Notice that in the above example, the truncated Huffman code gave a good compression ratio due to a clever choice of the cutoff point for clubbing the symbols, i.e., we had clubbed the last four and not the last five symbols. You might have been tempted to club E along with the symbols, F, G, H, and I, since it has the same probability as these symbols, but then that would have entailed an additional bit in the block code for each of the last five source symbols.

4.9 Nearly optimal codes

The truncated Huffman code is an example of a code that is not the most optimal but its advantage is that it involves less computation than the Huffman code. Other codes that are formulated along the same lines are the B code and the shift code. We present them below by considering an example.

4.9.1 B code

Consider a source with the probability of the source symbols being the same as that given in table 4.5.

In the B code, each codeword is made up of continuation bits, denoted C, and information bits, which are binary numbers. The only purpose of the continuation bits is to separate individual codewords, so they simply toggle between 0 and 1 for

Table 4.6. The source given in table 4.5 with the corresponding B code for each source symbol.

Source symbol	Probability	B_2 code
A	0.35	C00
B	0.15	C01
C	0.15	C10
D	0.1	C11
E	0.05	C00C00
F	0.05	C00C01
G	0.05	C00C10
H	0.05	C00C11
I	0.05	C01C00

each new codeword. The B code shown here (in table 4.6) is called a B_2 code because two information bits are used per continuation bit.

The continuation bit toggles between 0 and 1. By convention we can initially have C as 0. At the start of a new word the value of C toggles from 0 to 1. For example, if the message to be conveyed is AGEBABCABCADCAFHIDAA, then the encoded message will be

$$00010011000000010100010101010000111100001$$
$$11010100000001100111001000111000100.$$

The average word length is 3.75 bits per source symbol, which is much more than what was obtained by the truncated Huffman code. However, we have to remember that the B code is a mixture of a fixed length code and a variable length code, and the use of the continuation bit spoils the compression ratio to a great extent. On the other hand, you can realize that the amount of computation involved in generating the B code is negligible since, unlike the Huffman code, it does not involve sorting of the probabilities.

The B code compares very favorably with the fixed length binary code. Since there are nine source symbols for this source, we would have required 4 bits per symbol, whereas for the B_2 code we require only 3.75 bits per source symbol.

4.9.2 Shift codes

The philosophy behind shift codes is very similar to that of the B code. We split the source symbols into blocks of a certain size. The source symbols within a block are assigned codewords according to some rule (either fixed length binary codewords or Huffman codes). A string that is not used for any of the other source symbols is then used as a shift-up or shift-down symbol. For example, consider the source given in table 4.5. We can split them source symbols into two blocks. The first seven source symbols, which are in the first block, are assigned fixed length binary codes from 000 to 110. Then 111 is used a prefix for the remaining two source symbols. The prefix 111 indicates that the codeword refers to the source symbol in the second block. The table given below shows the codeword assignment in this case.

Source symbol	Probability	Binary shift code
A	0.35	000
B	0.15	001
C	0.15	010
D	0.1	011
E	0.05	100
F	0.05	101
G	0.05	110
H	0.05	111 000
I	0.05	111 001

The average length of the shift codes shown above is 3.3 bits per source symbol. For this example, the shift code is more efficient than the B code. This is also true in general, as the B code uses continuation bit(s) for all codewords while the shift uses a 'shift' symbol only for some codewords.

Another type of code on almost the same lines is the Huffman shift code. In this code, we club together all the source symbols that have a very small probability to form a compound symbol EI. Then we generate the Huffman code for the source that consists of this compound symbol and the other source symbols. Following the normal procedure for generating the Huffman code, we get the following.

Source symbol	Probability	Huffman shift code
A	0.35	00
EI	0.25	10
B	0.15	11
C	0.15	010
D	0.1	011

Now we use 10 which is the codeword for EI as a prefix and the codewords for the other words as a suffix to generate the Huffman shift code. The complete list of Huffman shift codewords is shown below.

Source symbol	Probability	Huffman shift code
A	0.35	00
B	0.15	11
C	0.15	010
D	0.1	011
E	0.05	10 00
F	0.05	10 11
G	0.05	10 010
H	0.05	10 011
I	0.05	10 10 00

The average length of the codewords in this case is 2.95 bits per source symbol.

Certain arbitrariness is involved in the design of the various 'nearly optimal' codes like the B code and the shift code. This is because we have to choose to split the source symbols into various blocks and the final output may depend crucially on how we implement the splitting of the symbols into blocks. For example, in the case of the Huffman shift code we have just discussed, can we achieve a better compression ratio by choosing the number of source symbols in a block in a slightly different manner? The reader is encouraged to explore this aspect on their own.

4.9.3 Shannon–Elias–Fano coding

This algorithm has the advantage that, unlike the Huffman code or its nearly optimal variants, the probabilities need not be sorted and arranged in descending order. Instead of using the probabilities of the source symbols, it uses the cumulative probability distribution (CPD) function. The cumulative probability corresponding to a certain source symbol (or gray level) is obtained by adding the probabilities of all the source symbols up to and including the source symbol x under consideration, i.e.,

$$F(x) = \sum_{r \leqslant x} P(r). \tag{4.17}$$

Instead of directly using the cumulative distribution function defined above (equation (4.17)), the algorithm uses a modified cumulative distribution function that is obtained by adding half of the probability of the current symbol to the sum of the probabilities of earlier symbols:

$$\overline{F}(x) = \sum_{r \leqslant x} P(r) + \frac{1}{2} P(x). \tag{4.18}$$

We round off the modified CPD to a certain number of bits and use the rounded CPD as a codeword. We will prove that if we round off the modified CPD to l bits, where l is chosen as per

$$l(x) = \left\lceil \log \frac{1}{P(x)} \right\rceil + 1 \tag{4.19}$$

then the resulting code is uniquely decodable as we are within the bounds set by entropy.

Proof of the above statement is as follows.

By the definition of rounding off,

$$\overline{F}(x) - \lfloor \overline{F}(x) \rfloor_{l(x)} < \frac{1}{2^{l(x)}}. \tag{4.20}$$

By substituting $l(x)$ from equation (4.19) into equation (4.20), we have

$$\overline{F}(x) - \lfloor \overline{F}(x) \rfloor_{l(x)} < \frac{P(x)}{2}. \tag{4.21}$$

This implies that the modified (and rounded) CPD function lies within the step corresponding to x and that $l(x)$ bits are sufficient to describe the source symbol x.

We now present a numerical example to clarify the procedure to be followed for Shannon–Elias–Fano coding. We will also show through this example that this method does not require us to sort the probabilities.

We consider five source symbols with probabilities as given in the table below. The table also shows the procedure for obtaining the codewords.

Symbol	Probability	$F(x)$	$\overline{F}(x)$	$\overline{F}(x)$ binary	$l(x)$	Codeword
x_1	1/2	0.5	0.25	0.01	2	01
x_2	1/8	0.625	0.5625	0.1001	4	1001
x_3	1/8	0.75	0.6875	0.1011	4	1011
x_4	1/8	0.875	0.8125	0.1101	4	1101
x_5	1/8	1.0	0.9375	0.1111	4	1111

You might be a bit skeptical about this coding scheme because we have arranged the source symbols in the descending order of probabilities. So to convince you, we now change the order in which the source symbols are placed and study the effect of that on the results we obtain.

Symbol	Probability	$F(x)$	$\overline{F}(x)$	$\overline{F}(x)$ binary	$l(x)$	Codeword
x_1	1/8	0.125	0.0625	0.0001	4	0001
x_2	1/8	0.25	0.1875	0.0011	4	0011
x_3	1/8	0.375	0.3125	0.0101	4	0101
x_4	1/8	0.5	0.4375	0.0111	4	0111
x_5	1/2	1.0	0.75	0.1100	2	11

Notice that in either case, i.e., irrespective of the ordering of the source symbols, we get an IDC with the same average word length. Hence, this scheme has an advantage over the Huffman code in that we do not need to sort the source symbols according to their probabilities. This will obviously reduce the number of computations required.

However, how good is the compression ratio obtained by this scheme? In the above example, the average length of the codewords is 3 bits/source symbol. This compares rather unfavorably with the entropy of the source, which is 2 bits/source symbol.

If you work out the Huffman code for this source, you will notice that in fact we touch the limit set by entropy since the average length of the Huffman code for this source turns out to be 2 bits per source symbol. We notice from the above table, that the rightmost bit of all the codewords is the same (it is '1' for all the codewords). Since this is redundant, we might as well drop the rightmost bit of all the codewords of the Shannon–Elias–Fano code; this in fact gives us the Huffman code. However, this is a coincidence, and in general there is no easy way of obtaining the Huffman code from the Shannon–Elias–Fano code. In general, the Shannon–Elias–Fano code gives us less compression than the Huffman code.

4.10 Reducing interpixel redundancy: run-length coding

So far, we have only looked at codes that reduce coding redundancy. In fact, the Huffman code assumes a zero-memory source, which essentially implies no interpixel redundancy. However, we know from experience that there is lot of interpixel redundancy in images. For example, a page of text, when viewed as an image, has lot of interpixel redundancy. The white spaces on a page of text can be viewed as an example of interpixel redundancy. Many human languages also have a fair degree of interpixel redundancy. As mentioned before, q is always followed by u. Moreover, some combinations of characters, like 'ing', are more common than 'uvw'.

How do we go about reducing interpixel redundancy? There are many algorithms, but the feature that is common to all of them is that only the 'new' information in a pixel is encoded while the 'redundant' information is conveyed only once (since it repeats).

The simplest scheme for reducing interpixel redundancy is run-length coding. Run-length coding can be applied directly only on binary images. In the case of grayscale or color images, one has to first do bit-plane slicing and then do run-length coding separately for each plane.

In any binary image one would expect a long string of 1s or 0s. For example, look at the figure given below, which shows a part of a binary image.

0000100000001
0000111110001
1111000001110

The information about the above image can also be conveyed in the following manner:

(0, 4), (1, 1), (0, 7), (1, 1), (0, 4), (1, 5), (0, 3), (1, 5), (0, 5), (1, 3), (0, 1).

The first number of a pair in parentheses tells us whether we are talking about a 'run' of 0s or a run of 1s, while the second number is the run-length. This method can be made more efficient by realizing that the 0s and 1s are anyway alternating, and thus we can just encode the run-lengths alone. However, we need to know whether the first run-length corresponds to a run of 0s or 1s. This is usually done by having a convention according to which the first run-length encoded corresponds to a run of 1s. If the first run happens to be a run of 0s, then 0 is taken as the run-length for 1. According to this convention, the run-lengths for the above image will be 0 4 1 7 1 4 5 3 5 5 3 1.

Further compression is achieved by doing a Huffman encoding of the run-lengths.

However, the run lengths are not as long as we would like them to be due to a property of the binary representation of a decimal number. When there is a transition from 127 to 128, then all the bits undergo a transition from 0 to 1, or vice versa. The number 127 written in binary using 8 bits is 01111111, while 128 is 10000000. Hence if a pixel has a gray level of 127 and the neighboring pixel has gray level of 128, then there is a disruption of the run in all the bit planes. Even in other cases, there may be a change in many of the bit planes. To avoid this problem, the gray code representation is normally preferred over the normal binary representation. In the gray code, the representation of adjacent gray levels will differ only in one bit (unlike binary format) where all the bits can change.

The gray code representation can be obtained from the binary representation, in the following manner

Let $g_{m-1}\ldots\ldots g_1 g_0$ represent the gray code representation of a binary number. Then,

$$g_i = a_i \oplus a_{i+1} \quad 0 \leqslant i \leqslant m - 2$$
$$g_{m-1} = a_{m-1}.$$
$$(4.22)$$

Here, $\oplus$ indicates the EXCLUSIVE OR (XOR) logic operation.

In gray code,

$$127 = 01000000$$
$$128 = 11000000.$$

Decoding a gray-coded image is done in the following manner.

The MSB is retained while the other bits undergo an XOR operation in the following manner:

$$a_i = g_i \oplus a_{i+1} \quad 0 \leqslant i \leqslant m - 2$$
$$a_{m-1} = g_{m-1}.$$
$$(4.23)$$

4.10.1 Other methods for reducing interpixel redundancy

What are the other methods for reducing interpixel redundancy? In all images the gray levels of adjacent pixels usually have some relationship. Normally, the gray levels of adjacent pixels can be expected to be close to each other (unless we encounter the edge of an object). Hence, the difference between the gray levels of adjacent pixels can be expected to be small. If we now calculate the entropy of the 'difference' image, it is expected to be less than the entropy of the original; thus, Huffman coding will give rise to a larger amount of compression in this case. Theoretically, the difference between adjacent values can lie anywhere between −255 and +255 (for an 8-bit image), but the actual range of the difference values are found to be much less, as seen from figure 4.11.

From the histogram, we can calculate the probability (frequency) of occurrence of the gray levels, and hence the entropy. In this case, the first-order entropy turns out to be 7.0754 bits/pixel (figure 4.9).

The difference image for the image in figure 4.8 is shown in figure 4.10. The difference image was generated by subtracting the gray level of each pixel from the gray level of the pixel to the right (in the same row). This operation of course is not

Figure 4.8. A gray scale image with an entropy of 7.0754 bits/pixel.

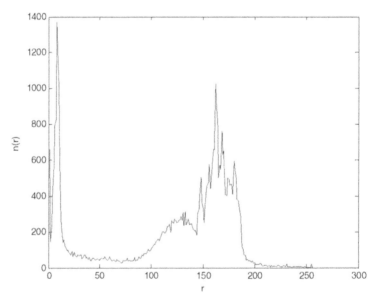

Figure 4.9. Histogram of the image in figure 4.8.

performed for the leftmost column; if it is, the original image cannot be regenerated from the difference image.

The histogram for the difference image is shown in figure 4.11.

The entropy of the difference image is found to be 0.3725 bits/pixel. Hence, enormous amounts of compression can be achieved simply by applying Huffman coding on the difference image.

The method discussed above, wherein we encoded the difference image, is a special case of what is in general known as 'predictive coding'. In predictive coding, we encode only the difference between the predicted value and the true value of a

Figure 4.10. Difference image for the image in figure 4.8.

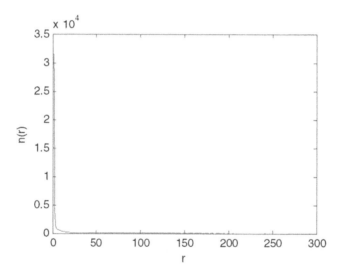

Figure 4.11. Histogram for the image in figure 4.10.

pixel. In the case of the difference image, we are essentially taking the predicted value of a pixel to be equal to the gray level of the preceding pixel.

In some situations, this may not lead to the lowest entropy. For example, if in an image we have a quadratic variation in the intensity, then the differences will not be a constant and hence the entropy of the difference will not be small. However, we can 'predict' a value for a pixel based on the value of the two pixels immediately preceding the current pixel. In such a case, the difference between the predicted and the true value will be very small, and more compression can be achieved.

4.11 LZW coding

We now describe a very elegant coding technique that attempts to reduce interpixel redundancy. The advantage of this technique is that it does not require, *a priori*, the probability of occurrence of the source symbols. Hence, encoding can be done 'on the fly'.

This technique was first described by Lempel and Ziv in 1977. The algorithm was modified by Welch in 1984. Hence, it is known as the LZW code[4]. In this technique, we find out which 'sequences' of gray levels are occurring in an image. Once a new sequence is detected, it is stored in a 'dictionary'. Whenever, a sequence is detected in an image, we check whether it exists in our dictionary. In case it is already present in the dictionary, we refer to the sequence by its dictionary location. This is very similar to the idea of pointers in C language. When using a pointer, we refer to a variable by its memory location.

If the sequence is not present in the dictionary, it is entered in a new location in the dictionary.

Let us understand the working of the algorithm by a simple numerical example. We consider a simple grayscale image with three rows and six columns as shown below.

22	12	33	12	12	42
22	42	42	22	12	12
33	33	12	33	12	12

The algorithm reads the pixel values one by one, scanning from left to right. When the end of a row is reached, we proceed to the beginning of the next row. The last pixel is combined with the first pixel in the next row to generate a sequence. The working of the algorithm can be easily understood by looking at table 4.7.

At each step, the encoder concatenates the contents of column 1 and column 2. If the resulting sequence is already found to exist in the dictionary, then the encoder does not give any output at this stage. Instead it reads the next pixel and concatenates it with the currently recognized sequence. This process continues until a new sequence that does not exist in the dictionary is found. At that point, the encoder sends the dictionary location of the contents of column 1 as output.

We reserve the locations 0 to 255 in the dictionary for the gray levels 0 to 255. The sequences are stored in locations 256 onwards.

An important decision that has to be made before beginning the encoding process is determining the number of bits to be used for sending the encoded output. It is obvious that this will have a direct impact on the compression ratio. If we are very ambitious and choose a very small number of bits, then we run the risk of incurring a dictionary 'overflow'. In the example given in table 4.7, we need a minimum of 9 bits to send the encoded output. However, choosing 9 bits implies that we can store at most 256 sequences in the dictionary (locations 256 to 511). This may not be enough for very big images. Alternately, we can play it safe and use more bits, in which case, we can store more sequences. But then this would mean a much lower compression ratio.

---

[4] The reader can refer to Salomon D 2007 *Data Compression: The Complete Reference* 4th edn (Springer) for more details. The algorithm discussed here is just one of a class of such algorithms.

Table 4.7. Encoding using the LZW algorithm.

Currently recognized sequence	Pixel being processed	Encoded output	Dictionary location (codeword)	Dictionary entry
	22			
22	12	22	256	22–12
12	33	12	257	12–33
33	12	33	258	33–12
12	12	12	259	12–12
12	42	12	260	12–42
42	22	42	261	42–22
22	42	22	262	22–42
42	42	42	263	42–42
42	22			
42–22	12	261	264	42–22–12
12	12			
12–12	33	259	265	12–12–33
33	33	33	266	33–33
33	12			
33–12	33	258	267	33–12–33
33	12			
33–12	12	258	268	33–12–12
12		12		

How much compression have we achieved by using the LZW encoding process?

In table 4.7, we have to send 14 9-bit words as output. Therefore, we would be requiring $14 \times 9 = 126$ as opposed to the $8 \times 18 = 144$ bits for the original image.

Hence, the compression ratio is an unimpressive $144/126 = 8/7 = 1.143$.

However, this technique promises to attain much higher compression ratios for bigger images.

Have we forgotten something? In my calculation of the compression ratio, I have only taken into account the number of bits used to store the encoded output. What about the number of bits used to store the dictionary? Should we not take that into account?

Amazingly, the answer to this question is, no! The dictionary is not required to be transmitted to the receiving end for the decoding process. The decoder builds up the dictionary during the decoding process and, as shown below, that dictionary is identical to the dictionary of the encoder.

The decoding process is very similar to the encoding process and is shown in table 4.8.

The decoder receives the encoded value. If the value is less than 256, the decoder recognizes that the encoded value refers directly to the gray level of the pixel and outputs the encoded value itself as the output. If the encoded value is greater than

Table 4.8. Decoding of the LZW code.

Currently recognized sequence	Encoded value	Decoded output	Dictionary location (codeword)	Dictionary entry
	22	22		
22	12	12	256	22–12
12	33	33	257	12–33
33	12	12	258	33–12
12	12	12	259	12–12
12	42	42	260	12–42
42	22	22	261	42–22
22	42	42	262	22–42
42	261	42–22	263	42–42
261	259	12–12	264	42–22–12
259	33	33	265	12–12–33
33	258	33–12	266	33–33
258	33	33	267	33–12–33
33	259	12–12	268	33–12

255, then the decoder immediately recognizes that the encoded value refers to the dictionary location and searches in the dictionary for the corresponding gray level sequence. The decoder builds up a dictionary during the decoding process in a manner that is very similar to that of the encoder. The only difference is that if the encoded value is a dictionary location, the decoder concatenates the contents of the first column and the first part of the sequence referred to in the second column.

For certain images, the algorithm discussed above can lead to a piquant situation (see exercise 25 at the end of this chapter.).

4.12 Arithmetic coding

We now discuss a new type of code that does not generate either fixed length or variable length codewords. In arithmetic coding, a one-to-one correspondence between source symbols and codewords does not exist. Instead, an entire sequence of source symbols (or message) is assigned a single arithmetic codeword.

The codeword itself defines an interval of real numbers between 0 and 1. As the number of symbols in the message increases, the interval used to represent it becomes smaller and the number of information units (say, bits) required to represent the interval becomes larger. Each symbol of the message reduces the size of the interval in accordance with the probability of occurrence of the source symbol.

From the viewpoint of information theory, initially, we are totally uncertain about the message. Our ignorance is reflected by the fact that the codeword can be anywhere in the range 0 to 1. As we read the symbols in a sequential manner, our

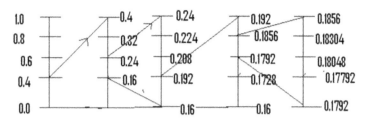

Figure 4.12. Arithmetic coding.

knowledge about the source increases and hence the range [0, 1] narrows. An end-of-message character is used to terminate the encoding process. We explain the working of the algorithm for the encoding with an example.

Let the source symbols be A, B, C, and D. The probabilities of these source symbols are as given below.

Source symbol	Probability
A	0.4
B	0.2
C	0.2
D	0.2

Let the message to be encoded be ABACD. Here, D is actually a character used to indicate the end of the message (figure 4.12).

We divide the interval from 0 to 1 according to the ratio of the probabilities. As each character in the message is read, the interval is subdivided accordingly as follows.

Since A has a probability of 0.4, it is allotted the range 0–0.4. B is allotted the range 0.4–0.6, C the range 0.6–0.8, and D 0.8–1.0.

Since the first symbol in the message is A, we narrow down the interval to 0 to 0.4 and subdivide this interval as per the probability of the symbols. As each successive symbol in the message is read, we go on subdividing the range in the ratio of the probabilities. This process continues until we encounter D, which indicates the end of the message. Finally, we represent the message by any number in the interval 0.18304 to 0.1856. For example, the number chosen can be 0.184 or 0.185. We notice that we are using three digits to represent a message having five symbols. Hence, we are using 0.6 digits per source symbol. This compares favorably with the entropy of 0.5786 digits/source symbol.

For very long messages, we can approach the bound set by entropy. In practice, the efficiency of this method is limited by the maximum number of digits that the computer can handle.

4.13 Transform coding

Transform coding is one of the powerful coding schemes used currently for compression. It is widely used in compression standards like Joint Photographers Experts Group (JPEG).

While discrete cosine transforms (DCTs) and wavelet transforms are more popular, we can understand the basics of transform coding using the Fourier transform. Recall that most of the information in a typical image is concentrated in and around the zero-frequency component (section 3.7 and figure 3.7). Hence, we can achieve lot of compression by transmitting/storing only the low-frequency components in an image. In transform coding, the compression achieved is associated with a loss of information. However, this loss (which is in the high-frequency region) does not lead to any significant degradation in the quality of the image, at least not to the human eye. The essential steps in transform coding are shown in the flow chart in figure 4.13.

Quantization of the transform coefficients essentially involves rounding off the transform coefficients. From the definition of the DFT, we know that, in general, the transform coefficients can be complex and the coefficients need not be integers even if the intensities of the pixels are integers.

The advantage of the DCT over the DFT is that it is not complex. Just as in the case of the DFT, there are minor variations in the definition of the DCT. We define the DCT as

$$Y(k, l) = \sum_{i=0}^{N-1}\sum_{j=0}^{M-1} 4y(i, j)\cos\left(\frac{\pi k}{2N}(2i + 1)\right)\cos\left(\frac{\pi l}{2M}(2j + 1)\right). \qquad (4.24)$$

Note that the DFT can be written as a sum of cosine and sine functions. However, the DCT, as seen from the above definition, is not simply the real (cosine) part of the DFT.

To explore the significance of the DCT, let us study the 1-D DCT.

In one dimension, the DCT would be defined as

$$Y(k) = \sum_{i=0}^{N-1} 2y(i)\cos\left(\frac{\pi k}{2N}(2i + 1)\right). \qquad (4.25)$$

The zero-frequency component of the DCT would be equal to

$$Y(0) = \sum_{i=0}^{N-1} 2y(i). \qquad (4.26)$$

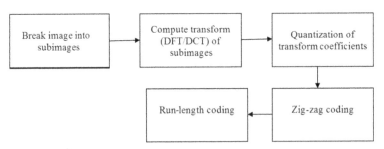

Figure 4.13. Flow chart for transform coding.

It can be seen that the zero-frequency component of the DCT is $2N$ times the average value of the function $y(i)$.

Is the DCT periodic like the DFT? Since it involves a cosine function, one would naturally expect it to be periodic. It can be easily shown that the DCT has a period of $4N$ (see exercise 26).

Exercises

1. If a code satisfies Kraft's inequality can we conclude that it is an UDC? If your answer is no, give a counter-example.
2. Suppose that 8 bits are used per pixel to store the image of a chessboard. The black squares have a gray level of 0 and the white squares have a gray level of 255. What are the types of redundancies present in the image?
3. How many distinct instantaneous codes can be constructed in which the lengths of the codewords are the same as that for the code in table 4.3? That is, the lengths of the codewords are 1, 2, 3, and 4, respectively. Give the complete list of all such codes.
4. A person is told that the 12th of June falls on Monday for a particular year. However, he is not told the year to which this information corresponds. If he is then told the day corresponding to the 12th of June of the succeeding year, how much extra information (in bits) is conveyed (on average) by this second piece of information?
5. Hargreaves and Raman are two mathematicians who are in communication with each other. Raman has already informed Hargreaves that he will be sending a 2×2 matrix whose elements are either 0 or 1. If now Raman informs Hargreaves that the matrix he is going to send has an inverse, then what is the information content of this statement?
6. The Monty Hall Problem: A contestant in a TV game show is shown three cubicles numbered one to three and closed off by curtains—one of which conceals a car. If the contestant can correctly guess the location of the car, they win the game. At random, the contestant picks cubicle number 1. The host, who knows where the car really is, now opens cubicle number 2, showing that it is empty.
    a) Should the contestant change their choice in light of the new information divulged by the host?
    See http://www.wiskit.com/marilyn.gameshow.html for a discussion of this problem.
    b) How much information did the host of the game show divulge by opening cubicle 2?
7. For what range of values is the inequality $\log_2 x \leqslant x - 1$ not valid?
8. Do the words of the English language form an IDC? Why?
9. What is the correct order for the following sequence of operations?
    Huffman coding, gray coding, run-length coding, bit-plane slicing

10. A 1-D image is defined as

$$f(x) = x \quad \text{for } x = 0 \text{ to } 255.$$

a) Draw the histogram for this image.
b) If the MSB of each pixel is set to zero, draw the resulting histogram.
c) Compare the entropy of the original image and the image resulting from the operation described in b).

11. A power law transformation is applied to a digital image.

a) If the contrast of the image improves as a result of the application of the transformation, will the entropy also increase? Why?
b) The histogram equalization technique is applied to a digital image. Compare the entropies of the input and output images.

12. You are downloading encoded images from two websites A and B. The image files are large and the capacity of the channel you are using is limited, and hence the file takes a long time to download. In both cases, the web-browser you are using decoders and display the part of the image file that has been received up to that point. In the case of website A, only the top few rows of the image are initially displayed and the number of rows on display gradually increases with time. In the case of website B, the display is of the same size as the original image, but initially the image is not sharp. The displayed image gets progressively sharper with time. What kind of coding scheme is used by the two websites? Explain the observed features on the basis of the coding scheme adopted in each case.

13. An object is executing periodic motion between the points A and B as shown below.

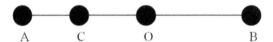

The instantaneous displacement, $x(t)$, of the object from the point O is given by

$$x(t) = x_o \cos t$$

where x_o is the distance OA, and C is the midway point between A and O.

Now suppose that the object is photographed at a certain time. The information about the location of the object (with respect to O) is conveyed in parts as follows:

a) The functional form of $x(t)$ is conveyed but the exact time when the photograph was taken is not conveyed. Instead, the information given is that the object was to the left of point O when the photograph was taken. What is the information content of this statement?
b) If later on it is revealed that the object was between O and C, what is the additional information conveyed?
c) What is the total information content of the statements in a) and b) and how much information is left to be conveyed?

14. A source generates random integers in the range of 0 to 9. Calculate the entropy of this source, assuming that it is an ideal random number generator.

15. If a source has a probability of zero, then the corresponding term in the calculation of the entropy is $0\log_2(0)$. Show that this term is zero. Hint: Use L'Hospital's rule.

16.   a) Starting from the definition of entropy, determine the entropy of an m-bit image that has a completely uniform/equalized histogram.
   b) Can variable length coding achieve compression for such an image? Explain.
   c) What kind of coding can achieve compression in this case?

17. The codewords for a ternary code are as given below.

Source symbol	Codeword
0	0
1	1
2	20
3	21

How many different instantaneous codes can be constructed such that the lengths of the codewords for each source symbol are as given in the table shown above? Give the complete list of all such codes.

18. How many unique binary Huffman codes are there for a three-symbol source (where all the symbols have different probabilities)? Construct them.

19.   a) Is the code given below instantaneous? Give reason(s) for your answer.
   b) Is it possible to find an instantaneous code with the same length of codewords?
      Give your reason(s).

Source symbol	Code symbol
1	01
2	011
3	10
4	1000
5	1100
6	0111

20.   i) Under what circumstances will a Huffman code include a codeword of length 1?
   ii) Under what condition does the average word length for an instantaneous code become equal to the entropy?

21. Determine a ternary Huffman code for the source given below and calculate the average word length of that code.

Source symbol	Probability
A	0.4
B	0.2
C	0.1
D	0.1
E	0.1
F	0.1

Note: Ternary code means that the code alphabets will be 0, 1, and 2. Modify the binary Huffman code algorithm in a suitable manner for this case.

22. Let a binary image have entropy H_1. The run lengths are now treated as source symbols and the entropy of this new source is H_2. Will H_2 be less than, greater than, or equal to H_1? Why? Do run-length coding for the bit stream

11101100110001000101, and calculate H_1 and H_2 for this case.

23. In practice, does the histogram equalization procedure increase or decrease the entropy of an image? Explain.

24. For which kind of source is it recommended to go for a B_3 code as opposed to a B_2 code?

25. The LZW algorithm described in section 4.12 can sometimes land us in a strange situation.

Consider the image given below.

22	12	33	12	12	42
22	42	42	22	12	12
33	33	33	33	12	12

i) Implement the LZW algorithm discussed in section 4.12.
ii) Decode the output obtained in a).
   Did you encounter a problem in decoding? The problem would have occurred in the entries corresponding to the last row (four successive 33s). In fact, this kind of problem occurs whenever a gray level repeats more than twice on its first occurrence in an image.
iii) How would you handle this problem? Suggest a modification to the normal LZW algorithm to take care of such situations.
iv) Do you foresee any other problems with the LZW algorithm?

26) Show that the period of the DCT is 4N, i.e., $Y(k + 4N) = Y(k)$.

Programming assignment

1. Write a program in MATLAB®/pseudo-code to compute the nth-order entropy (n is given as user input) of a binary image. Hint: Use binary-to-decimal conversion. The program should proceed along the following lines:

   a) At first the program converts the input 2-D array of gray levels into a 1-D array.

   b) Next it determines the nth-order entropy using binary-to-decimal conversion.

IOP Publishing

A Course on Digital Image Processing with MATLAB®

P K Thiruvikraman

Chapter 5

Image analysis and object recognition

5.1 Image analysis

Which task do you think is easier: playing a game of chess or recognizing faces? Normally we would think that playing a game of chess is much tougher. However, while we have been able to design computer programs that can beat the best chess player[1] in the world, the seemingly easy task of recognizing faces can be surprisingly complicated.

While computers may be far from matching the effortlessness with which humans recognize faces and objects, lot of progress has been made in this field. The area of automated analysis of images is known as computer vision, machine vision, and pattern recognition. Pattern recognition is actually a much broader field that includes not only recognition of patterns in images, but also the application of statistical techniques for pattern recognition in data, sound, and text.

Recently the field of image analysis has acquired a lot of practical importance because of the possibility of using automated systems for face recognition, fingerprint recognition, iris recognition, and also other means of biometric recognition for security purposes. Automatic recognition and interpretation of handwritten documents is also another exciting possibility. Optical mark readers have also become quite commonplace.

The successful design of systems for biometric recognition may involve specialized knowledge about features such as fingerprints and irises. Hence, we will not be discussing these in much detail. Instead we focus on some general concepts that are widely used in the field of image analysis.

We begin with a discussion about the detection of low-level features such as points and lines.

---

[1] In a widely publicized match in 1997, a computer known as Deep Blue, developed by Scientists at IBM, defeated the then reigning world chess champion Gary Kasparov.

5.2 Detection of points and lines

While a global perspective is important in object recognition, identification of simple features like points or lines may be crucial in aiding the process of recognition. One simple way to detect the presence of lines or points is to convolve the image with masks. For example, the Laplacian mask (section 2.6) will be useful in detecting isolated points. Suppose that we convolve an image with the laplacian mask shown below.

0	1	0
1	−4	1
0	1	0

We will obtain a strong response if the center of the mask coincides with an isolated point. Regions of constant or slowly varying response will give much weaker responses, which can be removed by thresholding. A much stronger response can be obtained with the mask given below.

1	1	1
1	−8	1
1	1	1

The advantage of this mask apart from its stronger response is that it is isotropic. Sometimes the weight of the central pixel in the mask is made positive while all other weights are made negative.

Proceeding on a similar logic, we can come up with masks for detecting horizontal and vertical straight lines.

−1	−1	−1
2	2	2
−1	−1	−1

−1	2	−1
−1	2	−1
−1	2	−1

2	−1	−1
−1	2	−1
−1	−1	2

2	−1	−1
−1	2	−1
−1	−1	2

Clockwise from the top-left: masks for detecting horizontal, vertical, and diagonal straight lines.

One feature that is common to the Laplacian mask and to the mask mentioned above for line detection is that the sum of the weights is zero. While these masks are conceptually simple, and easy to formulate and implement, they involve a lot of computation. How do we reduce the amount of computation while designing an algorithm of equal efficiency?

5.3 The Hough transform

The Hough transform[2] is a widely used algorithm for feature extraction in machine vision/image analysis. The Hough transform is a computationally efficient procedure for detecting straight lines in a binary image. Hence, grayscale images have to be thresholded before applying this technique.

The computational advantage of this technique can be understood as follows. Assume that there are N foreground points in an image. To identify which of these points lie on a given straight line, we would have to first look at $N(N-1)/2$ straight lines (one straight line for each pair of points) and then determine whether any of the remaining $N-2$ points lie on this line. Hence, the number of computations involved in this brute force approach will be of the order of N^3.

Hough proposed to deal with this problem in the parameter space. In Hough's original method, the two parameters were the slope and intercept of a straight line. We go from the normal Cartesian space, where we use the coordinates x and y, to the parameter space, which will have slope (m) and intercept (c) along each of the axes. In practice, this would mean that we maintain 'bins' or 'accumulator cells' for each possible value of (m, c). For a given image, the range of values of c would be limited by the dimensions of the image. On encountering a foreground point (x, y), we notice that it can lie on any line that satisfies the equation $y = mx + c$, and we increment all the bins that correspond to allow solutions for m and c of the above equation. To do this, we start with the lowest possible value of c, calculate the corresponding value of m (for a given (x, y)) from the equation of the straight line, and increment the corresponding bin. We would have to repeat this for all allowed values of c. We can see that the number of computations involved in the Hough transform will be of the order of nk, where k is the number of possible values of c.

In practice, the above method has a serious complication. While the range of values of c is limited by the dimensions of the image, there is no such restriction on the slope m. In principle, it can range from $-\infty$ to ∞. Hence, the number of bins we would need is actually infinite.

To avoid this problem, instead of the slope–intercept form for the straight line, we use the normal (ρ, θ) representation:

$$\rho = x \cos \theta + y \sin \theta. \tag{5.1}$$

---

[2] While the method was originally proposed by Hough, the algorithm that is presently used was proposed by Duda and Hart 1972 *Commun. ACM* **15** 11–15.

Here, ρ is the length of the perpendicular drawn from the origin to the line, and θ is the angle the perpendicular makes with the x-axis.

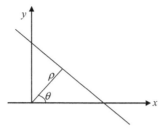

The following are important features of the Hough transform:
1) A point in the Cartesian plane corresponds to a sinusoidal curve in the parameter space.
2) A line in the Cartesian plane corresponds to a point in the parameter space.
3) If two points lie on the same line, then the corresponding sinusoidal curves will intersect at a point in parameter space.
4) Points lying on the same curve in parameter space correspond to lines passing through the same point in Cartesian (image) space.

We now summarize the implementation of the Hough transform:
(i) We construct a 2-D array that corresponds to the parameter space. From equation (5.1), we notice that ρ can be negative for certain values of x, y and θ. Hence, we set the range for ρ as $-\rho_{max}$ to $+\rho_{max}$. The range for θ is normally taken to be $-90°$ to $+90°$. Note that if we rotate a straight line by an angle greater than this it will be redundant.
(ii) We initialize all the array elements to zero.
(iii) We scan the entire image from the top-left corner until we reach a foreground point.
(iv) We substitute the coordinates (x, y) of this point in equation (5.1) with the lowest possible value for θ ($-90°$). Then we calculate the corresponding value of ρ from (5.1), and increment the accumulator cell corresponding to (ρ, θ).
(v) Repeat the previous step, i.e., calculation of ρ, for all values of θ.
(vi) When the entire range of θ values has been scanned, the value of each accumulator cell gives the number of points lying on a line with the corresponding values of ρ and θ.

One of the drawbacks of the Hough transform is that it considers two points to be on the same straight line even if there are some background pixels between them. This makes the Hough transform unsuitable for certain applications. For example, for many applications in machine vision, we would be interested in identifying straight lines. In such applications, we want to consider two disconnected segments of the same straight line (i.e., two line segments having the same slope and intercept, but having a gap between them) as two distinct straight lines. However, the Hough transform would identify the pixels in both segments as belonging to the same accumulator cell. Recent methods have tried to rectify this drawback[3].

Hough transform for circles and other curves

Even though the Hough transform was originally designed for detecting straight lines, it can easily be modified to detect any curve of the form $f(x, y) = c$.

To detect a circle, we use the equation for a circle, i.e.,

$$(x - a)^2 + (y - b)^2 = c^2. \tag{5.2}$$

The equation given above represents the equation of circle having radius c and its center at (a, b). In this case, we would require a three-dimensional (3-D) parameter space. If the image has $N \times N$ pixels, then we would require $(N - 2)$ possible values each for a and b and $N/2$ values for c. Here we assume that the center of the circle can be anywhere within the image, except along the edges, and that the radius can be at most half the width of the image. In effect, we are assuming that the complete circle is within the image. If we need to detect circles that do not lie entirely within the image, we would require a greater number of accumulator cells.

Similarly, we can use the Hough transform to detect the presence of any curve for which we are able to write down an equation of the form $f(x, y) = c$.

5.4 Segmentation: edge detection

The process of object recognition consists of many steps. Segmenting an image, i.e., splitting it into many different regions, is usually one of the first steps in this process. Segmentation can be defined as the process of splitting an image into a number of regions, each having a high level of uniformity in some parameter such as brightness, color, or texture. Edge detection and/or thresholding are used for segmentation. Usually, edge detection and thresholding are used together (the order in which we implement them is not very crucial).

Edge detection is usually accomplished by applying a mask on the input image (figure 5.1). The mask is designed such that it is highly sensitive to changes in image

Figure 5.1. A binary image.

---

[3] A recent algorithm by Khalid Daghameen and Nabil Arman detects only connected segments. The article entitled 'An efficient algorithm for line recognition based on integer arithmetic' can be accessed from https://pdfs.semanticscholar.org/4677/18c8e7aad1abdb03a3389bf8b237ecd3a7a5.pdf.

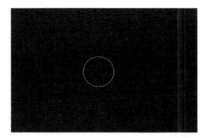

Figure 5.2. Result of the application of a Laplacian mask on figure 5.1.

intensity. Any mask that uses the gradient (first derivative) or higher derivatives of an image is ideally suited for this purpose.

Consider applying the Laplacian mask (refer to section 5.2) on a grayscale image. The output will be zero for the regions having constant intensity (figure 5.2).

If the input image is a grayscale image, then regions of slowly varying intensity (which are not edges) may also give rise to a nonzero response upon application of the Laplacian. In such cases, we have to threshold the output so that only the edges are visible.

While using derivatives for edge detection we have to remember that derivatives accentuate the noise in an image. Hence, it is customary to smooth an image and reduce the noise before going in for edge detection.

5.4.1 The Marr–Hildreth edge detection algorithm

It is clear that we have to use the Laplacian or the gradient for detecting edges, but it is also clear that derivatives accentuate noise in an image. Therefore, all edge detection algorithms have standard procedures for reducing or removing the noise before computing the derivatives.

The Marr–Hildreth algorithm convolves an image with a Gaussian smoothing filter before applying the Laplacian. An alternative method is to convolve the image with the Laplacian of Gaussian (LoG), ($\nabla^2 G$). The size of the Gaussian is chosen in such a way that small details of interest are not smoothed by its application.

Let us recall a few of the concepts related to the Laplacian and Gaussian masks. As has been the practice, we will initially look at continuous functions. Once we are clear about the concepts involved, we will design discrete masks for these operators.

The 2-D Gaussian function $\nabla^2 G$ can be computed from the definition given below.

$$
\nabla^2 G(x, y) = \frac{\partial^2 G(x, y)}{\partial x^2} + \frac{\partial^2 G(x, y)}{\partial y^2}
$$

$$
= \frac{\partial}{\partial x}\left[\frac{-x}{\sigma^2}\exp\left(-\frac{x^2 + y^2}{2\sigma^2}\right)\right] + \frac{\partial}{\partial y}\left[\frac{-y}{\sigma^2}\exp\left(-\frac{x^2 + y^2}{2\sigma^2}\right)\right]
$$

$$
= \left[\frac{x^2}{\sigma^4} - \frac{1}{\sigma^2}\right]\exp\left(-\frac{x^2 + y^2}{2\sigma^2}\right) + \left[\frac{y^2}{\sigma^4} - \frac{1}{\sigma^2}\right]\exp\left(-\frac{x^2 + y^2}{2\sigma^2}\right)
$$

$$
\nabla^2 G(x, y) = \left[\frac{x^2 + y^2 - 2\sigma^2}{\sigma^4}\right]e^{-\frac{x^2+y^2}{2\sigma^2}}
$$

The LoG is plotted in the figure given below.

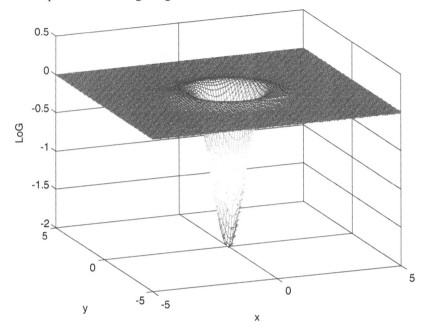

For plotting this figure, we have taken $\sigma = 1$.

We can now sample the function shown in the above figure to generate the mask required for the LoG. Alternately, we can come up with a mask that has integer values for the coefficients and closely approximates the properties of the LoG.

The main property of the LoG is that its average value is zero. This property can be proved by evaluating the volume under the surface from $-\infty$ to ∞ (for both x and y) and showing that the volume is zero. The average value of a 1-D function $f(x)$ from $x = a$ to $x = b$ is simply the area under the curve from a to b divided by $(b - a)$. For the case of a 2-D function we would have to evaluate the volume under the surface. The integral can easily be evaluated by converting to plane polar coordinates.

We also note that the value of the function is negative up to a certain radius from the origin and then becomes positive. Hence, the following mask is a suitable candidate for the LoG.

0	0	1	0	0
0	1	2	−1	0
1	2	−16	−2	1
0	1	2	1	0
0	0	1	0	0

Note that the sum of the coefficients of this mask is zero. This follows from the property that the average value of this function is zero. Another way of looking at it is that the mask will give a zero response in regions of constant intensity, which is the desired property of an edge detector.

After convolving the above mask with an image, the edges are detected as the points of zero crossing. However, as is seen from the above mask, the edges will form closed loops in that case. Hence, this is known as a spaghetti effect.

5.4.2 The Canny edge detector

The Canny edge detector tries to improve on the Marr–Hildreth edge detector. Instead of using the LoG, it uses the gradient. The image is initially convolved with the Gaussian mask before applying the gradient. In other words, we compute $f_s(x, y)$:

$$f_s(x, y) = G(x, y) \otimes f(x, y).$$

Here, $G(x, y)$ is the 2-D Gaussian function mentioned earlier.

We then take the gradient of $f_s(x, y)$ and compute its magnitude $M(x, y)$ and phase angle $\alpha(x, y)$. The gradient gives rise to thick edges, so we thin it by using nonmaxima suppression.

Let d_1, d_2, d_3, and d_4 denote the four basic edges.

The following is the nonmaxima suppression scheme for a 3×3 region:

1. Find the direction d_k that is closest to $\alpha(x, y)$.
2. If the value of $M(x, y)$ is less than at least one of its two neighbors along d_k, let $g_N(x, y) = 0$;
   otherwise, $g_N(x, y) = M(x, y)$.
3. Threshold $g_N(x, y)$ to reduce false edge points.
4. To avoid false positives (low threshold) and false negatives (high threshold) Canny's algorithm uses two thresholds: T_L and T_H.
5. The thresholding operation creates two additional images.

   These two images may be denoted as G_{NH} and G_{NL}:

   $$g_{NH}(x, y) = g_N(x, y) \geqslant T_H$$

   $$g_{NL}(x, y) = g_N(x, y) \geqslant T_L.$$

   Finally, we modify G_{NL} as follows:

   $$g_{NL}(x, y) = g_{NL}(x, y) - g_{NH}(x, y).$$

   What will be the result of this operation?

The nonzero pixels in $g_{NH}(x, y)$ *and* $g_{NL}(x, y)$ may be viewed as 'strong' and 'weak edges', respectively. Mark all the strong edge points. Typically there are some gaps in the strong edge points.

Gaps are closed using the following procedure:

1. Locate the next unvisited edge pixel, p, in $g_{NH}(x, y)$.
2. Mark as valid edge pixels all the weak edge pixels in $g_{NL}(x, y)$ that are connected to p, using 8-connectivity.
3. If all nonzero pixels in $g_{NH}(x, y)$ have been visited, go to step 4; else, return to step 1.
4. Set to zero all pixels in $g_{NL}(x, y)$ that are not marked as valid edge pixels.

The pros and cons of the Canny edge detector are discussed below.
- Pros: the quality of lines with regard to continuity, thinness, and straightness is superior.
- Cons: more complex implementation means a larger execution time.

Therefore, the Canny edge detector is not very suitable for real-time image processing.

For real-time processing, the thresholded gradient is used. Sometimes, the edges obtained after nonmaxima suppression are thicker than 1 pixel. Edge-thinning algorithms are used for such cases.

The following figure will help us to compare the performance of the Canny edge detector and the detector that uses the LoG.

Original image

Output using the Canny edge detector

Output using LoG

It is usual to have a thresholding operation preceding or succeeding the edge detection. Hence, we now discuss the process of thresholding.

5.5 Thresholding

Thresholding is the process by which a grayscale image is converted into a binary image. The range of gray levels for an 8-bit image is from 0 to 256. However, this does not imply that we should always choose 128 as the threshold value. The threshold value should be chosen such that the input image is segmented or separated into a background and foreground. Many methods have been suggested for thresholding. We discuss briefly some of the simpler methods.

We should also note that thresholding may sometimes fail, as in the case of a sphere lit from one side. There will be a continuous variation in intensity from one side of the sphere, which will be bright, to the other, which will have the background intensity.

The most frequently employed technique for determining the threshold for an image is analyzing the histogram and identifying the minimum between the foreground and the background peaks (figure 5.3).

Difficulties encountered in this method are as follows:
1. The valley may be so broad that it is difficult to locate a significant minimum.
2. There may be no clearly visible valley in the distribution because of excessive noise or due to variation in the background lighting.
3. There may be a number of minima because of the type of detail in the image, and selecting the most significant one will be difficult.
4. Noise within the valley may inhibit location of the optimum position.
5. Either of the major peaks in the histogram (usually the background) may be larger, and this will bias the position of the minimum.

Because of these problems, more sophisticated methods are used for thresholding. Some of these methods are listed below.

Variance-based thresholding
Entropy-based thresholding
Iterative thresholding

Variance-based thresholding

For a single threshold, the criterion to be maximized is the ratio of the between-class variance to the total variance.

Suppose that we select a threshold $T(k) = k$, where k is such that $0 < k < L - 1$. We use this threshold to separate the image into two classes C_1 and C_2.

The probability $P_1(k)$ that a pixel is assigned to class C_1 is

$$P_1(k) = \sum_{i=0}^{k} p_i. \tag{5.3}$$

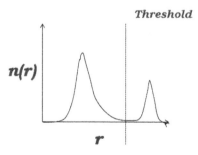

Figure 5.3. Using the minimum between the foreground and background peaks.

Similarly, the probability of class C_2 occurring is

$$P_2(k) = \sum_{i=k+1}^{L-1} p_i = 1 - P_1(k). \tag{5.4}$$

The mean intensity value of the pixels assigned to classes C_1 and C_2 are

$$m_1(k) = \frac{\sum\limits_{i=0}^{k} ip_i}{\sum\limits_{i=0}^{k} p_i} \qquad m_2(k) = \frac{\sum\limits_{i=k+1}^{L-1} ip_i}{\sum\limits_{i=k+1}^{L-1} p_i}. \tag{5.5}$$

The average intensity of the entire image is

$$m_G = \sum_{i=0}^{L-1} ip_i. \tag{5.6}$$

This can also be written as

$$P_1 m_1 + P_2 m_2 = m_G. \tag{5.7}$$

To evaluate the 'goodness' of the threshold at level k, we use the normalized, dimensionless metric:

$$\eta = \frac{\sigma_B^2}{\sigma_G^2}$$

where $\sigma_G^2 = \sum\limits_{i=0}^{L-1} (i - m_G)^2 p_i$ is the global variance, and $\sigma_B^2 = P_1(m_1 - m_G)^2 + P_2(m_2 - m_G)^2$ is the between-class variance.

By simplifying the above expression, we get

$$\sigma_B^2 = P_1 P_2 (m_1 - m_2)^2. \tag{5.8}$$

We see that maximizing this quantity maximizes the difference between the classes.

Iterative thresholding

An initial threshold is selected and the image is segmented into two parts. The pixels below the threshold are labeled as p_1 while those are above it are labeled as p_2. The average value of the pixels belonging to the groups p_1 and p_2 are calculated. If these averages are found to be T_1 and T_2, respectively, then the new threshold is taken to be $T_{\text{new}} = (T_1 + T_2)/2$. The image is now again divided into two groups p_1 and p_2, based on the new threshold T_{new}, and the whole process is repeated. This iterative procedure is repeated until T_{new} and T_{old} differ only marginally.

5.6 A global view of image analysis and pattern recognition

Before proceeding further, it may help us if we obtain a global perspective about image analysis and pattern recognition. This may help you to appreciate some of the algorithms that are going to be presented in the next few sections.

We have up to now discussed some methods for detecting low-level features like points, lines, and edges. We have also discussed the Hough transform, which can be used to detect any object having a regular shape. All these methods are based on using the shape or geometry of the object of interest. In some cases, one could also use color to recognize the presence of certain objects in an image. Template matching is another very direct method.

Template matching involves comparison of the image with a template existing in the database. Before matching with a template, we need to segment the given image to extract the object of interest.

Template matching, which might involve pixel-by-pixel comparison or calculation of the correlation between an image and a template, suffers from the following limitations:

- Difference in lighting between the image to be recognized and the template
- Rotation of an object (as compared to the template)
- Scaling (magnification used while capturing the image could be different from the magnification of the template)
- Translation of an object in the image as compared to its position in the template

Since direct matching with a template is beset with so many difficulties, we try to get a simple representation of an image/object and then try to compare this representation with the representation existing in the database.

5.7 Representation of objects

We can represent a region in terms of its external characteristics (e.g. its boundary) or in terms of its internal characteristics (i.e., color and texture of the pixels comprising the region). A simple description of the region is required for automatic recognition of an object.

The boundary can be described by features such as length, orientation of the straight lines joining its extreme points, and the number of concavities in the boundary. External representation is chosen when the primary focus is on shape characteristics.

We need to 'extract' the boundary of a region before we can describe it. We describe below the Moore's boundary tracking algorithm. Boundary extraction can also be performed through morphological operations.

Moore's boundary tracking algorithm:
- We are working with binary images in which object and background points are labeled 1 and 0, respectively.
- Initially we discuss only single regions.
- The aim is to obtain an ordered sequence of boundary points.
- We order the points in a clockwise direction.

1		1		1		
1				1	1	1
1						1
1						1
1		1		1	1	1

		c_1				
c_0	b_0	b_1	1			
	1			1	1	1
	1					1
	1					1
	1		1		1	1

The algorithm

1. Let b_0 be the uppermost, leftmost point in the image labeled 1. Examine the eight neighbors of b_0 starting at c_0 (western neighbor of b_0 and a background point).
2. Let b_1 denote the first neighbor encountered whose value is 1, and let c_1 be the background point immediately preceding b_1.
3. Store the locations of b_0 and b_1 for use in step 7.
4. Let $b = b_1$ and $c = c_1$.
5. Scan the eight neighbors of b, starting at c and proceeding in a clockwise direction. Let the neighbors be denoted as n_1, n_2,...,n_8. Find the first n_k labeled 1.
6. Set $b = n_k$ and $c = n_{k-1}$.
7. Repeat steps 5 and 6 until $b = b_0$ and the next boundary point found is b_1. The sequence of b points found when the algorithm stops constitutes the set of ordered boundary points.

So what do we do with this sequence of boundary points? We can represent them as a 'chain code'.

5.7.1 Chain codes

Chain codes are used to represent a boundary by a connected sequence of straight line segments of a specified length and direction. The direction of each segment is coded by using a numbering scheme. The sequence of directional numbers is called the Freeman chain code.

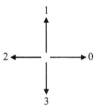

The chain code shown above is known as a 4-connectivity code. Essentially, the direction in which the boundary is oriented at each point is encoded into a string of numbers. We scan the image from the top-left corner until we arrive at the first foreground pixel. If the next foreground pixel is to the right of the first foreground pixel, then the corresponding chain code is 0. If the next foreground pixel is on top of the current pixel, the chain code is 1 and so on, as shown in the figure.

To give more detail, we can also use the 8-connectivity chain code as shown below.

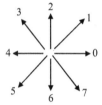

While it is convenient to us if Moore's algorithm precedes the assignment of the chain code, it is not absolutely essential, and one can have a program for assigning the chain code that also traverses the boundary following some convention.

For example, a chain code can be generated by following a boundary in, say, a clockwise direction and assigning a direction to the segments connecting every pair of pixels.

While the idea of a chain code is very simple and appealing, it has some disadvantages. What are the disadvantages?
- The chain code tends to be quite long in general.
- Any small disturbance due to noise causes changes in the code, thus impeding the process of recognition.

One way of making the chain code less susceptible to noise and also to make it shorter is to choose larger grid spacing.

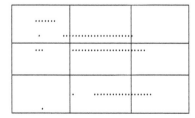

In the above figure, the dots represent the foreground pixels (against a white background). The horizontal and vertical lines form a 2-D grid. The distance between two grid points is much greater than the distance between two dots. Each dot is assigned to the nearest grid point. Since the number of grid points is much less than the number of foreground pixels in the original image, the chain code will be of a much shorter length. Notice that this procedure will also make the chain code immune to noise. This is because we expect the noise to shift the boundary by a few pixels. The shift in the boundary position is generally much less than the spacing of the grid.

We also have to make the chain code invariant with respect to rotation of the object. This is accomplished by considering successive differences in the chain code rather than the chain code itself.

For example, the chain code for the boundary shown in figure 5.4 is 0000000066644444444222 (assuming 8-connectivity).

Notice that the chain code is invariant under translations of the object. However, chain code will depend on the starting point chosen for the chain code. We can make it independent of the starting point by doing a cyclic permutation of the chain code until it has the smallest magnitude. Notice that in this particular case, it already has the smallest possible magnitude. By considering successive differences in the chain code values, we get 00000006006000000600. While taking successive differences, we have considered −2 to be equal to 6 (the minus sign can be interpreted to mean the opposite direction, and as per our convention 2 and 6 are in opposite directions).

We now do a cyclic permutation of the chain code until it attains the smallest magnitude. In the present case, it will become 00000000600600000006.

If the same image was photographed after the rectangle had been rotated by 90° (as shown in figure 5.5) in a clockwise sense, the chain code of the boundary will now read 0006666666644422222222. Taking successive differences will give us 00600000060060000000. A cyclic permutation gives us 00000000600600000006, which is the same as the chain code for the rectangle in figure 5.4. Hence, chain codes can be normalized with respect to rotations.

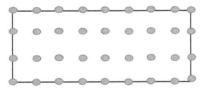

Figure 5.4. A binary image of a rectangle.

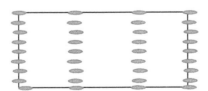

Figure 5.5. Rectangle shown in figure 5.4 rotated by 90° in a clockwise direction.

Size normalization is achieved by altering the size of the resampling grid (discussed earlier). These normalizations are exact only if the boundaries are invariant to rotation.

The same object digitized in two different orientations will have different boundary shapes (figure 5.6).

This effect can be reduced by

- Selecting chain elements that are long in proportion to the distance between pixels;
- Orienting the resampling grid along the principal axes of the object or along its eigenaxes.

A detailed discussion about principal axes/eigenaxes is given in section 5.10.

The chain code is an example of a boundary descriptor. The simplest boundary descriptor is the length of the boundary.

For a chain code curve with unit spacing in both directions, the number of vertical and horizontal components plus $\sqrt{2}$ times the number of diagonal components gives its length.

The diameter of a boundary B is defined as

$$\text{Diam}(B) = \max \left[D(p_i, p_j) \right]_{i,j} \tag{5.9}$$

i.e., it is the maximum distance between any two points on the boundary.

The value of the diameter and the orientation of a line segment connecting the two extreme points that comprise the diameter (called the major axis) are useful descriptors. The line perpendicular to the major axis is known as the minor axis. The minor axis should be of such length that the bounding box completely encloses the boundary (figure 5.7).

The ratio of the length of the major to the minor axes is known as eccentricity.

Figure 5.6. A cuboid photographed from three different orientations.

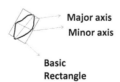

Figure 5.7. The boundary of an object with its major and minor axes.

5.7.2 Signatures

A signature is a 1-D functional representation of a boundary. The simplest way of obtaining the signature of a boundary is to plot the distance r from the centroid to the boundary as a function of the angle θ. To calculate the signature of a boundary, we compute the distance (r) of each point P from the centroid as a function of the angle made by a line joining the centroid to the point in question with the horizontal (see figures 5.8 and 5.9).

We now compute the signature of a circle and a right-angled triangle

Signatures and chain codes are 1-D representations of 2-D objects (boundaries). What about normalization of the signature with respect to rotation, translation, and scaling?

Signatures are automatically normalized with respect to translation (since they are with respect to the centroid). We can normalize them with respect to rotation by choosing the same starting point independent of the orientation of the object.

How do we do this?

Choose the starting point to be the point that is farthest from the centroid! This is fine provided that the point is unique! Another way is to choose the point on the

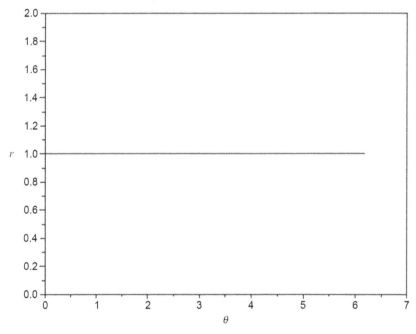

Figure 5.8. Signature of a circle of unit radius.

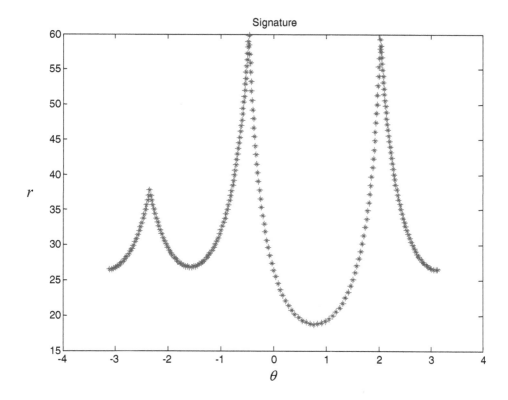

Figure 5.9. Signature of a right-angled triangle.

eigenaxis that is farthest from the centroid. This method requires more computation, but is more rugged since the direction of the eigenaxis is determined by all points on the contour.

How do we make the signature scale invariant?

One way to normalize is to scale all the functions so that they always span the same range [0,1]. This is susceptible to noise since the scale factor depends only on the minimum and maximum (which may be affected by noise). A better approach is to divide by the variance, provided it is nonzero!

5.7.3 Statistical moments

The shape of boundary segments (and of signature waveforms) can be described by statistical moments such as:

- Mean;
- Variance;
- Higher-order moments.

We can define the boundary by a function $g(r)$ as shown below. Consider the boundary shown below on the left. The function $g(r)$ is shown below on the right.

How was $g(r)$ obtained from the boundary segment?
- Join the endpoints of the boundary by a straight line.
- Rotate this line to align with the horizontal axis.

Treat the amplitude of g as a discrete random variable v and form an amplitude histogram $p(v_i)$.

Then, the *nth* moment of v about its mean is

$$\mu_n = \sum_{i=0}^{A=1} (v_i - m)^n p(v_i) \tag{5.10}$$

where the mean m is given by

$$m = \sum_{i=0}^{A-1} v_i p(v_i). \tag{5.11}$$

Generally, only the first few moments are required to differentiate between signatures of clearly distinct shapes. An alternative approach is to calculate the moments of r_i (distance of the ith boundary point from the centroid).

In this case, the moments are

$$\mu_n(r) = \frac{1}{K} \sum_{i=0}^{K-1} (r_i - m)^n$$

where m is given by

$$m = \frac{1}{K} \sum_{i=0}^{K-1} r_i. \tag{5.12}$$

In the expression for the mean, K is the number of points on the boundary. The advantage of using moments is that they are insensitive to rotation. Size normalization can be achieved by scaling.

We reproduce below a few geometrical objects and the moments of their signature:

Notice that, as expected, all moments are very small for the circle. Hence, the moments of the signature can be used to distinguish a circle from other shapes. In figures 5.10–5.12, $<r>$ denotes the average value of r. In order to show that the normalized moments are not sensitive to the size of the object, we show below the moments for a square that is much larger than the one shown above (figure 5.13).

Compare the normalized moments for the two squares and notice that they are not too different. Finally, we give below the moments for an elongated object (figure 5.14). Expectedly, the moments have large values in this case.

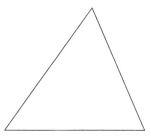

Figure 5.10. <*r*> = 40.3095; second moment/(square of mean) = 0.0529; third moment/(cube of mean) = 0.0055; fourth moment/(cube of mean) = 0.0057.

Figure 5.11. Square with <*r*> = 60.6903; second moment/(square of mean) = 0.0122; third moment/(cube of mean) = 7.8117×10^{-4}; fourth moment/(cube of mean) = 3.0185×10^{-4}.

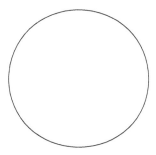

Figure 5.12. <*r*> = 39.6791; second moment/(square of mean) = 5.3115×10^{-4}; third moment/(cube of mean) = 8.6126×10^{-6}; fourth moment/(cube of mean) = 6.8792×10^{-7}.

Figure 5.13. Square with <*r*> = 111.0183; second moment/(square of mean) = 0.0153; third moment/(cube of mean) = 2.3964×10^{-4}; fourth moment/(cube of mean) = 4.7756×10^{-4}.

Figure 5.14. Elongated object with $<r> = 48.1681$; second moment/(square of mean) = 0.2907; third moment/(cube of mean) = 0.0042; fourth moment/(cube of mean) = 0.1439.

5.7.4 Regional descriptors

Having discussed the description of the boundary, let us look at regional descriptors. The area (number of pixels in the region) and perimeter (length of the boundary) can be used as regional descriptors, but these are sensitive to size.

Therefore, the following descriptors are better:
1. Compactness = (perimeter)^2/area
2. Circularity ratio (R_c): ratio of the area of a region to the area of a circle having the same perimeter

$$R_c = \frac{4\pi A}{P^2} \tag{5.13}$$

The value of the circularity ratio is 1 for a circle and $\pi/4$ for a square.

The circularity ratio is dimensionless and hence insensitive to scaling and rotation.

5.8 Texture

Description of images based on their texture has been receiving lot of attention recently. No formal definition of texture exists, but we intuitively feel that it provides a measure of properties such as smoothness/coarseness and regularity.

Three approaches are normally used to quantify texture:
statistical, structural, and spectral.

Statistical approaches yield characterizations of textures as smooth, coarse, grainy, etc.

Structural techniques deal with structural features (straight lines, etc) in an image.

Spectral techniques look at the Fourier spectrum to detect periodicities in the image.

Statistical approaches

In this approach, we look at statistical moments of the intensity histogram of an image or a region:

$$\mu_n(z) = \sum_{i=0}^{L-1} (z_i - m)^n p(z_i) \tag{5.14}$$

z denotes pixel intensity.

μ_n is the nth moment of z about the mean m.

The second moment, i.e., the variance, is of importance for texture description.

It is a measure of contrast that may be used to establish descriptors of relative smoothness.

For example, the measure

$$R(z) = 1 - \frac{1}{1 + \sigma^2(z)} \tag{5.15}$$

is 0 for areas of constant intensity and approaches 1 where the variance has a large value.

We divide the variance by $(L - 1)^2$ before using it in the above formula. The third moment is a measure of skewness.

The concept of entropy can also be used to quantify information about the texture of an image. Recall from chapter 4 that entropy is a measure of randomness (and also a measure of information content in an image).

The entropy of an image can be calculated once we have the histogram of an image. However, histograms carry no information about the relative positions of pixels having a certain intensity value. The information about the relative positions of pixels is important when describing the texture of an image. The information about relative positions of pixels is of course contained in the higher-order entropy of an image, but it is much more easily extracted from the co-occurrence matrix G.

The co-occurrence matrix G is a matrix whose (i, j) th element g_{ij} is the number of times that pixel pairs with intensities z_i and z_j in an image f in the positions specified by an operator Q.

We now give below a numerical example to clarify the concept of the co-occurrence matrix.

Consider a 3-bit grayscale image whose pixel values are stored in matrix A shown below.

$$A = \begin{matrix} 1\ 2\ 3\ 4\ 5\ 6 \\ 1\ 2\ 3\ 4\ 5\ 6 \\ 1\ 2\ 3\ 4\ 5\ 6 \\ 1\ 2\ 3\ 4\ 5\ 6 \\ 1\ 2\ 3\ 4\ 5\ 6 \end{matrix}$$

We now calculate the co-occurrence matrix for matrix A using the operator Q, where Q is defined as 'one pixel immediately to the right'.

The co-occurrence matrix G for matrix A is shown below.

$$G = \begin{array}{c} 1\,2\,3\,4\,5\,6\,7 \\ 1\,0\,5\,0\,0\,0\,0\,0 \\ 2\,0\,0\,5\,0\,0\,0\,0 \\ 3\,0\,0\,0\,5\,0\,0\,0 \\ 4\,0\,0\,0\,0\,5\,0\,0 \\ 5\,0\,0\,0\,0\,0\,5\,0 \\ 6\,0\,0\,0\,0\,0\,0\,0 \\ 7\,0\,0\,0\,0\,0\,0\,0 \end{array}$$

It can be seen from matrix A that 2 is always followed by 3, and there are five instances of this combination. Therefore, $G(2, 3) = 5$. The intensity 7 does not occur anywhere in the image, and therefore $G(7, k) = 0$ for all k.

The calculation of the co-occurrence matrix is not an end in itself. Various descriptors are used to describe the co-occurrence matrix. All these descriptors are defined in terms of the probability of the occurrence (p_{ij}) of a certain combination of intensity values z_i and z_j. The probability of occurrence of a certain combination can be calculated from the co-occurrence matrix G using the following equation:

$$p_{ij} = \frac{g_{ij}}{n}. \tag{5.16}$$

Here, n is the total number of combinations, which is also equal to the sum of all the elements of G.

By using the values of p_{ij}, we can calculate the values of m_r and m_c as follows:

$$m_r = \sum_{i=1}^{K} i \sum_{j=1}^{K} p_{ij} \tag{5.17}$$

$$m_c = \sum_{j=1}^{K} j \sum_{i=1}^{K} p_{ij}. \tag{5.18}$$

From equations (5.17) and (5.18), it is seen that m_r and m_c are the mean values of the intensity calculated along the rows and columns, respectively.

For the example under consideration, $m_r = 3$ and $m_c = 4$. Can you see why m_c is greater than m_r?

The standard deviations can also be calculated in two different ways:

$$\sigma_r^2 = \sum_{i=1}^{K} (i - m_r)^2 \sum_{j=1}^{K} p_{ij} \tag{5.19}$$

$$\sigma_c^2 = \sum_{j=1}^{K} (j - m_c)^2 \sum_{i=1}^{K} p_{ij}. \tag{5.20}$$

For the example under consideration, both σ_r and σ_c turn out to be equal to 2. This is because summing along the columns (as in equation (5.19)) gives a smaller number, but then this is compensated for by the smaller value of m_r, which is subtracted in equation (5.19).

By using the standard deviations and the mean values defined above, we can define a quantity called correlation, which describes how much a pixel is correlated with its neighbor. Correlation for an arbitrary image can vary from 1 (perfect correlation) to −1 (perfect anti-correlation).

Correlation is defined as

$$c = \sum_{i=1}^{K}\sum_{j=1}^{K} \frac{(i - m_r)(j - m_c)P_{ij}}{\sigma_r \sigma_c}. \tag{5.21}$$

Equation (5.21) can be used to calculate the correlation only if both standard deviations are nonzero.

For matrix A, which we are considering, the correlation turns out to be +1 because there is a perfect correlation between a pixel and its neighbor. If the intensity of a pixel is equal to 2, it is always followed by 3, 3 is always followed by 4, etc.

Another measure of the relation between an element of the co-occurrence matrix and its neighbor is known as contrast. As is apparent from the name, a greater difference between a pixel and its neighbor implies a higher contrast.

Contrast is defined as

$$C_t = \sum_{i=1}^{K}\sum_{j=1}^{K}(i - j)^2 P_{ij}. \tag{5.22}$$

The minimum value of C_t is 0 (for a constant image), and the maximum is equal to $(K - 1)^2$.

A quantity that is diametrically opposite to contrast is uniformity, which is defined as

$$U = \sum_{i=1}^{K}\sum_{j=1}^{K}P_{ij}^2. \tag{5.23}$$

Since all the values of P_{ij} are less than or equal to 1, the maximum value of U is 1 (for a uniform image) and the minimum value occurs when all P_{ij}s have the same value.

The minimum value is equal to $1/K^2$.

We can also use the concept of entropy in the context of the co-occurrence matrix. Following the definition of entropy given in chapter 4, we can define the entropy of a co-occurrence matrix as

$$H(G) = -\sum_{i=1}^{K}\sum_{j=1}^{K}P_{ij} \ln P_{ij}. \tag{5.24}$$

Similar to what we observed in chapter 4, the minimum value occurs when all values of P_{ij} are zero except for one (which is equal to 1). The maximum value occurs when all the P_{ij}s are equal. From equation (5.24), it is seen that $H(G)$ turns out to be equal to $2\ln K$ in such a case.

We calculate the co-occurrence matrix and the related statistical quantities mentioned above for four different images to see how these statistical concepts are able to bring out the difference in texture of these images (figure 5.15).

Texture	Mean	Standard deviation	R (defined in equation (5.15)) and normalized	Uniformity (equation (5.23))	Entropy (equation (5.24))
Smooth (figure 5.15(a))	177.39	10.78	0.0018	0.0258	5.874
Uniform (figure 5.15(b))	139.97	45.51	0.0309	0.0018	10.6031
Coarse (figure 5.15(c))	132.70	84.06	0.098	0.0027	11.5183
Uniform (figure 5.15(d))	66.76	63.67	0.0587	0.0405	9.1717

(a)   (b)

(d)   (c)

Figure 5.15. Different kinds of images. The various statistical parameters calculated for these images are discussed below. These four figures are labeled (a), (b), (c), and (d) in a clockwise manner starting from the top-left corner.

As expected, it is seen from the above table that the entropy of an image that has a coarse texture is greater than the entropy of images having a smooth or uniform texture. It is seen that all images score somewhat low on the scale of uniformity; however, we can still see that the images with a smooth and uniform texture have a higher uniformity than the images with a coarse texture. One or more of the statistical parameters mentioned above maybe used to classify images based on their texture.

5.9 Skeletonization or medial axis transformation (MAT)

Many of the representations and descriptors of images that we have considered in the previous sections were not true images; they were numbers and statistical quantities that could be extracted from images.

We now look at a simplified representation of an image known as a skeleton. A skeleton of an image is especially useful in object and character recognition.

The most intuitive definition of a skeleton is in terms of an MAT. The process of extracting the skeleton from an image consists of identifying those pixels that lie on the medial axis of the image.

A pixel is on the medial axis if it is equidistant from at least two pixels on the boundary of the object. This definition gives rise to easily identifiable and intuitive skeletons. Image skeleton extraction algorithms generally possess the following characteristics:

(i) Connectivity of the image skeleton must be consistent with the original image. This means that in an image, holes, objects, or the relation between holes and objects, must not change.

(ii) The width of the skeleton must be one pixel. As already mentioned, this characteristic of a skeleton makes it ideally suited for applications like character recognition.

(iii) The skeleton must be as close as possible to the center line (axis) of the original image.

(iv) The skeleton must possess as much of the detail of the original image as possible.

Since the skeleton of an image is defined in terms of the 'boundary points', it is obvious that the boundary of objects in an image have to be identified before we can implement an algorithm to extract the skeletons of these objects.

The boundaries of objects in an image may be extracted by applying various segmentation techniques (for example, edge detection). We will also discuss, in chapter 6, morphological techniques for extracting boundaries of objects.

In the further discussion about skeletonization algorithms, it is assumed that we have segmented an image into foreground and background pixels. The foreground pixels are assumed to be part of the object for which we are trying to extract the skeleton.

Figure 5.16. The figure on the left shows the skeleton of an object obtained by generating waves/fires from the boundaries of an object. The figure on the right shows the skeleton of an object obtained by using the maximum disk method.

There are certain models that intuitively explain how a skeleton can be obtained from its parent image (figure 5.16). These include the following.

(i) Prairie fire method—Consider a situation in which all the points on the boundary of an image are lit at the same moment, $t = 0$, and the flame spreads toward the interior of the image at the same speed along the perpendicular to the boundary. The line along which the fires from different surfaces meet is the medial axis skeleton. Instead of a fire, we can also obtain the same result by imagining that waves are generated from the boundary.

(ii) Maximum ball/disk method—Imagine that a disk is drawn in the interior of an object with an arbitrary point as the center. We gradually increase the radius of this disk until it is tangential to the boundaries of the image at a minimum of two points. If on increasing the radius we find that the disk becomes tangential to the boundary at only a single point, it is to be understood that the center of such a disk is not on the medial axis. The collection of the midpoints of disks that are tangential to the boundary at a minimum of two points would give the skeleton of the image. It is also to be noted that the disks are drawn in such a manner that they do not intersect with each other.

(iii) Peeling or iterative method—It can be easily seen that the prairie fire method and the maximum disk method, while being easy to understand and appreciate, are both computationally intensive because the points on the medial axis are obtained by trial and error (in the case of the method of maximal disks) and by a large number of iterations (until the paths of the fires cross) in the case of the prairie fire method. The 'peeling' or 'iterative thinning' method involves the iterative peeling of each layer of the object until there is only the skeleton left. This method is computationally less intensive than the prairie fire method and the maximum disk method, and hence has been widely adopted in practice for skeletonization.

There are several thinning algorithms for skeletonization that are currently in use. These fall into two main categories:

(i) Those that provide a step-wise algorithm and apply the test for deletion at each step (subiteration algorithms).

(ii) Those that apply a test of whether the pixel under consideration can be deleted by considering where the pixel lies on the image grid (subfield algorithms).

The algorithms mostly follow the method of template matching in order to identify the pixels that are to be deleted and the ones that are to be retained. These algorithms apply a 3 × 3 mask on the image and mark the point for deletion if certain criteria are satisfied. Parallel skeletonization algorithms apply the deletion operation to the whole image in one iteration, i.e., the new value of a pixel in the nth iteration depends on its own value as well as the value of its neighbors in the $(n - 1)$th iteration.

One of the earliest methods for obtaining the skeleton of an object by iterative thinning was proposed by Zhang and Suen[4]. It is basically a fast parallel-thinning algorithm. In this algorithm, the main point to be considered is that endpoints and pixel connectivity are preserved. This is taken care of in the various steps of the algorithm. Each pattern is thinned down to a skeleton of unitary thickness. In this method, all the pixels that do not form a part of the skeleton are removed. Several passes are done over the source image in order to mark and delete the foreground points that do not form a part of the final skeleton.

There are certain intuitive criteria that must be satisfied by the foreground pixel in order for it to be marked for deletion. These are as follows:

(i) It must be a pixel that lies on the edge of the image.
(ii) It must not be an endpoint, i.e., it must not lie on the extremities of the skeleton.
(iii) Deletion of the point must not alter the connectivity status of the object.
(iv) Its deletion must not cause excessive erosion.

The neighborhood of each pixel is evaluated to check whether the aforementioned criteria are satisfied before the point is marked for deletion. Note that a point satisfying the above criteria is only marked for deletion and not deleted immediately. All points marked for deletion are actually deleted only at the end of each iteration (i.e., after one complete pass over the entire image).

In order to understand the exact working of Zhang and Suen's thinning algorithm, we define the neighborhood of a pixel by the following diagram.

P_9	P_2	P_3
P_8	P_1	P_4
P_7	P_6	P_5

The neighborhood of each pixel with a value of 1 (i.e., a foreground pixel) is examined iteratively, and if it satisfies the conditions given below the value of the

[4] Zhang T Y and Ching Y S 1984 A fast parallel algorithm for thinning digital patterns *Commun. ACM* **27** 36–39.

pixel (marked P_1 in the neighborhood specified above) is changed to 0. This goes on until there are no foreground pixels that satisfy these conditions.

At the nth iteration of the algorithm a foreground pixel is marked for deletion if

(i) $2 \leqslant B(p) \leqslant 6$, where $B(p)$ represents the number of neighbors of the pixel P_1 that have a value of 1, i.e. are in the foreground;

(ii) $T(p) = 1$, where $T(p)$ is the number of 0 to 1 transitions in pixel value when traveling from P_2 to P_9 in the clockwise manner.

(iii) If n is odd, then P_1 is marked for deletion if $p_2 \cdot p_4 \cdot p_6 = 0$ and $p_4 \cdot p_6 \cdot p_8 = 0$. Here, $\cdot$ refers to the normal multiplication operation.

   If n is even, $p_2 \cdot p_4 \cdot p_8 = 0$ and $p_2 \cdot p_6 \cdot p_8 = 0$.

Each step in the algorithm takes care of a particular constraint of skeletonization:

1. The condition given in step (i) ensures that the endpoints of the skeleton are not erased (corresponding to $B(p) = 1$). The other extreme of $B(p) = 7$ or 8 corresponds to pixel P_1 being in the interior of the object and therefore it should not be marked for deletion.

2. Step (ii) ensures that connectivity is preserved, and that points in between the extremities of the skeleton are not deleted.

3. The conditions given in point (iii) ensure that in the odd-numbered iterations only the south and east border and the northwest corner points are removed; meanwhile, in the even-numbered iterations, the north and west boundary points and the south-east corner points are removed. This is because in the odd-numbered iteration the solution for the condition is ($p_4 = 0$ or $p_6 = 0$) or ($p_2 = 0$ and $p_8 = 0$). When ($p_4 = 0$ or $p_6 = 0$), point P_1 is either an east border point or a south border point, as seen from the figure of the Moore neighborhood. On the other hand, when ($p_2 = 0$ and $p_8 = 0$), P_1 is a northwest corner point. The same logic applies in the case of even iterations in which the logical AND and OR operations are exchanged and the point must be either a north or west border point, or a southeast corner point.

We now reproduce (figure 5.17) some binary images with their corresponding skeletons (obtained by implementing the Zhang–Suen algorithm).

The skeletons obtained for some of the images in figure 5.17 are seen to be easily recognizable and intuitive, and give results that closely approximate the medial line of the objects that are given as input. However, in certain cases in figure 5.17 some discrepancies are observed. Skeletons of some shapes are indistinguishable from each other due to the deletion of the border points, as seen in the case of the rectangle and the oval. In the case of well-defined images such as letters, which have curves and shapes that are specific to each character, the skeletons include arcs that define each character properly. These results distinguish the Zhang–Suen algorithm from a shrinking algorithm. Another drawback is the fact that certain figures and shapes are completely eliminated if certain safeguards are not employed. These include figures that are simplified into a 4 × 4 square of pixels in the penultimate iteration.

From figure 5.17, it is seen that the implemented algorithm finds a good approximation of the skeleton of the object in most cases, barring a few in which

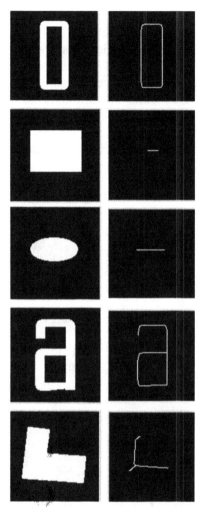

Figure 5.17. Some simple images (on the left) with their corresponding skeletons (on the right).

there is either no difference between different figures, or in which the input figure gets completely eliminated. The origin of the problem seems to lie in step (iii), which eliminates some of the corners of the image, thus leading to undesirable erosion.

As per the definition of a medial axis, one would expect that the diagonals of a rectangle would form its skeleton. However, the skeleton of a rectangle obtained by Zhang and Suen's algorithm bears no relation to the expected skeleton.

Some modifications[5] have been proposed to the above algorithm. One possible modification is to adjust step (i) of the algorithm so that a foreground pixel is eliminated if $4 \leqslant (p) \leqslant 6$.

---

[5] The results presented in figures 5.15 and 5.16 and the modified algorithm described here are extracted from the work done by Nitin Suresh.

By comparing figures 5.17 and 5.18, we see that the modified algorithm gave almost the same results as the original algorithm in the case of well-defined characters and digits. However, in certain cases, we observe from figure 5.18 that the modified algorithm gives results superior to those of the original algorithm. For example, we see that the skeleton of a rectangle satisfies the MAT described earlier. The only disadvantage of the modified algorithm is that the skeleton exhibits more complexity in this case, i.e., there are more branches in the skeleton when we approach corners (for example, look at the skeleton of the letter L in figure 5.18).

We see from figure 5.19 that the skeleton of an ellipse consists of its major and minor axis as is to be expected of an MAT. One undesirable feature of the

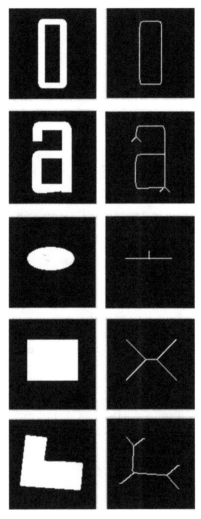

Figure 5.18. Some simple images and the corresponding skeletons obtained by using the modified criterion that a foreground pixel is deleted if $4 \leqslant (p) \leqslant 6$.

skeletonization algorithms discussed here (both the original Zhang–Suen algorithm and the modified algorithm) is that these algorithms are susceptible to noise. Noise can slightly alter the shape of boundaries. The skeletons of such noisy images will exhibit some extra branches due to perturbations in the boundary of objects. These will complicate the process of object recognition and limit the performance of algorithms designed for object recognition based on matching the skeletons of objects with those of templates.

The question may still linger in your mind about how methods of object or character recognition will proceed after obtaining the skeleton of an object. After all, a skeleton is only a simplified representation of an object, which is the meat of the object recognition algorithm.

As mentioned earlier, the process of skeletonization is supposed to simplify the process of object or character recognition. Through skeletonization, we have simplified the image to be recognized. The simplification has gotten rid of one variable in the images to be recognized, i.e., variations in the thickness of strokes. However, we still have to solve the problem of variations in the scale (magnification) of the image and its orientation.

We describe in the next section a method that seeks to overcome the problems posed by variations in the orientation and scale of an image. This is the method of principal component analysis (PCA), which has become very popular in recent years.

Figure 5.19. Some results obtained from the modified skeletonization algorithm.

5.10 Principal component analysis (PCA)

PCA is a powerful technique that can be used for both image recognition as well as compression. It can be used for both these purposes because it essentially it gives us a compact way of describing an object.

Recall the following concepts of vector spaces:

- Any vector in a vector space can be written as a linear combination of a set of basis vectors.
- For a matrix, the set of its eigenvectors can be used as a basis.

We want representation and description to be independent of size, translation, and rotation. PCA provides a convenient way to do this.

The points in a region (or its boundary) may be treated as 2-D vectors.

All the points on the boundary constitute a 2-D vector population that can be used to compute the covariance matrix C_x and the mean vector m_x.

The covariance matrix is defined as

$$C_X = E\{(X - m_X)(X - m_X)^T\} \quad \text{where} \quad X = \begin{bmatrix} x_1 \\ x_2 \\ \vdots \\ x_n \end{bmatrix}. \tag{5.25}$$

Here x_1, x_2,....x_n are the components a n-dimensional vector. We have one vector associated with each point in the image. In image recognition, X stands for the 2-D position vectors of the foreground points in a binary image. Later we will see how PCA can be used for color images. In the case of a color image, X is a set of 3-D vectors that have the red, green, and blue (RGB) values of the pixels. The components of these 3-D vectors are the RGB values of the pixels.

In equation (5.25), E stands for the expected value (or average value).

The mean vector, by definition, is

$$m_X = \frac{1}{K} \sum_{k=1}^{K} X_k. \tag{5.26}$$

The covariance matrix can be written as

$$C_X = \frac{1}{K} \sum_{k=1}^{K} X_k X_k^T - m_X m_X^T. \tag{5.27}$$

We have expanded (5.26) to obtain (5.27).

One eigenvector of C_x points in the direction of maximum variance (data spread) of the population, while the second eigenvector is perpendicular to the first.

PCA automatically takes care of rotation. Size variation is taken care of by dividing by the eigenvalues.

A numerical example would help us to understand the technique of PCA.

Consider a binary image that is made up of just four foreground points, as shown below.

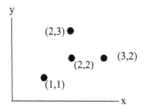

The mean vector is (2, 2).

By substituting the coordinates of all the points and the mean vector in (5.27), we obtain

$$C_x = \begin{pmatrix} 1/2 & 1/4 \\ 1/4 & 1/2 \end{pmatrix}.$$ (5.28)

Notice that the covariance matrix, by definition, will always be symmetric.

The eigenvalues of the covariance matrix are found to be 3/4 and 1/4.

The corresponding eigenvectors are (1 1) and (−1 1).

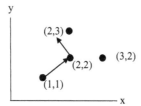

The eigenvectors are shown in the above figure using arrows.

Notice that the eigenvectors are the axes about which the Y-shaped object (made of the four points) is symmetric. The eigenvectors of a symmetric matrix will always be mutually orthogonal. The eigenvectors are also known as the eigenaxes or principal axes of the object. The concept of principal axes has many applications in science and engineering. One of the nice applications of principal axes is that if the principal axes are chosen as the basis vectors then the covariance matrix will be diagonal.

Before we show that the covariance matrix is diagonal if the principal axes are chosen as the basis, we show how the Hotelling transform can be used to aid PCA.

The Hotelling transform proceeds as follows:

- First subtract the mean vector from the position vector of each point.
- The eigenvectors of the covariance matrix form the rows of A.
- Now transform the position vectors x to y as follows:

$$y = A(x - m_x).$$

Subtracting the mean shifts the origin to the centroid.

But what does multiplying by A amount to?

Remember that the rows of A are the eigenvectors. Therefore, multiplying $(x - m_x)$ by A will give us the projection of the eigenvectors along the position vectors (or vice versa).

In the present example, matrix A is found to be

$$A = \begin{pmatrix} 0.707 & 0.707 \\ -0.707 & 0.707 \end{pmatrix}. \tag{5.29}$$

Here, we have normalized the eigenvectors so that they have unit magnitude.

The vectors y are given below.

$$y_1 = \begin{pmatrix} 0.707 & 0.707 \\ -0.707 & 0.707 \end{pmatrix} \left[\begin{pmatrix} 1 \\ 1 \end{pmatrix} - \begin{pmatrix} 2 \\ 2 \end{pmatrix} \right] = \begin{pmatrix} -1.414 \\ 0 \end{pmatrix}$$

$$y_2 = \begin{pmatrix} 0.707 & 0.707 \\ -0.707 & 0.707 \end{pmatrix} \left[\begin{pmatrix} 2 \\ 2 \end{pmatrix} - \begin{pmatrix} 2 \\ 2 \end{pmatrix} \right] = \begin{pmatrix} 0 \\ 0 \end{pmatrix}$$

$$y_3 = \begin{pmatrix} 0.707 & 0.707 \\ -0.707 & 0.707 \end{pmatrix} \left[\begin{pmatrix} 2 \\ 3 \end{pmatrix} - \begin{pmatrix} 2 \\ 2 \end{pmatrix} \right] = \begin{pmatrix} 0.707 \\ 0.707 \end{pmatrix}$$

$$y_4 = \begin{pmatrix} 0.707 & 0.707 \\ -0.707 & 0.707 \end{pmatrix} \left[\begin{pmatrix} 3 \\ 2 \end{pmatrix} - \begin{pmatrix} 2 \\ 2 \end{pmatrix} \right] = \begin{pmatrix} 0.707 \\ -0.707 \end{pmatrix}$$

$$\tag{5.30}$$

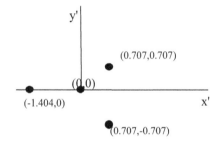

In effect, the Hotelling transform corresponds to rotating the object (and the coordinate axes) so that the eigenaxes are oriented in the horizontal and vertical directions. Hence, the Hotelling transform takes care of rotations of the object. Normalization with respect to scaling can be achieved by dividing by the eigenvalues. In practice, the image is shifted after the application of the Hotelling transform so that all the coordinates are positive. In the above example, this would imply adding 1.404 to the x coordinates of all the foreground points and 0.707 to the y coordinates of all the points.

5.10.1 PCA for color images

Let x_1, x_2, and x_3, respectively, be the values of a pixel in each of the three RGB component images. The three values can be expressed in the form of a column vector:

$$X = \begin{bmatrix} x_1 \\ x_2 \\ x_3 \end{bmatrix}. \tag{5.31}$$

If we are capturing images with sensors that are operating in different parts of the electromagnetic spectrum, we can have a greater number of dimensions.

PCA then proceeds in a similar way as before.

From the above analysis, it is clear that the original image can be reconstructed from the principal components. When we apply PCA to color images we have three eigenvalues.

5.10.2 Image reconstruction from principal components

We can get back the xs and hence the original image starting from the ys.

The inverse Hotelling transform is given by

$$x = A^T y + m_x. \tag{5.32}$$

Here we have used the fact that matrix A, which diagonalizes the symmetric covariance matrix, will be an orthogonal matrix that satisfies $AA^T = I$. Hence, the inverse of an orthogonal matrix will be equal to its transpose[6]. An interesting idea is to use only the largest eigenvectors to reconstruct x. This has significance in image compression. We normally use RGB representation for color images.

Suppose a given image has only two colors, say, green and orange. To describe the two colors we will need all three color components (RGB), but if we switch over to the eigenvector representation we need only two!

What is the magnitude of error in the reconstruction?

$$e_{ms} = \sum_{j=1}^{n} \lambda_j - \sum_{j=1}^{k} \lambda_j = \sum_{j=k+1}^{n} \lambda_j \tag{5.33}$$

The mean square error is given by:

We will now show that choosing the eigenaxes as the basis vectors will diagonalize the covariance matrix. When we make a change of basis, then C_x will be transformed to $S^{-1}C_xS$, where S is a matrix whose columns are the eigenvectors of C_x. Such a transformation of C_x is known as a similarity transformation.

For the covariance matrix given in (5.28), the matrices S and S^{-1} would be

$$S = \begin{pmatrix} 1 & 1 \\ 1 & -1 \end{pmatrix} \text{ and } S^{-1} = \frac{-1}{2}\begin{pmatrix} -1 & -1 \\ -1 & 1 \end{pmatrix}. \tag{5.34}$$

The similarity transformation of C_x would lead to

$$C'_x = S^{-1}C_xS = \frac{-1}{2}\begin{pmatrix} -1 & -1 \\ -1 & 1 \end{pmatrix}\begin{pmatrix} 1/2 & 1/4 \\ 1/4 & 1/2 \end{pmatrix}\begin{pmatrix} 1 & 1 \\ 1 & -1 \end{pmatrix} = \begin{pmatrix} 3/4 & 0 \\ 0 & 1/4 \end{pmatrix}. \tag{5.35}$$

From equation (5.35), it is seen that the similarity transformation diagonalizes the covariance matrix. The diagonal elements are the eigenvalues of the covariance matrix. This is in fact true in general. The elements of the diagonalized matrix are

---

[6] For a thorough discussion about orthogonal matrices and matrix diagonalization, refer to Gilbert Strang's *Introduction to Linear Algebra*, 4th edition.

the eigenvalues of the original matrix. It may also be mentioned that the trace (i.e., the sum of the diagonal elements) and determinant of a matrix are invariant under a similarity transformation. This fact may also be used to obtain the diagonal form of a matrix.

5.10.3 Application of PCA for optical character recognition (OCR)

We will now see how PCA is useful for OCR. Recall from section 5.9 that skeletonization is one of the ways of obtaining a simple representation of an image.

Once the skeleton of a single character has been obtained, we can use PCA for recognizing the characters.

For the sake of completion, we describe below the various steps involved in using OCR and its various applications.

OCR is widely used for example in the postal system of many countries, for sorting mail according to the addresses given on the covers of envelopes and packages. The accuracy of this system is not yet 100%, especially for handwritten addresses. For the purpose of letter sorting, there is an image acquisition unit, a video coding unit, and an OCR unit. A human element is required to sort the letters that are not sorted through automatic OCR, and for this the cost is higher and the efficiency lower. For improving this situation, further research is required on the OCR module.

Preliminary processing of images is required before we can attempt to recognize the characters because we need images that match the standard training sets as much as possible. The various steps involved in the processing are listed below.

1. Conversion from RGB to grayscale—The input images from the acquisition unit are usually RGB (color) images and since the color information is not very useful for the purposes of character recognition and can in certain cases lead to unnecessary complications, the input RGB image is converted to a grayscale image with 256 levels.

2. Digital filtration—To improve the quality of the image, emphasize details, and make processing of the image easier, the input image is convolved with a suitable filter. For example, to remove noise, a 3×3 median filter maybe utilized.

3. Segmentation—The input image is segmented, and individual characters are extracted from it. This process is especially complicated in the case of handwritten characters written in cursive style.

Once the above steps have been implemented, we have to deal with variations in the input characters. In all OCR systems, a database is maintained with many sample images incorporating all possible minor variations in the characters. This set of images is known as the training set. Any new unknown character that has to be recognized will be compared with the training set.

The next step is to apply PCA to the training set. Here again, we have two options. One option is to form a 'mean' image of all images in the training set that correspond to a particular character, and apply PCA to that. This is the procedure that is widely followed in the literature.

We reproduce below some 'mean' images obtained from a training set (figure 5.20). To reduce unnecessary complications, it is better to thin these images before implementing PCA. Notice that the mean images are blurred. The blurring may affect the quality of the skeletons obtained from these images. To overcome this problem, one option is to threshold the mean images and convert them to binary images before we compute the skeleton.

Once the skeletons have been obtained, we can apply PCA to the training set. PCA is also applied to the test image of a character, and the Euclidean distances of the principal components of the test image from the characters in the training set are computed. The test image is assigned to the character that has the minimum Euclidean distance from it.

The other option is to implement PCA separately for each individual image in the training set. Recall that we end up with the eigenvectors of an image during the process of computing its principal components. The eigenvectors can be represented by a point in a four-dimensional space eigenspace (there are two eigenvectors for a 2-D image, each having two components).

All the images in the training set that correspond to a single character will form a cluster of points in the eigenspace. The character will be represented by the centroid of this cluster of points. PCA is applied to the test image and is assigned to the centroid with the minimum Euclidean distance. You will appreciate this method of classification more after reading about the techniques of pattern recognition in section 5.11.

5.11 Pattern recognition

Once a simplified description of an object/image is available in the form of a chain code or in terms of any other descriptor that we have discussed in the earlier sections, the next stage is to use statistical techniques to classify them.

We start with a few basic definitions:
- A pattern is an arrangement of descriptors.
- A pattern class is a family of patterns that share some common properties.
- Pattern recognition by a computerized system involves techniques for assigning patterns to their respective classes—automatically and with as little human intervention as possible.
- Commonly used pattern arrangements are vectors (for quantitative descriptions) and strings and trees (for structural descriptions).

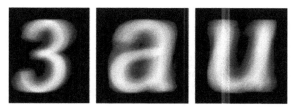

Figure 5.20. Mean images of the characters '3', 'a', and 'u' obtained from a training set.

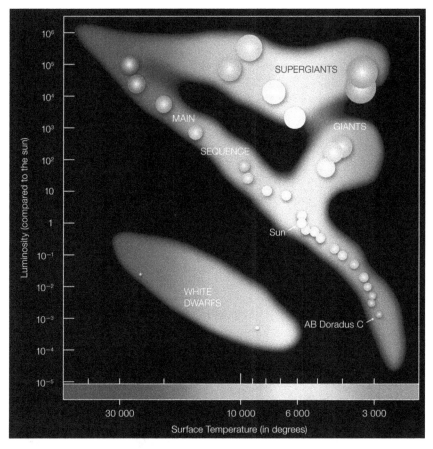

Figure 5.21. The Hertzsprung Russel diagram used to classify stars. Our sun is part of the cluster known as the main sequence[7].

One of the pioneering efforts in this field was done by Fisher in 1936. He measured the length and width of three varieties of iris flowers and created a plot with petal length along the x-axis and petal width along the y-axis. He found that the data for the three classes of flowers formed three clusters. In fact, if the correct descriptors are found, this method of classification can be applied to any field.

A similar technique is used in astronomy to classify stars. It is found that if the absolute luminosity of stars is plotted against their surface temperatures, then the stars fall into certain classes, as shown in figure 5.21.

Once we have created such a plot, we can use clustering techniques to classify objects in an automatic way.

Recognition based on clustering techniques
Clustering techniques are based on discriminant functions.

---

[7] Photo credit: European Space Observatory https://www.eso.org/public/unitedkingdom/images/eso0728c/.

Let $x = (x_1, x_2, x_3, \ldots, x_n)^T$ represent an n-dimensional pattern vector. In the case of the classification of stars or flowers mentioned above, x would be 2-D. However, in certain cases, we may have more attributes and the pattern vector would have more dimensions. For example, we may use height, weight, chest size, and waist size to classify individuals as thin, obese, healthy, etc.

In general, we could have W pattern classes $w_1, w_2, \ldots, w_n$.

The basic problem in pattern recognition (using the clustering approach) is to find W decision functions $d_1(x), d_2(x), d_3(x)\ldots d_w(x)$ with the property that if a pattern x belongs to class w_i, then

$$d_i(x) > d_j(x) j = 1,2, \ldots W; j \neq i. \tag{5.36}$$

An unknown pattern is assigned to the class to which it is closest in terms of a predefined metric. The simplest metric possible is the minimum (Euclidean) distance classifier.

The mean vector of the patterns of a class is given by

$$m_j = \frac{1}{N_j} \sum_{x \in \omega_j} x_j. \tag{5.37}$$

N_j is the number of pattern vectors from class w_j.

To determine the class membership of an unknown pattern vector x, we assign it to the class of its closest prototype. We use the Euclidean distance measure for this:

$$D_j(x) \left\| x - m_j \right\| j = 1, 2, \ldots W. \tag{5.38}$$

Selecting the smallest distance is equivalent to evaluating the functions

$$d_j(x) = x^T m_j - \frac{1}{2} m_j^T m_j j = 1,2,\ldots W. \tag{5.39}$$

We will now show that selecting the smallest distance to a class is equivalent to evaluating the functions $d_j(x)$.

We want to find the class for which the distance of x from the mean of the class is a minimum.

That is, we minimize

$$D_j^2 = \left\| x - m_j \right\|^2 = (x - m_j)^T (x - m_j) = x^T x - 2x^T m_j + m_j^T m_j. \tag{5.40}$$

This can be rewritten as

$$D_j^2 = x^T x - 2\left(x^T m_j - \frac{1}{2} m_j^T m_j \right). \tag{5.41}$$

Therefore, minimizing D_j^2 is equivalent to maximizing the term in brackets.

The decision boundary between classes w_i and w_j for a minimum distance classifier is

$$d_{ij}(x) = d_i(x) - d_j(x) \tag{5.42}$$

$$= x^T(m_i - m_j) - \frac{1}{2}(m_i - m_j)^T(m_i + m_j) = 0. \qquad (5.43)$$

The surface given by the above equation is the perpendicular bisector of the line joining m_i and m_j.

Proof: The first term is the projection of x along (m_1-m_2) since it is the dot product of x and (m_1-m_2).

Similarly the other term is the projection of $(m_1 + m_2)/2$ along (m_1-m_2). These two projections are equal only if x lies on the perpendicular bisector of the line joining m_1 and m_2 (figure 5.22).

The decision boundary need not always be a straight line, as the following example shows.

Example 5.1:

A class ω_1 contains the vectors (2, 0), (−2, 0), (0, 4), and (0, −4) while the class ω_2 contains the vectors (8, 0), (−8, 0), (0, 12), and (0, −12). Are these vectors linearly separable? What is the shape of the decision boundary for these classes?

If we plot the points (see figure 5.23), we notice that the set of points belonging to w_1 and w_2 are situated symmetrically with respect to the origin; moreover, all the points belonging to the former class are closer to the origin than those of the latter class. Hence, the decision boundary cannot be a straight line in this case, and thus the vectors are not linearly separable. We also see that the distances of the points from the origin are not same along the x- and y-axes. Hence, we might conjecture that the shape of the decision boundary will be an ellipse in this case.

Matching by correlation

A straightforward way of conducting object or pattern recognition is to match an unknown pattern/image with a pre-existing template (also known as a mask) by calculating the correlation between the image and the mask.

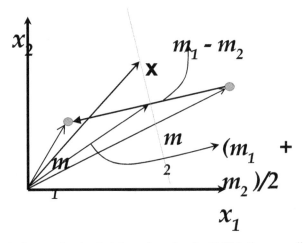

Figure 5.22. Schematic diagram showing that the surface given by (5.43) is the perpendicular bisector of the line joining the mean vectors.

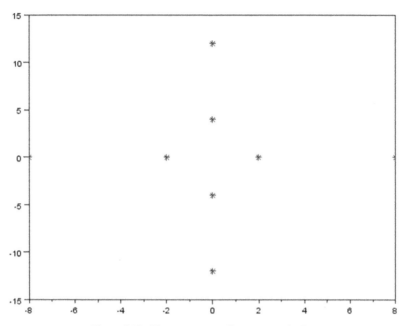

Figure 5.23. Figure corresponding to example 5.1.

The correlation of a mask $w(x, y)$ of size $m \times n$ with an image $f(x, y)$ may be expressed as

$$c(x, y) = \sum_s \sum_t w(s, t) f(x + s, y + t).$$

To make the correlation scale-free, we use the following normalized correlation coefficient:

$$\gamma(x, y) = \frac{\sum_s \sum_t [\omega(s, t) - \bar{\omega}] \sum_s \sum_t [f(x + s, y + t) - \bar{f}(x + s, y + t)]}{\left\{ \sum_s \sum_t [\omega(s, t) - \bar{\omega}]^2 \sum_s \sum_t [f(x + s, y + t) - \bar{f}(x + s, y + t)]^2 \right\}^{1/2}}.$$

Here, $\bar{\omega}$ and $\bar{f}$ are average values of the template and the function f, respectively.

$\gamma(x, y)$ has values in the range $[-1, 1]$. The maximum values occur when f is identical to the template. We look for the locations where $\gamma(x, y)$ has the maximum value.

The correlation coefficient is already normalized for changes in intensity values, but how do we normalize for size and rotation? Normalizing for size requires that we know the distance from which the image is taken (assuming a certain viewing angle). In remote sensing, the image can be put in the proper orientation if the direction of flight is known.

Normalizing for size and rotation in an arbitrary context may be very difficult.

In this chapter, we have tried to present some of the simple techniques used in image analysis and pattern recognition. In recent years, many other techniques, based on neural networks, have become very popular.

Exercises

1. a) Derive the equation (r as a function of θ) for the signature of the equilateral triangle ABC (see figure below) that is applicable for $\theta = 0°$ to $120°$. The coordinates of B are $(3, 0)$ while A and C lie on the y-axis and are equidistant from the origin.

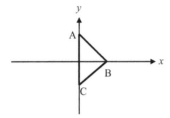

   b) Modify the equation for the signature obtained in a) to obtain the equation of the signature for the range $\theta = 120°$ to $240°$.

2. A number of stones are projected at various angles to the horizontal with different velocities. The coordinates of the stones at different points in their trajectory are recorded, and an image is obtained that shows the complete trajectory of all the stones until they hit the ground. All the stones are projected from the same point, which is designated as the origin. The horizontal coordinate is designated by x and the vertical coordinate by y. It is proposed to use the Hough transform for detecting the trajectories of all the stones.

   a) Write down the general form of the equation for the trajectory of a stone.

   b) What will be the dimension of the parameter space used for the Hough transform?

3. The RGB intensity values for each pixel in an RGB image can be represented by a 3-D vector x. The image has N rows and N columns.

   How many additions and multiplications are required in evaluating the Hotelling transform? You need not consider the operations that are part of the steps preceding the Hotelling transform.

4. The signature of an object having a regular shape is shown below. Identify the shape and also the dimensions of the object from the figure given below. If θ is measured with respect to the horizontal axis, show the orientation of the object with respect to the horizontal.

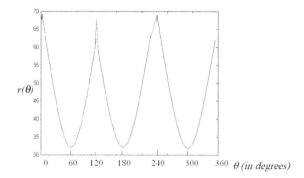

5. a) You are asked to use the Hough transform to detect circles in a binary image of size 100×100 (pixels). Assuming that all the circles lie completely within the image, what will be the minimum size of the parameter space you will be choosing in order to detect circles of all possible radii? How many accumulator cells should there be for detecting circles of all possible radii?

    b) If the Hough transform is being used for detecting straight lines in a binary image of size 100×100, how many accumulator cells will be required if θ is incremented in steps of $1°$ and the distance ρ is calculated up to an accuracy of 1 pixel units.

6. Assume that you have designed a system to identify objects from the shape of their boundaries. You have photographed objects that are either spheres or circular disks of the same radii. The light is incident normal to the surface of the disk. In the image, which is 2-D, the boundary will be circular in the case of the disk as well as the sphere. Since the shape of the boundary is the same in both cases, what other information can you use from the image in order to distinguish between the two objects?

7. You are asked to use the Hough transform for detecting ellipses in a binary image of size 100×100 (pixels). Assuming that all the ellipses lie completely within the image, what will be the dimension of the parameter space you will be choosing in order to detect ellipses? Give the range for each of the parameters. How many accumulator cells should there be for detecting all possible ellipses?

8. In the recognition of handwritten characters, one important step is to determine the slant of the letters. For example, the letters in '*slant*' are inclined while the letters in 'slant' are not. Based on concept(s) you have learned in this chapter, explain how you will determine the angle of inclination of the handwritten characters? Assume that you have binary images of the handwritten document.

9. Nowadays, it has become common practice to use OMR sheets for conducting examinations. In an OMR form, there are four open circles (or ellipses) for each question and the student has to darken the circle corresponding to the correct answer. Four dark squares (typically of area

1 cm × 1 cm or less) are placed at the corners of the OMR sheet (one at each corner). These squares are very crucial for the process of correctly detecting the coordinates of the darkened circles. Why?

10. The LoG is used in many edge detection algorithms. Show that the average value of the Laplacian of a Gaussian operator is zero. Here, G is the continuous 2-D Gaussian function given by

$$G(x, y) = e^{-\left(\frac{x^2+y^2}{2\sigma^2}\right)}.$$

11. In each of the following cases, place the operations in the proper order:
    a) calculation of signature, determination of centroid, thresholding, edge detection;
    b) determination of eigenvectors, determination of eigenvalues, thresholding, edge detection;
    c) edge detection, thresholding, chain code, Moore's boundary tracking algorithm.

12. Assume that you have to design an image processing system that will monitor a chessboard (as the game is progressing). The system takes still photographs whenever a move has been completed. The task for the system is to now detect which squares on the board have chess pieces and which ones are empty. Hint: Chess squares that do not contain any piece are uniformly white or uniformly dark.

Programming assignments

1. Write a program to calculate the signature of an object. The program should also calculate the moments of the signature.

   Hint: While calculating the signature, you will be calculating θ using the fact that $\theta = \tan^{-1}(y/x)$. Use the *atan2* function available in MATLAB® instead of the *atan* function. The function *atan2* calculates θ over the range $-\pi/2$ to $+\pi/2$, while the *atan* function calculates θ over the range $-\pi$ to $+\pi$ and is multivalued.

2. Write a program to perform PCA. The program should calculate the covariance matrix of an input binary image. Use the inbuilt MATLAB® functions to determine the eigenvalues and eigenvectors of the covariance matrix and apply the Hotelling transform to the image.

3. Write a program to perform PCA on a color image. The program should calculate the covariance matrix of an input color image. Use the inbuilt MATLAB® functions to determine the eigenvalues and eigenvectors of the covariance matrix and apply the Hotelling transform to the image. Reconstruct the image using two of the largest eigenvalues. Compare the reconstructed image with the original.

4. Given below is part of a program for implementing variance-based thresholding. (Only the important parts of the program are printed here.)
   1. A=imread('filename.bmp','bmp');
   2. A=double(A);
   3. Rows=size(A,1);
   4. Columns=size(A,2);
   5. for i=1:256
   6. histr(a(i,j)+1)=histr(a(i,j)+1)+1; 'histr was already initialized';
   7. end

Now continue the development of the program. The program has to calculate the between-class variance *sigmab* for various values of threshold t starting from $t = 1$ to $t = t_{max}$, where t_{max} is the value of t for which *sigmab* has the maximum value. The program has to stop running once t_{max} has been reached.

Sigmab = $P_1 P_2 (m_1 - m_2)^2$ where P_1 and P_2 are the probabilities of a pixel to belong to the classes 1 and 2, and m_1 and m_2 are the mean values of the two classes (the calculation of these quantities should also be shown in the program).

IOP Publishing

A Course on Digital Image Processing with MATLAB®

P K Thiruvikraman

Chapter 6

Image restoration

This is a photograph of the night sky. But what are those white arcs you see in this photograph?

You will be able to answer this question after you have finished reading this chapter.

We have mentioned that remote sensing is one area where the techniques of image processing have been applied extensively. Remote sensing satellites (unlike geostationary satellites) move relative to the surface of the Earth. Due to the relative motion, they can capture images of different parts of the Earth's surface.

However, we know that if we capture the image of an object that is moving relative to the camera, then the object will appear to be blurred (see figure 6.1). This is so because the boundaries of the object would have moved during the time the shutter of the camera was open.

Motion blur is one of the degradations that an image can suffer. Images can also be degraded due to noise or other reasons such as improper focusing of the camera. Undoing the effects of these degradations is known as image restoration. Image

Figure 6.1. A photograph taken from a moving aircraft.

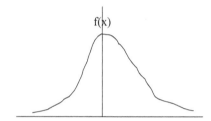

Figure 6.2. Representation of the intensity variation $f(x)$ in a 1-D image.

restoration is a very crucial step since all algorithms for image recognition can be implemented only after the image has been restored to its original state.

In remote sensing, apart from motion blur, atmospheric turbulence is another cause for image degradation. Atmospheric turbulence also affects the quality of astronomical images obtained from ground-based telescopes[1]. We will now look at certain techniques for image restoration.

6.1 Analyzing motion blur

To understand motion blur, let us consider what happens when we photograph a 1-D image that is moving with respect to the camera. We assume that the motion is along a direction perpendicular to the line of sight. This is certainly true of remote sensing, where the satellite is revolving around the Earth while maintaining a constant distance from its surface.

Let the image be modeled by a 1-D function $f(x)$ (figure 6.2). The motion of the object is also along the x-direction.

Let us say that we are moving from left to right while the picture is being acquired, i.e., the motion of the observer is perpendicular to the line of sight. Such a situation arises in remote sensing.

---

[1] The apparent twinkling of stars is also due to turbulence in the Earth's atmosphere.

In such a situation, at a given instant of time t, the observed image is $f(x')$, where

$$x' = x - v_x t.$$

What we capture in the camera is the summation of all such images, since the shutter is open for a finite time T.

Therefore, the captured (degraded) image is given by

$$g(x) = \frac{1}{T} \int_0^T f(x') dt. \tag{6.1}$$

Let us look at this problem in the Fourier domain:

$$G(u, v) = \frac{1}{T} \int_{-\infty}^{\infty} \int_{-\infty}^{\infty} \int_0^T f(x - vt, y) dt \, \exp(-2\pi j u x) \exp(-2\pi j v y) dx \, dy. \tag{6.2}$$

Here we have considered a 2-D image. However, the motion is still along only one dimension, i.e., along the x-axis.

We can rewrite this as

$$G(u, v) = \frac{1}{T} \int_0^T \int_{-\infty}^{\infty} \int_{\infty}^{\infty} f(x', y) \exp\left(-2\pi j u x'\right) \exp(-2\pi j v y') dx' dy'$$
$$\times \exp(-2\pi j u v_x t) dt. \tag{6.3}$$

Here, we have substituted for x in terms of x'.

$$G(u, v) = \frac{1}{T} \int_0^T F(u, v) \exp(-2\pi j u v_x t) dt \tag{6.4}$$

Hence, the Fourier transform of the degraded image is identical to that of the original (undergraded image), except for a phase factor. The integration over time can be easily carried out, giving

$$G(u, v) = \frac{1}{T} \int_0^T F(u, v) \exp(-2\pi j u v_x t) dt \tag{6.5}$$

$$G(u, v) = \frac{1}{T} \left(\frac{\exp(-2\pi j u v_x t)}{-2\pi j u v_x} \right)_0^T F(u, v) \tag{6.6}$$

$$G(u, v) = \frac{1}{T} \left(\frac{\exp(-2\pi j u v_x T) - 1}{-2\pi j u v_x} \right) F(u, v) \tag{6.7}$$

$$G(u, v) = \frac{\exp(-\pi j u v_x T)}{T} \left(\frac{\exp(-\pi j u v_x T) - \exp(\pi j u v_x T)}{-2\pi j u v_x} \right) F(u, v). \tag{6.8}$$

Let $v_x = a/T$ (where a is the distance moved by the object during the time T). Therefore,

$$G(u, v) = \exp(-\pi jua)\left(\frac{\exp(-\pi jua) - \exp(\pi jua)}{-2\pi jua}\right)F(u, v) \qquad (6.9)$$

$$G(u, v) = \exp(-j\pi ua)\frac{\sin(\pi ua)}{(\pi ua)}F(u, v) \qquad (6.10)$$
$$= F(u, v)H(u, v).$$

$H(u, v)$ is the Fourier transform of the degradation function (also known as the point-spread function).

Since the effect of degradation is multiplicative in the Fourier domain, in the spatial domain

$$g(x, y) = h(x, y)*f(x, y). \qquad (6.11)$$

In the presence of additive noise,

$$g(x, y) = h(x, y)*f(x, y) + \eta(x, y)$$

or

$$G(u, v) = H(u, v)F(u, v) + N(u, v). \qquad (6.12)$$

The discussion given above is not valid for the case when motion is not perpendicular to the line of sight or when only one object is moving in the field of view (instead of the observer moving).

Such a situation arises in photographing sports events (for example), where we are photographing a moving sportsman against a stationary background.

6.2 Inverse filtering

We now discuss how we can restore an image that has degraded due to the motion of the camera (section 6.1).

From equation (6.12), we have, in the absence of noise,

$$F(u, v) = G(u, v)/H(u, v). \qquad (6.13)$$

Hence, we can restore the image if we know the Fourier transform of the degradation function.

However there are some problems with inverse filtering:

1. Usually noise is present, and we require information about the Fourier spectrum of the noise (which is usually difficult to obtain).
2. $H(u, v)$ can become zero for certain values of u and v.

$H(u, v)$ becomes zero when $u = 1/a$ or multiples of this number.

Here, a is the length moved in time T (practically, this length is given in terms of number of pixels). Usually this problem is tackled by doing inverse filtering excluding the frequencies where zeros are encountered. Thus, this is like applying a low-pass filter on top of the inverse filter.

We can generalize our discussion of degradation to include degradation due to causes other than uniform motion. It turns out that it is easy to restore an image if it is subject to linear, position-invariant degradations. The degradation due to motion (equation (6.1)) is clearly a linear degradation since it involves an integral that is a linear transformation. The degradation due to motion also satisfies the condition of position invariance since the entire image is subject to the degradation and the degraded value of a pixel is independent of the position.

It can be shown that, in general, if the response of the degradation function to an impulse is known, its response to any image can be worked out.

To prove this, we note that equation (6.1) can be written as a convolution of two functions as shown below:

$$g(x) = \int_{-\infty}^{\infty} f(x - \alpha)h(\alpha)d\alpha \tag{6.14}$$

where $h(\alpha) = 1/T$ over the interval during which the image is being acquired. We note that $h(\alpha)$ is a rectangular function, and its Fourier transform is the sinc function.

In fact, we can show that the degraded image $g(x, y)$ is always equal to the convolution of the image $f(x, y)$ and the degradation function $h(x, y)$, provided the degradation satisfies the conditions of linearity and position invariance.

The degraded image $g(x, y)$ can be represented as

$$g(x, y) = H[f(x, y)] + \eta(x, y). \tag{6.15}$$

Here, H is a degradation operator that acts on the image and transforms it into the degraded image. We ignore noise for the time being and rewrite $f(x, y)$ as

$$f(x, y) = \int_{-\infty}^{\infty} \int_{-\infty}^{\infty} f(\alpha, \beta)\delta(x - \alpha, y - \beta)d\alpha d\beta. \tag{6.16}$$

If H is a linear operator, then

$$\begin{aligned} g(x, y) &= H \int_{-\infty}^{\infty} \int_{-\infty}^{\infty} f(\alpha, \beta)\delta(x - \alpha, y - \beta)d\alpha d\beta \\ &= \int_{-\infty}^{\infty} \int_{-\infty}^{\infty} H[f(\alpha, \beta)\delta(x - \alpha, y - \beta)d\alpha d\beta]. \end{aligned} \tag{6.17}$$

H acts only as a function of the coordinates (x, y), and therefore, equation (6.17) can be written as

$$g(x, y) = \int_{-\infty}^{\infty} \int_{-\infty}^{\infty} f(\alpha, \beta)H[\delta(x - \alpha, y - \beta)]d\alpha d\beta. \tag{6.18}$$

If H is position-invariant, i.e., the response at any point in the image depends only on the value of the input at that point, not on its position, then

$$H[\delta(x - a, y - b)] = h(x - a, y - b). \tag{6.19}$$

The RHS of this equation is called the impulse response of H.

Therefore, from the above derivation we see that if the response of H to an impulse is known, the response to any input $f(\alpha, \beta)$ can be calculated. Notice from equation (6.18) that the effect of the degradation due to H is a convolution of the impulse response and the original image. One way of undoing the degradation is to deconvolve the degraded image. Another way is to model the degradation (as we have done for the case of uniform motion) and calculate the impulse response. Once the impulse response has been obtained, we can obtain the Fourier transform of equation (6.18). In the Fourier domain, $G(u, v)$ will be equal to the product of the Fourier transforms of the impulse response and the undegraded, original image. We can therefore use the technique of inverse filtering contained in equation (6.13) for all linear, position-invariant degradations.

Now, after the discussion of motion blur in sections 6.1 and 6.2, you are in a position to give a correct interpretation of the photograph printed at the beginning of this chapter (the photograph of the night sky).

This is an example of a photograph taken with a long exposure time, i.e., the shutter of the photograph is kept open for a long time. While the shutter is open, the Earth is rotating on its axis and as a consequence the stars and other heavenly bodies appear to move in the night sky. Thus, the image of a star will not be a point, but a small arc of a circle (also known as a star trail).

In the present case, the photograph[2] was created by combining 300 photographs clicked over a period of 3 h during a single night. The effect seen is equivalent to that obtained in the case of a long exposure photograph.

The center about which the stars appear to rotate is a point on the Earth's axis. In this case it is vertically above the North Pole.

Star trails will be seen in all astronomical photographs that have been subject to a long exposure time. A long exposure is very much required for many astronomical photographs in order to capture the image of very faint stars. Hence, restoring such images is very much required. However, the degradation model in this case will be different from that discussed in section 6.1 (which was for the case of uniform linear motion). Discussion of degradation of an image due to rotational motion is left as an exercise to the reader.

6.3 Noise

Noise is introduced into images during transmission and acquisition. It may be better to remove noise first, since inverse filtering in the presence of noise will be difficult to deal with (as seen from equation (6.12)).

Noise can be classified either based on its spectral properties or based on its statistical properties. Based on the spectral properties, noise can be classified as follows:

1. White noise (Fourier spectrum of noise is a constant).
2. Spatially periodic noise (can be removed by filtering in the Fourier domain).

---

[2] The photograph mentioned here were taken by Mr. Vijay Narayan. I am very thankful to him for sending me the photograph.

Based on the statistical behavior of the gray level values in the noise component, we can classify the noise into:

- Gaussian;
- Rayleigh;
- Erlang (Gamma);
- Exponential;
- Uniform;
- Impulse (salt and pepper).

We now briefly discuss the probability distributions followed by the various kinds of noise mentioned above.

Gaussian noise is present in electronic circuits and in sensors due to high temperature. Mathematically, the Gaussian distribution is given by

$$p(z) = \frac{1}{\sqrt{2\pi}\sigma} \exp(-(z-\mu)^2/2\sigma^2). \tag{6.20}$$

Here, $p(z)$ is the probability density function for Gaussian noise. z is the noise level, whose mean value is μ and standard deviation is σ. It is a common mistake to assume that $p(z)$ can only take values in the range 0 to 1. This restriction applies only to the values of probability, which is given by $p(z)dz$. $p(z)dz$ is the probability that a pixel selected at random suffers from a noise level that is in the range z and $z + dz$. It is assumed that the noise is additive in nature, i.e., the noise value z adds on to the actual pixel value.

The Gaussian probability density function is plotted below (figure 6.3).

The probability density function for Rayleigh noise (figure 6.4) is

$$p(z) = \frac{2}{b}(z-a)\exp(-(z-a)^2/b) \quad \text{for } z \geqslant a \tag{6.21}$$
$$= 0 \qquad\qquad\qquad\qquad\qquad \text{for } z < a.$$

We now look at other possible probability density functions for noise.

The probability density function for exponential noise is given as follows:

$$p(z) = a\exp(-az) \quad \text{for } z \geqslant 0 \tag{6.22}$$
$$= 0 \qquad\qquad\quad \text{for } z < 0.$$

The probability density function for uniform noise is as follows:

$$p(z) = 1/(b-a) \quad \text{if } a \leqslant z \leqslant b \tag{6.23}$$
$$= 0 \qquad\qquad \text{otherwise.}$$

Another possible type of noise is the salt and pepper noise that occurs due to transient noise. Salt and pepper noise occurs due to sudden surges that may result from switching on or off heavy electrical equipment.

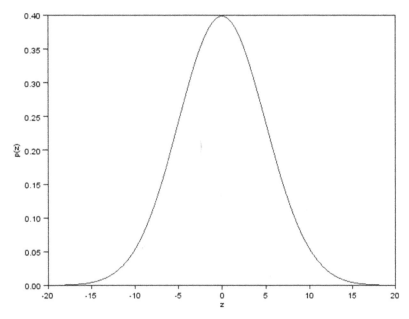

Figure 6.3. Gaussian probability density function with zero mean and a standard deviation of 5 units.

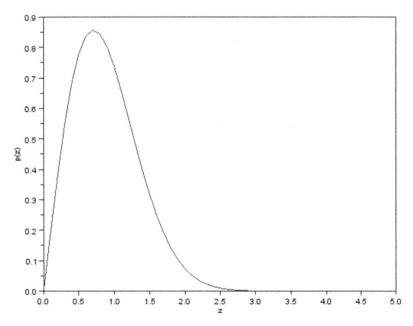

Figure 6.4. Rayleigh probability density function with $b = 1$ and $a = 0$.

The salt pepper and pepper noise has the following distribution:

$$p(z) = P_a \ \text{ for } z = a$$
$$= P_b \ \text{ for } z = b \qquad\qquad (6.24)$$
$$= 0, \ \text{ otherwise.}$$

The median filter is especially suited for removing salt and pepper noise. If an image is corrupted with salt and/or pepper noise, then the intensities of those pixels become either 0 or 255. Simple averaging would just smear or distribute the noise among the surrounding pixels.

To realize this, imagine a region of an image with a uniform background, where all the pixels have the same intensity of, say, 128. Some of the pixels may be affected by salt noise and some by pepper noise. If we now convolve the image with a simple averaging filter of size 3 × 3, then the value after averaging would be 143.875 (rounded to 144) if only one pixel within the mask is affected by salt noise. The averaged value would be higher if more than one pixel within the mask is affected by salt noise. Similarly, if the image is affected by pepper noise, the averaged value would be less than 128 (the original value).

Now consider applying a 3 × 3 median filter on the same noise-affected image. We calculate the median of all the pixel values within the mask and replace the central pixel in the mask with the median value. If we assume that the majority of the pixels are unaffected by noise, then the median value would be 128 and the noise would be completely removed. Hence the median filter is more effective than the averaging filter in removing salt and pepper noise.

In general, we would like to design different kinds of filters and study their effectiveness in removing the different kinds of noise we have discussed.

In order to test our algorithms, we deliberately corrupt a test image with artificially generated noise.

How can we generate noise of a particular kind and with desired parameters?

We can easily generate uniform noise using random number generators. The in-built function RAND in MATLAB® generates random numbers.

How can we obtain other probability density functions like Gaussian, exponential, etc?

In order to generate other noise probability density functions, we use the following relation:

$$p(z)dz = p(r)dr.$$

Here, $p(r)$ is the random distribution. Therefore, $p(r) = 1$ over the entire range.
Therefore,

$$r = \int_0^1 p(z)dz. \qquad\qquad (6.25)$$

Since $p(z)$ is given, we can invert this relation to get the required z values from r.

Example 6.1 Generate noise values z that follow the probability density function

$$p(z) = 10 \exp(-10z). \tag{6.26}$$

$$r = \int_0^z 10 \exp(-10z)dz = -\exp(-10z)|_0^z$$
$$= 1 - \exp(-10z) \tag{6.27}$$

We can invert this relation to get

$$z = (-1/10) \ln(1 - r).$$

If we want to generate a list of 100 values of z satisfying the exponential distribution, we generate 100 random numbers (r) and substitute them into the above equation. For each value of r, the above equation gives us a corresponding value of z.

6.4 Removal of noise by morphological operations

We have so far looked at removing noise by using filters like the averaging filter and the median filter. Another approach is to remove noise by morphological operations. Morphological operations can also be used for extracting the boundary of an object (for example).

Morphological operations are easily defined and implemented for binary images. Hence, the subsequent discussion pertains only to binary images.

In performing morphological operations, we use structuring elements or masks. Structuring elements are small subimages that are used to probe an image under study.

In figure 6.5, the pixels that are shaded have a value of 1 and the unshaded pixels have a value of 0. Other structuring elements are also possible. For example, we can choose a square mask of size 3×3 and choose all the pixels within it to have a value of 1. We can 'apply' or translate the structuring element over the entire image and define some operations. One of the simplest is erosion.

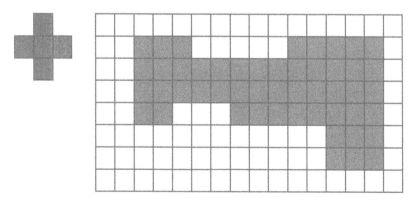

Figure 6.5. A binary image (right) and a structuring element (left) that is applied to the image.

6.4.1 Erosion

The erosion of A (image) by B (structuring element) is defined as

$$A \ominus B = \{z | (B)_z \subseteq A\}. \tag{6.28}$$

The above equation implies that the erosion of A by B is the set of all points z such that B, translated by z, is contained in A. Using the language of set theory, we can rewrite equation (6.21) as

$$A \ominus B = \{z | (B)_z \cap A^c = \varphi\}. \tag{6.29}$$

Equation (6.22) says that the erosion of A by B is such that the set of all points (pixels) satisfying the erosion operation are such that the intersection of those points with the complement of A is a null set.

We see that translating the structuring element all over the image will remove the pixels on the boundary of the shaded region since these points have an intersection with the complement of A (i.e., the background).

The resulting image (after one pass of the structuring element over the image in figure 6.5) will be as presented below.

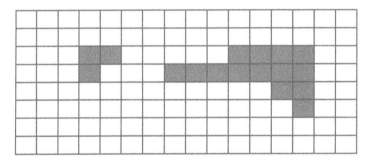

We see that erosion affected the connectivity of the object in this case. Repeated passes of the structuring element over the image will lead to further erosion. We now define the operation that is complementary to erosion. However, this operation will not undo the effect of erosion.

6.4.2 Dilation

If erosion erodes or thins objects, then dilation 'grows' or 'thickens' objects.

Hence, one important application is for bridging gaps. Sometimes gaps develop in boundaries due to noise. This can impede the performance of algorithms that attempt to 'recognize' the shape of the boundary. Hence, dilation may be helpful in these cases. Dilation is defined as

$$A \oplus B = \left\{z | (\hat{B})_z \cap A \neq \Phi\right\}. \tag{6.30}$$

6.4.3 Opening and closing

We now combine the operations of erosion and dilation. We can define two different operations when we combine them (depending on the order in which they are performed). The opening of set A by structuring element B, denoted $A \circ B$, is defined as

$$A \circ B = (A \ominus B) \oplus B. \tag{6.31}$$

Hence, it is erosion followed by dilation. Opening smoothens the contour of an object, breaks narrow isthmuses, and eliminates thin protrusions (figure 6.6).

In the above case, we have used a circular structuring element, which may not be practically feasible. However, more conventional rectangular or square structuring elements also lead to almost similar results.

In closing, the dilation is followed by erosion. Therefore,

$$A \cdot B = (A \oplus B) \ominus B. \tag{6.32}$$

Note:
- Outward-pointing corners are rounded while opening an object, while inward-pointing corners are unaffected.
- Inward-pointing corners are rounded while closing and outward-pointing corners are unaffected.

Opening satisfies the following properties:
1. $A \circ B$ is a subset (subimage) of A.
2. If C is a subset of D, then $C \circ B$ is a subset of $D \circ B$.
3. $(A \circ B) \circ B = A \circ B$

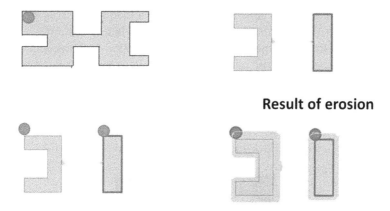

Result of erosion

Result after dilation

Figure 6.6. Opening of an image. Note that the effect of erosion is not completely undone by dilation.

Closing satisfies the following properties:
1. A is a subset (subimage) of $A \cdot B$.
2. If C is a subset of D, then $C \cdot B$ is a subset of $D \cdot B$.
3. $(A \cdot B) \cdot B = A \cdot B$

Note that opening and then closing an image removes almost all the noise, but some of the ridges contain breaks. Hence, additional processing is required to maintain connectivity.

There are many other practical uses of morphological operations. For example, erosion can be used to extract the boundary of an image. Since erosion removes the boundary of an image and gives us the 'bulk' of the image. Subtracting the result of erosion from the original image will give us the boundary of the object.

$$\beta(A) = A - (A \Theta B)$$

Morphological operations can also be used to 'label' objects in an image. Labeling is an important first step in many applications since we usually need to count the number of objects within an image. Instead of using morphological algorithms for labeling objects, we can use an alternative algorithm, which we describe in the following section.

6.5 Alternative method for extracting and labeling connected components

- Convert the image into a binary file (pixels will be 0 or 1).
- Scan (read) the pixels, one by one, starting from the top-left corner.
- If a nonzero pixel is encountered, label it as 2.
- Look at the neighbors of this pixel and then the neighbors of the neighbors and label all non-zero pixels as 2.
- All the neighbors that have a value of 1 are added to an array so that we can later look at the neighbors of these pixels in a later iteration.
- The total number of objects in the image will be $k - 1$, where k is the last label to be used (this is because of the fact that we have used the number '2' to label the first object).

Let us assume that we are required to count the number of ellipses in an image. Initially we have a binary image (figure 6.7) where all the foreground pixels are labeled 1. The result of the labeling operation is shown in figure 6.8.

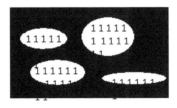

Figure 6.7. A binary image where the foreground pixels have a value of 1.

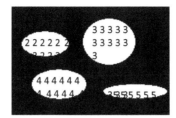

Figure 6.8. Result of the labeling operation.

Figure 6.9. A single beam of x-rays is incident on an object (white circle) from the left. The signal is proportional to the intensity absorbed by the object.

6.6 Image reconstruction from projections

6.6.1 CT scan

In this chapter, we have looked at how an image can be restored by removing noise or by removing the effects of degradation due to motion. We will now consider a topic of great importance in the field of biomedical imaging. The CT scan is widely used to obtain 3-D images of regions within the human body. The 3-D image is actually reconstructed from many images of the region taken from different angles. We will now look at how the reconstruction is accomplished.

In CT, x-ray beams are incident on the object from various angles. Detectors placed on the side opposite the source of x-rays record the intensity of the radiation transmitted through the object. It is generally assumed that the object absorbs the x-rays to a greater extent than the background. The intensity recorded by the detector will be equal to the difference between the original intensity of the source and the intensity absorbed by the object.

Let us consider a simple case so that we are able to analyze the entire process.

Let the object under investigation be as shown in figure 6.9.

Figure 6.9 shows a single x-ray beam that is incident on the object under investigation. In practice, multiple beams are used from different directions. A strip of detectors on the other side record the transmitted intensity. For convenience, we consider the signal to be proportional to the absorbed intensity, although in reality the signal is proportional to the transmitted intensity. The transmitted intensity is linearly related to the absorbed intensity. Therefore, this assumption can be considered as reasonable (they are related by a constant: see equation (6.34)).

The absorption signal in figure 6.9 was not obtained experimentally but was computed using some well-known laws of physics and some reasonable assumptions. The assumptions used in calculating the absorption signal in figure 6.9 were the following:

(i) The background does not absorb any radiation.
(ii) The circular object is homogeneous, and the intensity of the radiation transmitted through it is given by the well-known Beer–Lambert's law:

$$I = I_o \exp(-\lambda d). \tag{6.33}$$

Here, I_o is the intensity of the incident x-rays, λ is a constant characteristic of the absorption of the material, and d is the distance traversed by the ray. It is seen from figure 6.9 that since the object is circular, the distance traversed within the object will be different for different rays. The signal was computed by taking this into account, and was based on the equation

$$I_{abs} = I_o - I = I_o(1 - \exp(-\lambda d)). \tag{6.34}$$

For a nonhomogeneous object that will have different values of λ for different parts, we would have to suitably modify equation (6.33) and equation (6.34). For the sake of simplicity, we consider only homogeneous objects for the time being.

To reconstruct the object from the received signal, we project the ray back along the direction from which it was received. The process of projecting the ray backward is an imaginary one that will help us in reconstructing the object. The strength of the backprojected ray is equal to the strength of the received signal (which is proportional to the amount of absorption). We can now realize why we consider the received signal to be equal to the amount of absorption. This will help us in locating and quantifying the thickness of the object along the direction of the x-ray.

Of course, the shape of the object cannot be reconstructed from a single backprojection. We require signals from many directions in order to obtain a faithful reconstruction of the object.

If we backproject the received signal in figure 6.9, we would obtain the image in figure 6.10.

Figure 6.10 implies that since we are ignorant about the precise shape of the object, we assume that the received signal could have resulted from an object located anywhere along the path of the ray.

We can narrow down the shape of the object by superposing on figure 6.10 the backprojection of the signal received from other directions. For example, if we had sent a beam in a direction perpendicular to that used in figure 6.9, then the result of the backprojections from the two beams will give us further information about the shape of the object.

If instead of superposing the two backprojections we had looked at their overlap, we would have obtained figure 6.11.

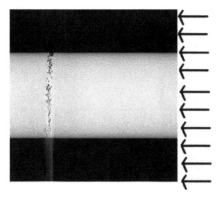

Figure 6.10. Result of projecting the received signal in the backward direction.

Figure 6.11. Superposition of the backprojection of beams sent in perpendicular directions.

In this case (figure 6.12), the reconstructed object is a square, whereas the actual object was circular in shape. It is clear that superposing many more backprojections will lead us to a reconstruction that is closer to the actual object.

In obtaining figure 6.12 from figure 6.11, we have deleted (considered as background) all those pixels that fall outside the overlap region. A simpler way of obtaining the same effect is to sum the backprojections and scale the maximum intensity to 255 (if we are dealing with 8-bit images). In that case, the regions outside the overlap region will be scaled down (relatively); and in the case of a large number of beams, the pixels outside the overlap region will be reduced almost to the level of the background. This effect is already observed in figure 6.11.

6.6.2 The Radon transform

The discussion in section 6.6.1 contained all the essential principles used in CT, but we now elaborate on the mathematical principles behind the reconstruction process.

Figure 6.12. Overlap of the backprojections of two perpendicular beams.

A beam of x-rays used in CT will consist of many parallel rays, and each of them can be represented by a straight line. It is convenient to use the normal form of the straight line (equation (5.1)), which was used for the Hough transform.

An arbitrary point in the projection signal is given by the sum of the absorbance along the line $x \cos \theta + y \sin \theta = \rho$.

The total absorbance along the line is given by

$$g(\rho, \theta) = \int_{-\infty}^{\infty} \int_{-\infty}^{\infty} f(x, y)\delta(x \cos \vartheta + y \sin \theta - \rho)dxdy. \qquad (6.35)$$

The impulse function used in equation (6.28) picks out the value of the function $f(x, y)$ along the line $x \cos \theta + y \sin \theta = \rho$.

It is understood that $f(x, y) = 0$ for the background pixels; within the foreground, it has a value that depends on the absorbance of the object at that point. Even though a double integral appears in equation (6.28), it is to be understood that we are performing the integration along a straight line (because of the impulse function) and not over an area.

In the discrete case of an image with $M \times N$ pixels, the integral in equation (6.28) is replaced by a summation:

$$g(\rho, \theta) = \sum_{x=0}^{M-1} \sum_{y=0}^{N-1} f(x, y)\delta(x \cos \theta + y \sin \theta - \rho). \qquad (6.36)$$

Note that equation (6.35) and equation (6.36) imply that the information we see seek, i.e., $f(x, y)$, is buried within an integral (or a summation). Equation (6.35) and equation (6.36) are mathematically correct statements of the signal obtained in the process of tomography. The method of backprojection discussed in section 6.6.1, while appealing to our intuition, is not mathematically correct as we can at most obtain approximate information about the shape of the object using that technique. In order to obtain precise information about the image, we need to extract $f(x, y)$ from equation (6.36). This may look like a formidable task, but fortunately, our old friend, the Fourier transform, comes to our rescue once more.

6.6.3 The Fourier slice theorem

Let us consider the 1-D Fourier transform of a projection with respect to ρ:

$$G(\omega, \theta) = \int_{-\infty}^{\infty} g(\rho, \theta) \exp(-2\pi j\omega\rho)d\rho. \tag{6.37}$$

By substituting $g(\rho,\theta)$ from equation (6.35) into equation (6.37), we obtain

$$G(\omega, \theta) = \int_{-\infty}^{\infty}\int_{-\infty}^{\infty}\int_{-\infty}^{\infty} f(x, y)\delta(x\cos\vartheta + y\sin\theta - \rho)dxdy \exp(-2\pi j\omega\rho)d\rho. \tag{6.38}$$

Then, by changing the order of the integration, we have

$$G(\omega, \theta) = \int_{-\infty}^{\infty}\int_{-\infty}^{\infty} f(x, y) \\ \times \left[\int_{-\infty}^{\infty} \delta(x\cos\vartheta + y\sin\theta - \rho)\exp(-2\pi j\omega\rho)d\rho\right]dxdy. \tag{6.39}$$

Using the property of the impulse function, we evaluate the integral over ρ to obtain

$$G(\omega, \theta) = \int_{-\infty}^{\infty}\int_{-\infty}^{\infty} f(x, y)\exp(-2\pi j\omega(x\cos\theta + y\sin\theta))dxdy. \tag{6.40}$$

The RHS of equation (6.40) can be identified as the Fourier transform of $f(x, y)$ if we define $u = w\cos\theta$ and $v = w\sin\theta$.

Therefore, equation (6.40) can be written as

$$G(\omega, \theta) = F(u, v). \tag{6.41}$$

Equation (6.41) is known as the Fourier slice theorem. The interpretation of equation (6.41) is that the 1-D Fourier transform of a projection is a slice of the 2-D Fourier transform of the region from which the projection was obtained.

Equation (6.41) also implies that we can obtain $f(x, y)$ by performing an inverse Fourier transform on $G(\omega, \theta)$.

In the present discussion, we have assumed that the x-ray system we are using employs a parallel beam of rays. In practice, most CT systems use a fan-beam system[3].

Exercises

1. It is desired to generate
   a) Gamma noise that has the probability density function

$$p(z) = a\,2\,z\exp(-az) \quad \text{for } z \geqslant 0$$
$$= 0 \quad\quad\quad\quad\text{for } z < 0$$

---

[3] See Gonzalez and Woods 2009 *Digital Image Processing* 3rd edn (Pearson) for details.

b) noise having the distribution

$$p(z) = \frac{2}{b}(z - a)\exp\left(-\frac{(z - a)^2}{b}\right) \quad \text{for } z \geqslant a$$
$$= 0 \quad \text{for } z < a.$$

How will you accomplish this using the method discussed in example 6.1?

2. It is required to generate 100 values of a variable z. The probability density for z is given by

$$p(z) = \frac{A}{1 + z^2} \quad \text{for } 1 \geqslant z \geqslant 0.$$

a) What should be the value of A?

b) How would you generate the values of z, given 100 random numbers r that lie in the range of 0 to 1?

3. A 1-D image that has M pixels is defined in the following manner:

$$f(x) = 255 \text{ for } x = 0 \text{ to } L - 1$$
$$= 0$$

i.e., we have a white rectangle that has a length of L pixels and a width of 1 pixel.

The rectangle starts moving in the positive x-direction (the dark background does not move) and moves a distance of a pixels during the time of image acquisition T. Calculate the gray level $g(x)$ of the pixels in the image (which is degraded due to the motion).

4. Somebody photographs a blank featureless wall, but the photograph turns out to be as shown below (figure 6.13). The photographer suspects the observed features to be some kind of noise.

Classify the noise on the basis of its statistical properties and on the basis of its Fourier spectrum. Which spatial domain filter will you use to remove the noise?

Figure 6.13. Image affected by noise.

5. A camera is used to photograph the object (white circle against a dark background) shown below.

Initially the image of the circle is of radius R and all pixels within the image have gray levels of 255 (all the pixels outside the circle have gray levels of 0). As the photograph is being taken, the circle starts moving directly toward the camera with a velocity v. The object is initially at a distance D_o from the camera and the total distance moved by the object during the time the image was acquired is small compared to D_o.

   a) How would the size of the image vary with D (distance of the object from the camera)?

   b) Use this relation and the facts stated above to show that the radius of the image (R) varies linearly with time (derive an expression for R in terms of D_0, v, and t).

   c) Using these results, plot a graph of gray level versus radial distance for the acquired image (ignore quantization effects).

6. The intensity of a 1-D image $f(x)$ varies as follows.

$$f(x) = 0 \quad \text{for } x < 0$$
$$f(x) = x \quad \text{for } 0 < x < 255$$
$$f(x) = 0 \quad \text{for } x > 255$$

x can take only integer values. If the image moves along the positive x-direction by a distance equal to 5 pixels during image acquisition, then derive the intensity variation $g(x)$ in the blurred image. Ignore quantization effects. Calculate $<f(x)>$ and $<g(x)>$ ($< >$ indicates average). Are they equal? Why?

Programming assignments

1. Write MATLAB® programs to implement erosion, dilation, opening, and closing of an image. Modify the program written for erosion to extract the boundary of an object.

2. Write a program to generate a set of numbers distributed as per the probability density function given in exercise 1 above.

3. Write a MATLAB® program to label the number of objects in a binary image. Use the algorithm discussed in section 6.5.

IOP Publishing

A Course on Digital Image Processing with MATLAB®

P K Thiruvikraman

Chapter 7

Wavelets

7.1 Wavelets versus the Fourier transform

The Fourier transform is a widely used tool in image processing. It has been applied to a wide variety of tasks ranging from filtering to image compression. While the Fourier transform is an elegant and powerful tool, an even more powerful mathematical tool, known as the wavelet transform, has emerged in recent years.

To appreciate and understand how the wavelet transform is superior to the Fourier transform, we recapitulate some of the features of the Fourier transform discussed in chapter 3. In particular, we draw your attention to the image in figure 3.8 and its Fourier transform. Recall that the magnitude of the Fourier transform was independent of the position of the line, but the information about the position of the line is embedded in the phase part of the Fourier transform.

It is sometimes stated incorrectly that the Fourier transform has information about the frequencies present in a signal or an image, but has no information about when (or where) these frequencies occurred. We see from the discussion in chapter 3 that such a statement is incorrect. However, it is also true that for very big images the phase of the image has to be calculated to a very high precision. For example, in the case of the image in figure 3.8, the possible values of the phase are multiples of $(2\pi/5)$. The number 5 in the denominator is related to the size of the image (the number of rows in this case). If the image were bigger, then the phase would have to be calculated to a higher precision[1].

An easier way of appreciating the drawback is as follows. We are representing a finite image by using sine and cosine functions, which are of infinite extent. At face

---

[1] A more detailed explanation can be obtained from the article by G Strang in *Bulletin of American Mathematical Society*, vol 28, no. 2. 1993.

value, it is not a very efficient process. We would be better off if we used functions of finite extent to represent finite images. It turns out that images (which have many edges or sudden discontinuities) are more efficiently represented by wavelets, while an audio signal, especially music (which is more continuous), is more efficiently represented by its Fourier coefficients. Wavelets are localized functions. Therefore, the positional information about the occurrence of various frequencies is built into them in a natural way. While the Fourier transform uses only two functions—sine and cosine functions—wavelets come in many varieties. We will confine our discussion about wavelets to the Haar wavelet, which is the simplest of the wavelets.

As the reader may know, in Fourier analysis of a function, we represent a function $f(x)$ in terms of an orthogonal set of basis functions (the sine and cosine functions). This is exactly analogous to the representation of an arbitrary vector in terms of a linear combination of orthogonal sets of basis vectors. To make it more specific, we can represent any 3-D vector as a linear combination of the three unit vectors along the x-, y-, and z-axes.

7.2 The Haar wavelet transform

Instead of choosing a set of sine and cosine functions (of various frequencies) as a basis set, we can choose a set of localized functions as a basis.

The Haar wavelets are defined as follows.

We first define a mother wavelet $\psi(x)$ as

$$
\begin{aligned}
\psi(x) &= 1 && \text{for } 0 \leqslant x < \tfrac{1}{2} \\
&= -1 && \text{for } \tfrac{1}{2} < x \leqslant 1 \\
&= 0 && \text{otherwise.}
\end{aligned}
\tag{7.1}
$$

Using this function, we can define daughter wavelets $\psi_{jk}(x)$ as follows:

$$
\psi_{jk}(x) = \psi(2^j x - k).
\tag{7.2}
$$

From this definition, it is clear that the factor 2^j (here j is a non-negative integer) is a scale factor, and the subtraction of k implies a shift to the right. The original mother wavelet is simply the function $\psi_{00}(x)$.

The first few daughter wavelets are shown below.

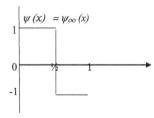

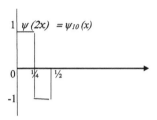

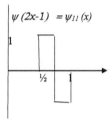

The first few wavelets are represented below.

$$\psi_{00} = \psi(x)$$
$$\psi_{10} = \psi(2x)$$
$$\psi_{11} = \psi(2x - 1)$$
$$\psi_{20} = \psi(4x) \qquad (7.3)$$
$$\psi_{21} = \psi(4x - 1)$$
$$\psi_{22} = \psi(4x - 2)$$
$$\psi_{23} = \psi(4x - 3)$$

It is to be noted that the shift k has to be in the range 0 to $2^j - 1$. This restriction is required in order to confine the function to the range of 0 to 1. The diagrammatic representation of ψ_{21}, ψ_{30}, ψ_{31}, etc. is left as an exercise to the reader.

A function $f(x)$ can be written as a linear combination of the wavelet defined above:

$$f(x) = c_0 + \sum_{j=0}^{\infty} \sum_{k=0}^{2^j-1} c_{jk}\psi_{jk}(x). \qquad (7.4)$$

Such an expansion is possible because the ψs form a set of orthogonal basis functions. The orthogonality of these functions can be seen from equation (7.5).

$$\int_0^1 \psi_{mn}(x)\psi_{jk}(x)dx = 0 \ \text{ if } m \neq j \text{ and } n \neq k \qquad (7.5)$$

We can use the orthogonality relations to compute the coefficients c_{jk}. To compute a particular coefficient c_{mn}, we multiply (7.4) by ψ_{mn} and integrate over the range of 0 to 1. This process leads to the following relations for the coefficients:

$$c_{mn} = 2^{m-1} \int_0^1 \psi_{mn} f(x) dx \tag{7.6}$$

$$c_0 = \int_0^1 f(x) dx. \tag{7.7}$$

Notice that the calculation of the coefficients is exactly analogous to the calculation of the Fourier coefficients, which also use the orthogonal nature of the sine and cosine functions.

Equation (7.6) is the continuous Haar wavelet transform. At this point, you may be interested in knowing the discrete version of (7.6).

Equation (7.4) can be written in matrix notation as

$$\mathbf{f} = \mathbf{WC} \tag{7.8}$$

where the matrix W has the basis wavelets as its columns

$$W = \begin{bmatrix} 1/2 & 1/2 & 1/\sqrt{2} & 0 \\ 1/2 & 1/2 & -1/\sqrt{2} & 0 \\ 1/2 & -1/2 & 0 & 1/\sqrt{2} \\ 1/2 & -1/2 & 0 & -1/\sqrt{2} \end{bmatrix}. \tag{7.9}$$

We have chosen the basis such that each column is a unit vector. This will help in the subsequent treatment.

Equation (7.8) can be easily solved for obtaining the coefficients C:

$$\mathbf{C} = \mathbf{W}^{-1}\mathbf{f}. \tag{7.10}$$

By definition, $\mathbf{W}$ is an orthogonal matrix (its columns are mutually orthogonal and its determinant is unity), and therefore the inverse of $\mathbf{W}$ is equal to its transpose. Therefore,

$$\mathbf{C} = \mathbf{W}^T\mathbf{f}. \tag{7.11}$$

It can be easily verified that the wavelet transform is invertible. We also notice one immediate advantage of the discrete wavelet transform. Unlike in the DFT, all the coefficients of the discrete wavelet transform are real. Hence, the number of coefficients that we have to deal with is effectively half of the number of coefficients when we use the DFT. Furthermore, it can be shown that most of the coefficients are zero in the case of the wavelet transform. Hence, we can reconstruct the original image from less coefficients. Since the DFT uses functions of infinite extent to represent localized functions (images), we can expect that many coefficients will be nonzero. For example, the Fourier transform of a rectangular function is the sinc function. This means that we require many Fourier coefficients to represent a rectangular function, whereas the same can be represented by very few coefficients if we use wavelets.

We now discuss this issue quantitatively by calculating the Fourier and wavelet coefficients for a rectangular function that is sampled at four points and has the following values:

0, 1, 1, 0. That is $f(0) = 0$, $f(1) = 1$, $f(2) = 1$ and $f(3) = 0$.

The 1-D Fourier transform $F(u)$ is readily calculated using equation (3.43) and found to be

$$F(0) = 0.5 \quad F(1) = -0.25 - 0.25i \quad F(2) = 0 \quad F(3) = -0.25 + 0.25i.$$

If we calculate the wavelet coefficients using equation (7.11), we obtain

$$C(0) = 1; \quad c(1) = 0; \quad c(2) = -0.7071; \quad c(3) = 0.7071.$$

Notice that one of the coefficients is zero. In general, the number of nonzero wavelet coefficients will be less than the number of Fourier coefficients (since the wavelet coefficients are all real, whereas the Fourier coefficients will in general have a real and an imaginary part). Hence, higher compression ratios can be achieved if we use a wavelet transform instead of the Fourier transform.

This can be appreciated even more if we take the function f to have the values 1, 1, 0, and 0.

In this case, the Fourier coefficients are

$$F(0) = 0.5 \quad F(1) = 0.25 - 0.25i \quad F(2) = 0 \quad F(3) = 0.25 + 0.25i.$$

The wavelet coefficients turn out to be

$$C(0) = 1 \quad C(1) = 1 \quad C(2) = 0 \quad C(3) = 0.$$

Hence, it is seen that, in general, considerable saving/efficiency can be achieved by using wavelets.

7.3 An alternative view of wavelets

Let us say that we want an alternative representation for a string of numbers, say,

$$A = [1, 11, 33, 23, 44, 34, 22, 32]. \tag{7.12}$$

We can represent this string of numbers by grouping them into pairs and looking at their averages and differences. This leads us to the following representation:

$$A1 = [6, 28, 39, 27, 5, -5, -5, 5]. \tag{7.13}$$

The first four elements of $A1$ are the average values of each pair (adjacent elements of A are treated as a pair), while the next four elements are the successive differences divided by 2. Therefore, $A1(5) = (A(2) - A(1))/2$ and $A1(6) = (A(4) - A(3))/2$, and so on. Here, $A1(5)$ represents the 5th element of $A1$.

It can be seen that we can reconstruct A from $A1$ by adding and subtracting the elements separated by a distance of four places.

We need not stop the process at this stage. We can apply the same procedure repeatedly. By applying the same procedure again, we end up with

$$A2 = [17, 33, 0, 0, 11, -6, -5, 5]. \tag{7.14}$$

At each stage we can reconstruct the row vector at the preceding stage by the appropriate addition and subtraction operations.

By continuing the operations one last time, we end up with $A3$, which is given by

$$A3 = [25, 0, 2.5, 0, 8, 0, -8.5, 5]. \tag{7.15}$$

These transformations are invertible, but what is their use?

Notice that we will require an extra bit (for the sign) to represent $A1$, $A2$, and $A3$ in comparison to A. However, in general, the elements of $A1$, $A2$, $A3$ are smaller than A. Can we exploit this for compression? Yes we can. The matrices $A1$, $A2$, and $A3$ contain elements that are in general smaller in magnitude than A. Hence, if we quantize the elements of $A1$, $A2$, $A3$, and $A4$, and then threshold the resulting values, we will end up with up with a matrix with many elements being zero. The spirit behind these series of transformations is similar to that of the procedure adopted in transform coding (refer to figure 4.13). Of course, quantization and thresholding of the elements will lead to lossy compression. But as in the case of transform coding, the errors involved are quite negligible.

We would also like see the equivalence between the approach specified above and the Haar wavelet. This can be readily done by writing the transformations described above in matrix form.

The transformation of (7.12) to (7.13) can be written in the matrix form as follows:

$$A1 = \begin{bmatrix} 1/2 & 1/2 & 0 & 0 & 0 & 0 & 0 & 0 \\ 0 & 0 & 1/2 & 1/2 & 0 & 0 & 0 & 0 \\ 0 & 0 & 0 & 0 & 1/2 & 1/2 & 0 & 0 \\ 0 & 0 & 0 & 0 & 0 & 0 & 1/2 & 1/2 \\ 1/2 & -1/2 & 0 & 0 & 0 & 0 & 0 & 0 \\ 0 & 0 & 1/2 & -1/2 & 0 & 0 & 0 & 0 \\ 0 & 0 & 0 & 0 & 1/2 & -1/2 & 0 & 0 \\ 0 & 0 & 0 & 0 & 0 & 0 & 1/2 & -1/2 \end{bmatrix} \begin{bmatrix} 1 \\ 11 \\ 33 \\ 23 \\ 44 \\ 34 \\ 22 \\ 32 \end{bmatrix}. \tag{7.16}$$

Notice that the columns of the transformation matrix used above are orthogonal to each other (similar to the matrix in equation (7.9)). The transformation matrix can also be easily inverted to obtain A from $A1$. The inverse of the transformation matrix is given by

$$\begin{bmatrix} 1 & 0 & 0 & 0 & 1 & 0 & 0 & 0 \\ 1 & 0 & 0 & 0 & -1 & 0 & 0 & 0 \\ 0 & 1 & 0 & 0 & 0 & 1 & 0 & 0 \\ 0 & 1 & 0 & 0 & 0 & -1 & 0 & 0 \\ 0 & 0 & 1 & 0 & 0 & 0 & 1 & 0 \\ 0 & 0 & 1 & 0 & 0 & 0 & -1 & 0 \\ 0 & 0 & 0 & 1 & 0 & 0 & 0 & 1 \\ 0 & 0 & 0 & 1 & 0 & 0 & 0 & -1 \end{bmatrix}. \tag{7.17}$$

Note that the inverse of the transformation matrix is obtained simply by transposing the transformation matrix and multiplying the transpose by 2. While the Haar wavelet is defined such that the determinant of W (see equation (7.9)) is 1, the transformation matrix in equation (7.16) is defined in a slightly different sense so that the determinant of the transformation matrix is not 1. Hence, it does not share all the properties of the Haar wavelet transform.

Exercises

1. Equation (7.9) gives a 4×4 wavelet transform. Obtain in a similar manner the 8×8 Haar wavelet transform.
2. Following equation (7.16), obtain the transformation matrix for the case where you have a column vector with four elements.
3. In case the number of elements in a column vector is not a power of 2, how would you do the transformation?
4. Using equation (7.16), obtain the transformation of a set of values with a linear variation. For example, $A = [1\ 2\ 3\ 4\ 5\ 6\ 7\ 8]$.

Programming assignments

1. Write a program that will the compute transformations from equations (7.12)–(7.15). The program can take the number of times the transformation is to be repeated as user input. The program can work iteratively or recursively. (Note: Some versions of MATLAB® have an upper limit on the number of recursions and hence it is not advisable to use recursion in MATLAB®).

IOP Publishing

A Course on Digital Image Processing with MATLAB®

P K Thiruvikraman

Chapter 8

Color image processing

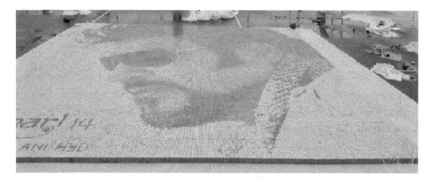

The above image was made entirely using Rubik's cubes (a total of 14160 cubes were used). The students[1] who achieved this were recreating a color photograph. As you may know, there are only six colors on a Rubik's cube while a normal color photograph may have many more colors. How did they manage to recreate the photograph? The answer lies within this chapter

---

[1] This feat was achieved in a record time of seven hours by a group of students belonging to the Hyderabad campus of Birla Institute of Technology and Science, Pilani. Hats off to them!

Up to now we have confined ourselves to grayscale images. We did this deliberately so that we could easily understand the various algorithms used in image processing and their implementation.

However, color images are used routinely in our daily life and the information concerning the color of an object is very crucial in object recognition. In fact, color and shape are the two main features used for object recognition, and the recognition of an object from the information about its color is easier than the recognition using information about its shape.

Before we proceed to discuss the various color models used, it is relevant to ask the following question: how do we modify the image processing algorithms that we have discussed up to now to make them suitable for processing color images? A simple answer may be that the various image processing algorithms can be implemented separately for each color. This usually involves repeating the operation for the various colors in an image. Since the most commonly used color format is RGB (red, green, and blue), we implement the algorithm (say, gray level transformation) separately for each of the three primary colors. However, in certain cases this may not give rise to the desired result. In this chapter we discuss the commonly used color models.

8.1 The RGB color model

In the RGB color model, red (700 nm), green (546.1 nm), and blue (435.8 nm) are used as primary colors. All other colors can be produced by a suitable linear combination of these colors.

The color model can be represented by the following 3-D plot.

In practice, each color component varies in the range of 0 to 255. It can be seen from figure 8.1 that while red, green, and blue are the primary colors, yellow, cyan,

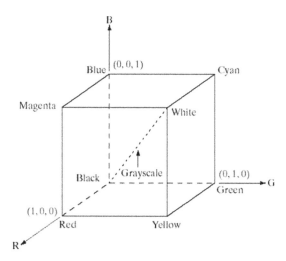

Figure 8.1. The RGB color model.

Figure 8.2. The red–green ($B = 0$), blue–red ($G = 0$), and green–blue ($R = 0$) planes.

and magenta can be viewed as the secondary colors that can be generated by combining two of the three colors.

We can gain more insight into the RGB model by looking at the variation of color within a given plane. For example, if we look at the blue–green plane, the variation is as given in figure 8.2.

The conversion from RGB to grayscale is also seen from figure 8.1. If red, green, and blue vary in the range (0, 255), then the conversion to the corresponding grayscale value is given by

$$I = \frac{1}{\sqrt{3}} \sqrt{R^2 + G^2 + B^2}. \tag{8.1}$$

Here, I is the grayscale intensity value of a pixel, and R, G, and B are the corresponding red, green, and blue values for that pixel. In general, we use 8 bits for representing the grayscale intensity value of a pixel. Hence, for a color image, 24 bits would be required for specifying the R, G, and B values. The total number of colors that can be generated in this model is.

$$(2^8)^3 = 16777216$$

However, many display devices may be unable to render in a faithful manner such a huge number of colors. Many systems in use today produce at most 256 different colors. Forty of these 256 colors are known to be processed differently by various operating systems[2]. The other 216 colors, also known as safe colors, are considered as standard especially for internet applications. Each of the 216 colors is formed from three RGB values as before, but each R, G, B value can only be 0, 51, 102, 153, 204, or 255.

8.2 The CMY and CMYK color models

Red, green, and blue are considered as the primary colors of light, but cyan, magenta, and yellow are the primary colors of pigments. It can be seen that cyan is a linear combination (in equal proportion) of blue and green. Therefore, when white light is incident on a pigment made of cyan, it will reflect cyan and absorb all other colors. In other words, the cyan pigment does not have any component of red because it absorbs the red color present in the incident light.

The CMY model uses cyan, magenta, and yellow as the primary colors. This is suitable for devices that deposit colored pigments on paper, such as color printers and copiers.

The conversion from the RGB to CMY model is straightforward and is given by

$$
\begin{bmatrix} C \\ M \\ Y \end{bmatrix} = \begin{bmatrix} 1 \\ 1 \\ 1 \end{bmatrix} - \begin{bmatrix} R \\ G \\ B \end{bmatrix}. \tag{8.2}
$$

For the case of light reflected from a cyan pigment, $R = 0$ while G and B are 1. Therefore, from equation (8.2), we see that in such a case, $C = 1$ while $M = Y = 0$.

According to equation (8.2), equal amounts of the primary pigments, cyan, magenta, and yellow, should produce black. In practice, combining these colors for printing produces a muddy-looking black. Thus, in order to produce true black, a fourth color, black, is added, giving rise to the CMYK color model.

8.3 The hue, saturation, and intensity (HSI) color model

The RGB and CMY color models are ideally suited for hardware implementation. The red, green, and blue components in the light incident on a camera can be extracted easily using filters placed in front of the camera. These are then super-imposed to produce a color image.

However, when humans view a color object, they describe it by its hue, saturation, and brightness. Hue is a color attribute that describes a pure color (pure yellow, orange, or red), whereas saturation is a measure of the degree to which a pure color is diluted by white light. Brightness is related to the overall intensity of the pixel. Hence, in the HSI model, the color information is decoupled from the intensity information; this is not the case with the RGB model.

---

[2] A detailed discussion can be found in *Digital Image Processing* 3rd edn by Gonzalez and Woods.

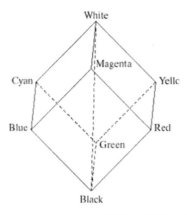

Figure 8.3. Relationship between RGB and HSI color models.

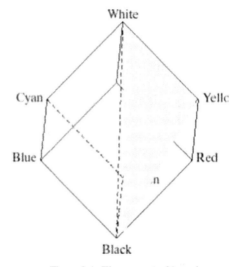

Figure 8.4. The concept of hue.

The conversion from the RGB model to the HSI model can be understood from figure 8.3.

In figure 8.2, the intensity axis is the straight line joining the vertices of the cube labeled 'black' and 'white'. To determine the intensity of a color point, we simply pass a plane that contains the color point and is perpendicular to the intensity axis. The intensity value is given by the point of intersection of this plane with the intensity axis. The saturation (purity) of a color increases as a function of distance from the intensity axis.

Hue is defined as the 'shade of a color'. Figure 8.4 helps us to understand this concept in a better way.

In figure 8.3, a shaded triangle has its vertices at white, black, and yellow. All the points contained in the plane segment defined by the intensity axis and the boundaries of the cube have the same hue (yellow in this case). By rotating the shaded plane about the vertical axis, we would obtain different hues.

The transformation from RGB to HSI can be derived by the following geometric construction: rotate the RGB cube in such a manner that the point corresponding to white is vertically above the black point. In such a case, the intensity axis will be vertical, as seen in the figure given below.

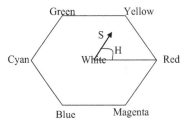

The above figure can be justified as follows. Since there are three primary colors, in a plane they will be lying 120° apart (by symmetry). The secondary colors will be equidistant from two adjacent primary colors. As mentioned before, the saturation S is the distance from the intensity axis and hue H is the angle between the line joining the color point to the intensity axis and the red axis. Saturation depends on the distance from the intensity axis. Using these two components we can derive the relations that relate RGB to HSI. These conversions are required in many situations since HSI is closer to the way we describe colors, whereas RGB is ideally suited for hardware implementation.

I suppose you are now in a position to answer the question posed at the beginning of this chapter (the question about the Rubik's cube). The colors on the faces of a Rubik's cube are white, red, blue, orange, green, and yellow. Any other color that is present on the original photograph has to be mapped onto one of these.

So what the students must have done was the following:

1. Since they used 14 160 cubes in all we can assume that the total number of pixels in the photograph was equal to this number (or a multiple of this number).

2. The RGB values for each pixel in the photograph can be thought of as three coordinates of a point P in 3-D space. The Euclidean distance of the point from each of the six colors (white, red, blue, orange, green, and yellow) can be worked out.

3. The color that has the minimum Euclidean distance from P is chosen to be the one that will represent the RGB values of the pixel under consideration. The cube is adjusted accordingly so that this color is displayed on one of the faces.

Exercises

1. Vegetation looks red in many satellite images. Find out the reason for this.
2. Convert (255, 255, 0) to the corresponding grayscale value.

Programming assignment

1. Write a program that will generate a yellow triangle. The vertices of the triangle are at black, white, and yellow in the HSI model. All the points in the triangle will have the same hue.

Chapter 9

Introduction to MATLAB®

9.1 Introduction

MATLAB®[1] is one of the most widely used software packages for the analysis and visualization of data in science and engineering. It is also well suited for implementing algorithms for image processing since it has a separate image processing toolbox. The image processing toolbox contains many built-in functions for implementing many of the algorithms we have discussed in this book. MATHEMATICA, which was originally developed for symbolic computation, also offers many built-in commands for image processing.

While MATLAB® is a very user-friendly package, it may take some time for a new user to get used to it. This short introduction is intended to familiarize the user with the MATLAB® environment and the commands required to run the programs listed as part of this project.

We will assume that you have installed MATLAB® on your computer. Once MATLAB® is installed, click on the MATLAB® icon on the desktop to run MATLAB®.

Once the icon is clicked, the entire MATLAB® package with all the toolboxes is loaded on to the memory of the computer. Most of the screenshots (figures 9.1–9.3) pertain to the version 'R2012b' of MATLAB®. If you are using a different version of MATLAB®, the appearance of the windows may be slightly different. However, the commands and programs given here should work as intended even if you are using other versions of MATLAB®.

MATLAB® commands can be typed directly in the 'command window', which opens when MATLAB® is loaded.

---

[1] MATLAB® is a product of Mathworks. Complete details about MATLAB® can be obtained from http://www.mathworks.in/products/matlab/.

Figure 9.1. MATLAB® icon 'R2012b' is the version of MATLAB® used while writing this book.

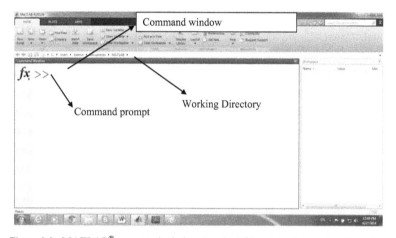

Figure 9.2. MATLAB® command window (on the left) and workspace (on the right).

Figure 9.3. Close-up of the MATLAB® command window. The current working directory is displayed above the command window.

The command window is shown in figure 9.2. The 'workspace', which is a separate window shown in figure 9.2 (it is to the right of the command window), displays the variables that are currently available.

Programs can be executed either by typing the name of the program file (without the .m extension) on the command prompt or by clicking the 'Run' icon when a .m

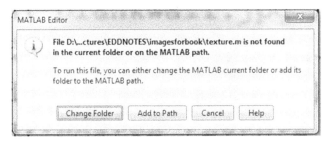

Figure 9.4. Message from MATLAB® that is displayed if you attempt to run a program that is not in the current folder (directory).

```
>> a=imread('cup_on_board.jpg');
Error using imread (line 368)
File "cup_on_board.jpg" does not
exist.
```

Figure 9.5. Error message displayed if the image file is not in the current folder.

file is open. New .m files can be created by clicking on 'new script' in the 'Home' tab (figure 9.3).

While running MATLAB® programs (.m files), ensure that the image or text files that the program is supposed to access are stored in the directory in which the program is stored. The current working directory is displayed above the command window (see figure 9.2 and also figure 9.3). If you wish to access a file in another directory, the entire path has to be specified. Before running a program, you have to change the working directory to the directory in which the program is stored. In recent versions of MATLAB®, you will be prompted to change the directory when you attempt to run a program that is outside the working directory. You can choose the 'Change Folder' option if presented with such a message (figure 9.4).

If you attempt to access an image file that is not in the current directory, MATLAB® will display an error message (figure 9.5).

9.2 Help with MATLAB®

There are some excellent books on using MATLAB®. The following is a short list of the many books available for this purpose:

1. *Getting Started with MATLAB®* by Rudra Pratap, Oxford University Press
2. *Mastering MATLAB®* by Duane C Hanselman and Bruce L Littlefield, Pearson
3. *MATLAB®: A practical approach* by Stormy Attaway, Butterworth–Heinemann (Elsevier), 2009
4. *Numerical Computing with MATLAB®* by Clive Moler, available online at http://www.mathworks.com/moler/chapters.html

5. *Digital Image Processing using MATLAB®* by Gonzalez, Woods and Eddins, Pearson Education

You can also get help with the syntax of any particular command by typing 'help' followed by a space and the name of the command in the command prompt. For example, typing 'help plot' will display the syntax for the plot command (which is used to plot 2-D graphs). Typing only 'help' displays all the help topics. For example, some of the help topics are 'general', 'elmat', and 'elfun'. Typing 'help general' will display all the general-purpose commands that are part of MATLAB®, while typing 'help elmat' will display elementary matrices and matrix manipulation. Typing 'help elfun' displays all the elementary math functions that are part of MATLAB®.

You can then choose any of the commands or functions and type 'help' followed by that command as described earlier.

9.3 Variables

The syntax of MATLAB® is very similar to the C programming language, but one major advantage of MATLAB® is that, unlike in C, one need not define variables before using them.

The basic data type in MATLAB® is an array. Even scalars are treated as arrays of size 1×1. There is no need to specify the dimensions of the array at the beginning of the program. MATLAB® automatically identifies the type of array being used. However, for efficiency and speed of implementation, it is suggested that we initialize and hence specify the dimensions of the array.

Unlike in C, the array indices start with 1.

To input a matrix, say,

$$A = \begin{bmatrix} 1 & 2 & 5 \\ 3 & 9 & 0 \end{bmatrix}$$

we type $A = [1\ 2\ 5;\ 3\ 9\ 0]$ on the command prompt (or in a .m file).

The semicolon indicates the start of a new row.

Hence, $u = [1\ 3\ 9]$ produces a row vector, and $v = [1;\ 3;\ 9]$ produces a column vector.

Matrix elements can be referred to as $A(i, j)$. $A(i, j)$ refers to the element in the ith row and jth column of the matrix (array) A.

$A(m:n, k:l)$—refers to rows m to n and columns k to l.

A(:, 5:20)—refers to the elements in columns 5 through 20 of all the rows of matrix A.

While assigning names to variables (and also .m files), it should be remembered that names of variables and files (or functions) have to begin with a letter of the alphabet. After that, the name can contain letters, digits, and the underscore character (e.g. value_1), but it cannot have a space. MATLAB® is case-sensitive, which means that there is a difference between upper- and lowercase letters. Therefore, variables called mynum, MYNUM, and Mynum are all different. We can use the command 'who' to obtain the names of variables currently loaded onto the memory of MATLAB®.

Sometimes we may wish to delete certain variables from MATLAB®. In such a case we can use 'clear variable name'.

Typing

```
>> clear Mynum
```

will clear, i.e., delete, Mynum from memory. Meanwhile, typing

```
>> clear
```

will delete all the variables from memory. It is good practice to use 'clear' at the beginning of each program so that we do not unwittingly reuse the values of some old variables. Of course, if we require access to the value of a variable that is stored in the memory, then we should not use this command.

While assigning names to variables, it is best to avoid names that are used for built-in functions. For example, 'i' is reserved for the square root of -1 in MATLAB®. If we use it to refer to another variable (for example let us say we type '$i = 2$' at the command prompt or in a MATLAB® program), then MATLAB® 'i' will no longer refer to $\sqrt{-1}$, but will be treated as being equal to the value that we have assigned. MATLAB® also understands 'pi' as being equal to 'π'. It is a good practice to use 'pi' in MATLAB® programs instead of '22/7' or '3.14' in our programs. Using 'pi' will improve the accuracy of our computations. Of course, we should remember that we should not use 'pi' to refer to any other variable. You should especially keep the aforementioned points about 'i' and 'pi' in mind while writing programs to compute the Fourier transform of an image (for instance) since the Fourier transform involves both 'π' and $\sqrt{-1}$. Note that we can also use 'j' instead of 'i' to refer to $\sqrt{-1}$ in MATLAB®.

The size of a matrix can be obtained by the command
s = size(A).
s(1) contains the number of rows.
s(2) contains the number of columns.

The size command is especially useful in image processing. For any image processing operation, we will initially read the gray levels of the pixels from an image file and store it in an array. The size command can then be used to obtain the number of rows and columns in the image. We usually apply many transformations to each pixel in the image. In such cases, we will run 'for' loops, which will apply the same transformation over all the rows and columns.

9.4 Mathematical operations

Most of the mathematical operations are represented in the usual fashion in MATLAB®. Examples are listed in the table below.

Addition	+
Subtraction	−
Multiplication	*
Division	/
Exponentiation	^

If A and B are matrices, then $A*B$ will multiply the matrices A and B. Sometimes, we are required to multiply the corresponding terms in two matrices. We would represent this as $A.*B$.

The '.' signifies that the first element in A has to be multiplied by the first element in B, and so on.

To summarize, if we have to perform matrix multiplication, we use the expression $A*B$. If we use the expression $A*B$, then the number of columns in A have to be equal to the number of rows in B. If we want to multiply the corresponding terms in A and B, the two matrices should have an equal number of rows and columns.

A '.' is used whenever we need to perform term-by-term operations.

Multiplication	.*
Division	./
Exponentiation	.^

While performing mathematical operations such as multiplication, division, addition, subtraction, etc, MATLAB® uses the well-known 'BODMAS' rule.

This rule is a convention that tells us the order in which these operations have to be performed.

BODMAS is actually an abbreviation, and is broken down as follows.

Brackets first (**B**). This implies that we compute the result of the operations within a set of brackets first.

Order (**O**)—Order, i.e., powers and square roots are computed next.

Division and multiplication (**DM**) are performed next. These are on equal footing, so the expression has to be evaluated from left to right.

Addition and subtraction (**AS**)—Addition and subtraction are also on equal footing, but the expression is to be evaluated from left to right.

Relational operations are represented in a manner similar to that in C with minor variations.

<	less than
<=	less than or equal to
>	greater than
>=	greater than or equal to
==	equal
~=	not equal

A single '=' (equal to) is an assignment operation, whereas '==' is used to check whether the variables on either side of this symbol are equal to each other.

Apart from relational operators, we also have logical operators in MATLAB®. Some of these operators are mentioned below.

&&—logical AND

||—OR

~—NOT

XOR—Exclusive OR

MATLAB® supports a number of data types:

- int (integer)—within this class, we can have int8, int16, int32, int64, and uint8. The numbers following 'int' refer to the number of bits used to store the variable. We obviously need a greater number of bits to store large numbers. 'unit8' means that the variable is stored as an unsigned 8-bit integer. This is the data type used to store the intensity values of pixels in an image. Unsigned integers used as intensity values are all positive.
- Float (real numbers)—single or double precision.
- Characters or strings—variables that are characters/strings are enclosed in single quotes. For example, >> c ='cash';.

Sometimes we may wish to take an input from the user at the beginning of a program. This is accomplished by the '*input*' command.

g = input('Enter a number: ')

By typing this command, the user will be prompted to enter a number. The number the user types will be stored in the variable g. The 'disp' command can be used to display the value of a variable. The value of a variable may also be displayed on the screen by simply typing the variable name without a semicolon at the end.

For example

$C = A*B$

Will calculate and display the value of the matrix C, while

$C = A*B$;

will calculate C but not display its value on the screen.

9.5 Loops and control statements

Sometimes we require that the same operation is repeated many times. For example, the same power law transformation has to be repeated for each and every pixel. In such cases, we introduce 'loops' in our program.

The syntax for creating 'for' and 'while' loops is very similar to that in *C*. For example, if we need to add 2 to all the odd-numbered elements in a 1-D array *A* having 101 elements, we use the following commands.

```
for i=1:2:101
A(i)=A(i)+2;
end
```

If it is required to add 2 to every member of the array *A*, the same may be accomplished without a 'for' loop. Simply type

A = A+2;

In the command for the 'for' loop, the general syntax is

```
for Initial value:Increment:Final value
```

If the increment is not specified in the statement of the 'for' loop, a default value of 1 is assumed by MATLAB®.

All the commands that lie between the 'for' statement and the corresponding 'end' will be executed multiple times, as specified in the 'for' loop command. 'For' and 'while' loops can be broken (when a certain condition is satisfied) by using the 'break' command.

On some occasions, we may need to change the flow of a program based on whether a particular condition is satisfied. On such occasions, we use the 'if' condition to check whether the given condition is satisfied and accordingly change the flow of the program.

The general form of the if statement is

```
if expression
  statements
ELSEIF expression
  statements
ELSE
  statements
END
```

We can use relational operators ('= =', '~ =' etc) in conjunction with logical operators in the expression of the 'if' condition. We can also use nested 'if's (an 'if' condition within another 'if' condition) in certain cases.

9.6 Built-in MATLAB® functions

It is not within the scope of this book to list and discuss all the built-in functions available in MATLAB® and its toolboxes. However, we will discuss below a few of the built-in functions that you are likely to use on a regular basis.

We list below some of these functions:

- abs(x): Calculates the absolute magnitude of x. For example, if $x = -5$, abs(x) = 5; if
  x is complex, then abs(x) will be equal to the modulus (magnitude) of the complex number.
- rem(x, y): Computes the remainder after dividing x by y. mod(x, y) also gives the remainder after division. However, 'mod' and 'rem' give different results if x and y have opposite signs.
- Trigonometric functions: sin(x) calculates the sine of x, where x is assumed to be in radians. In a similar manner, the cosine, tangent, cotangent, secant, and cosecant of an angle can be calculated.
- asin(x) gives the inverse sine or arcsine of x in radians. In a similar manner, all other inverse trigonometric functions can be calculated.
- sinh(x) gives the hyperbolic sine of x. All other hyperbolic functions may be computed in a similar manner.
- rand or rand() generates a pseudorandom number in the range of 0 to 1. rand (M, N) generates an $M \times N$ matrix of random numbers in the range of 0 to 1. 'rand' will only generate a pseudorandom number and not a 'truly' random number because a computer is a completely deterministic machine and it has been pointed out that it is impossible to obtain a string of truly random numbers using an instrument that is completely deterministic[2]. The generation of random numbers may be useful in various contexts: for example, when we want to simulate noise. If the distribution of noise is not uniform, we would have to convert the uniform (random) distribution to the required distribution by the methods described in chapter 6.
- min(A): Returns the minimum out of the set of values in the vector A. If A is a matrix, min(A) returns a column vector. If we desire to have the minimum out of a set of values in a matrix (for example an image), we should modify this command to min(min(A)).
- max(A): In a similar manner, max(A) returns the maximum out of a set of values in the vector A. If A is a matrix, we should use max(max(A)) to obtain the maximum value out of all the elements of the matrix A.

---

[2] It is relevant at this point to quote the famous mathematician Jon Von Neumann: 'Anyone who considers arithmetical methods of producing random digits is, of course, in a state of sin'.

- sum*(A)*: This built-in function returns the sum of all the components of the vector *A*. If *A* is a matrix, sum(*A*) will return a vector whose components are the sums of individual columns of *A*. If we require the sum of all the elements of the matrix *A*, we need to modify this command to sum(sum(*A*)).
- Mean(*A*) and std(*A*) will return the arithmetic mean and the standard deviation of *A*, respectively. If *A* is a matrix, we need to modify the commands as in the case of min, max, and sum.

9.7 Some more useful MATLAB® commands and programming practices

Sometimes we might need to read the values of variables from a file or write the values to a file. In such a case, we can use the commands 'fprintf' (for writing to a file) and 'fscanf' (reading from a file). Before reading from or writing to a file, we need to of course open the file using the 'fopen' command. 'fopen' will create a file with the specified name in the current folder if such a file does not already exist. An example is given below.

```
fid=fopen(âmydata.txtâ);
 A=fscanf(fid,â%dâ)â;
 fclose(fid);
```

Here, '%d' is used because the file 'mydata.txt' contains integers. 'fclose' is used to close the file after reading from it.

Writing to a file can be achieved as shown below.

```
fid=fopen(âtest.txtâ,âwâ);
fprintf(fid,â%6.2f /nâ,y);
fclose(fid);
```

In the above example, the command 'fprintf' stores the values of the variable *y* in the file 'test.txt'. '%6.2f' refers to the fact the data type of *y* is a float with a precision of 2 decimal places. Note that the MATLAB® syntax of both 'fprintf' and 'fscanf' are very similar to the syntax for these commands in the C language.

While writing programs, it is useful to write comments at appropriate locations. These comments will help us understand the working of the program and will be especially useful if we want to refer to the program after a long time has elapsed. Over time, we may have forgotten the logic behind the program!

Comments can be enclosed within single quotes as shown below.

'This is a comment';

If you want to comment out an entire section of the program, you can select that section and choose the 'comment' option after right-clicking the mouse (figure 9.6). Commenting out some part of a program is a useful tool for debugging it. If our program has a bug, i.e., a logical flaw, due to which it does not give the expected output, then we usually isolate the flaw by commenting out a part of the program that we suspect has a flaw. When we comment out a part of the program, MATLAB® will not execute that part. When we click the 'Run' button, MATLAB® will only execute the remaining (uncommented) part of the program. If the remaining part of the program is executed flawlessly, then we have succeeded in isolating the bug. As seen in figure 9.6, we can uncomment this part of the program once we have fixed the bug.

9.8 Functions

Like many programming languages, MATLAB® allows the user to define their own functions, which can then be called from within other programs or functions.

Functions are also stored as '.m' files, but the first line in such a file should have the word 'function' followed by the name of the function. The input and output arguments should also be mentioned (figure 9.7). Input arguments are the variables

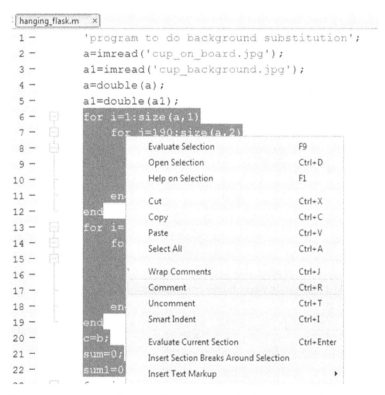

Figure 9.6. You can comment out entire parts of a program by selecting that part and right-clicking the mouse.

```
1    function [ output_args ] = Untitled2( input_args )
2    %UNTITLED2 Summary of this function goes here
3    %   Detailed explanation goes here
4
5
6    end
```

Figure 9.7. Definition of a function. You will see this figure if you click 'New function' in the home tab of MATLAB®.

```
minmax.m  x  readnumb.m  x
1 -    fid=fopen('numb.txt','r');
2 -    s=fscanf(fid,'%d');
3 -    [mn,mx,m]=minmax(s);
4
```

Figure 9.8. Program 'readnumb.m', which reads the array of numbers in the text file and stores them in an array. The program also calls a user-defined function.

```
minmax.m  x  readnumb.m  x
1    function [ mn,mx,m ] = minmax( a )
2    % Function to calculate the minimum, maximum and mean of a set of numbers;
3 -  mn=min(a)
4 -  mx=max(a)
5 -  m=sum(a)/size(a,1)
6
7
8
9 -  end
```

Figure 9.9. Example of a user-defined function. Note that it is best to have the name of the file be same as the name of the function.

that the function takes as input to calculate the output variables (which are specified in the output arguments).

We give below a simple example of a function that can be defined and used in MATLAB®. Let us assume that we have a 1-D array of numbers stored in a file named 'numb.txt' Let us say that we are required to compute the minimum, maximum, and the mean of this array of numbers. We accomplish this by writing a program that reads the array of numbers from the text file and then calls a function that calculates the required quantities.

The program and the function are reproduced in figures 9.8 and 9.9.

It is seen from figure 9.9, that the user-defined function '*minmax*' calculates the minimum and maximum of the set of values by using the built-in functions *min*, *max*, and *sum*.

The advantage of defining a function is that if later we are required to compute the same quantities (minimum, maximum, and mean) for another array named *S* (for example), then we need not modify the definition of the function. Rather, we need only to modify the argument of the function when it is called. Therefore, when the function is called from the program 'readnumb.m', we replace 'minmax(a)' with 'minmax(S)' to calculate the minimum, maximum, and mean of *S*.

It is interesting to note that descriptions of even user-defined functions can be accessed using the help command. In the example under consideration, typing 'help minmax' will cause the following lines to appear on the screen.

```
>> help minmax Function to calculate the minimum, max-
imum, and mean of a set of numbers;
```

The short description of the function supplied as a comment within the function will be displayed when we type 'help <function name>' at the command prompt.

It is good programming practice to break up a lengthy program into many functions. This enables us to check each function separately for bugs and also allows us (and others who happen to read the program) to understand the working of the program.

While using functions, it should be kept in mind that only the variables that appear as the output arguments of the function can be accessed from outside. You can easily confirm this by deleting the LHS of the assignment operation in line 3 of readnumb.m (figure 9.8). If you do that, you will notice that you can no longer access those variables from outside the function. If you want certain variables to be accessible from outside the function, you should include them in the output arguments of the function or define them to be global variables.

It is standard programming practice to use recursion while writing programs. Recursion refers to calling a function from within itself. You can see that recursion will be useful while implementing many algorithms in image processing. FFT and Huffman coding are two examples that readily spring to our minds when we think of recursion. However, MATLAB® has an upper limit on the number of times a function can be called recursively. Hence, it is better to avoid recursion while using MATLAB®. It is to be noted that a program that uses recursion can always be rewritten such that the recursion is replaced by iteration.

Programming assignments

1. Write a program that will decide whether a given number is prime or composite. The number is to be taken as input from the user (use the 'input' command). The program has to check whether the given number N is divisible by numbers up to $\sqrt{N}$. Can you see why we need to check the divisibility only up to the square root of N?

2. Write a program that will list all prime numbers from 1 to 100. Use the 'Sieve of Eratosthenes' to generate the list. The 'Sieve of Eratosthenes' consists of writing down all the numbers (here we store the numbers in a 1-D array) from 2 to 100. We know that 2 is a prime number. Every multiple of 2 is then struck off the list since they are not prime numbers. In a similar manner, all multiples of 3, 5, 7, ... etc are struck off the list. When the program has run up to 100, **the numbers that remain are the prime numbers**.

3. Write a program that will generate the famous Pascal's triangle. In case you have forgotten, Pascal's triangle is reproduced below.

```
                1
               1 2 1
              1 3 3 1
             1 4 6 4 1
           1 5 10 10 5 1
         1 6 15 20 15 6 1
       1 7 21 35 35 21 7 1
```

Notice that each element in Pascal's triangle is equal to the sum of the elements to the left and right of the element in the previous row. The nth row of the triangle consists of the coefficients in the binomial expansion of $(1 + x)^n$. You can use an array to store the triangle. Note that you will have zeros for the unused positions of the array (maybe you can avoid displaying the zeros).

For convenience, you want to display the Pascal's triangle as given below.

```
1
1 2 1
1 3 3 1
1 4 6 4 1
1 5 10 10 5 1
1 6 15 20 15 6 1
1 7 21 35 35 21 7 1
```

This maybe more convenient if you are using an array to store the elements of the triangle.

IOP Publishing

A Course on Digital Image Processing with MATLAB®

P K Thiruvikraman

Chapter 10

The image processing toolbox

10.1 Introduction

As seen from our discussion in chapter 9, MATLAB® is a powerful tool for data analysis and visualization. In addition, it has a number of toolboxes that facilitate its application in many fields. One of the toolboxes available with MATLAB® is the Image Processing Toolbox.

The Image Processing Toolbox consists of a large number of built-in functions that make it very easy for us to implement various algorithms used in image processing.

However, while using the toolboxes, one should not get carried away and overuse the built-in functions. Relying too much on built-in functions will not help us to understand the details of the various algorithms we use. Understanding the details of each algorithm is essential if we have to modify and make them more efficient. Writing our own programs (instead of using built-in functions) will also help us in situations where we cannot use MATLAB®.

Since MATLAB® is a high-level language whose commands have to be translated into lower-level languages by the computer, MATLAB® programs will not run as fast as programs written in languages like C. Therefore, it is not preferred for real-time applications. Furthermore, MATLAB® occupies a lot of memory space.

With these disadvantages you might well ask whether we are better off using a language like C. While it is true that MATLAB® has certain disadvantages, it has a number of advantages that has resulted in its widespread use in the field of image processing.

Developing programs in MATLAB® is much simpler than in languages like C. Even as simple a task as reading an image file and storing the pixel intensities in an image requires a very large program with hundreds of lines of code in C. If we eschew MATLAB® altogether, then we run the risk of making very slow progress and getting mired in the technicalities and syntax of programming languages.

doi:10.1088/978-0-7503-2604-9ch10

Hence, it is appropriate to use MATLAB® and employ a judicious mix of built-in and user-defined functions.

You can get a list of commands/built-in functions that are part of the Image Processing Toolbox by typing 'help Image' at the command prompt.

Some of the commands useful for image processing are actually part of the general MATLAB® environment.

10.2 Reading from an image file and writing to an image file

The first command that is generally used in any program for image processing is 'imread'.

The syntax for imread is

```
a=imread('filename.format','format')
```

This command reads the image file mentioned within single quotes, i.e., 'filename. format', and stores it in the array *a*.

The pixel values are stored as unsigned 8-bit integers. This format is referred to in MATLAB® as uint8. If it is a grayscale image, the array will be 2-D, whereas a color image will be stored as a 3-D array. A color image that is stored in an array *a* can be converted to grayscale by using the following command:

```
a=rgb2gray(a)
```

The size command can be used to determine the number of rows and columns in the image. The unsigned integer format is not useful for doing many mathematical operations on an array containing pixel values. Hence, it is better to convert the array elements to a double precision format using the following command:

```
a=double(a);
```

The built-in command *'hist'* can be used to obtain and plot the histogram of an image. The histogram can also be obtained by writing a few lines of code as shown below.

```
(% indicates a comment):
1   a=imread('filename.jpg','jpg');
2   a1=rgb2gray(a);
3   a1=double(a1);
```

```
4    sz=size(a1);
5    % rgb2gray converts a color image in rgb format to a
grayscale image.
6    for i=1:256
7    histr(i)=0;
8    end
9    % This initializes an array named histr for storing
the histogram.
10
11   for i=1:sz(1)
12   for j=1:sz(2)
13   histr(a1(i,j)+1)=histr(a1(i,j)+1)+1;
14   end
15   end
16   i=1:256;
17   plot(i,histr)
```

% sz(1) gives the number of rows, and sz(2) contains the number of columns present in the input image.

% Line number 13 accesses the *ith* row and *jth* column in the image, and increments the bin corresponding to the gray level a1(i,j). Since a1(i,j) can be zero and the array index for the histogram should start from 1, we add a 1 to a1(i,j).

The plot command in line 17 plots the histogram on the screen.

In many applications, for example, in the case of applying a power law transformation to an image, we modify the input image that is stored in the array *a* and store it as another array *b*. We might want to now store the array *b* as an image. This is accomplished by using the command 'imwrite', whose syntax is given below.

```
imwrite(b,'outputfilename.fmt','format')
```

However, before we can use the imwrite command, we have to convert the elements of array *b* to unsigned integer format. Hence, the following command should precede the imwrite command.

```
b=uint8(b);
```

For many applications, we may need to read many images from a single folder. Such a situation typically arises when you are looking for a particular feature in many images (to put it in a more familiar manner, you are looking for a needle in a haystack). You may have many images, each corresponding to a different portion of the haystack. What you would like to do is to read all the images in one go and store values in an array (or many arrays). A recent example of such a search for a needle in a haystack was the sad case of the Malaysian Airlines flight number MH370, which disappeared mysteriously in the Indian Ocean. Since the area within which the plane was likely to be found was too vast, search teams probably used automated means of searching for wreckage of the plane in satellite images. Unfortunately, to date the search remains inconclusive.

We now give below a function that will read all the images in a folder and store values in a single array.

```
function A = ReadImgs(Folder,ImgType)
    Imgs = dir([Folder '/' ImgType]);

% dir lists the files in the directory named 'Folder'
(which is one of the input arguments of the function).

    NumImgs = size(Imgs,1);

% This gets you the number of images in Folder.

    image = double(imread([Folder '/' Imgs(1).name]));
    A = zeros([NumImgs size(image)]);
% This initializes an array A where the RGB values of all
the images can be stored.
    for i=1:NumImgs,
        image = double(imread([Folder '/' Imgs(i).name]));

 A(i,:,:,:) = image;

% For grayscale images, this can be replaced by A
(i,:,:).

    end
    end
```

Let us assume that we have stored all the images that we need to read in a folder known as 'imagesfolder'. Then, we can call the above function from a MATLAB® script or another function (or by typing it in the command window) by using the following function call.

A = ReadImgs('imagesfolder','*.jpg');

All the .jpg images that were stored in 'imagesfolder' will be read by the function ReadImgs and stored in a four-dimensional array A. We can then access the pixel values of individual images by changing the first index of the array A, i.e., A(1,:,:,:)

will return the pixel values of the first image, A(2,:,:,:) will return the values corresponding to the second image, and so on.

While using functions, you should remember that only the output arguments (which in this case is the array A) are accessible to you from outside the function. The other variables used within the function (for example, NumImgs, image, etc in this case) will not be accessible to you from outside the function.

10.3 Fourier domain processing

In Fourier domain processing, extensive use is made of the DFT. To cut down on processing time, it may be advisable to use the FFT function available in MATLAB®.

Given below is a program which compares the time take by the MATLAB® FFT function to compute the Fourier transform of an image, with the time taken to compute the discrete Fourier transform without using the FFT algorithm.

```
clear;

t0=clock;
% Clock is a MATLAB® function that returns the system
time. We are using it here to determine the time required
to compute the DFT;

f = imread('fourier.bmp');
f=double(f);
r=size(f,1);
% r is the number of rows in the image;
% c is the number of columns in the image;
c=size(f,2);

for x=1:r
    for y=1:c
        sum1(x,y)=0+0i;
    end
end
% Initializing an array sum1 to store the Fourier coef-
ficients. 'i' in line
% 13 is the square root of -1. Remember that Fourier
coefficients are
% expected to be complex;

for x = 1:r
    for y = 1:c
```

```
        for n= 1:r
           for m = 1:c
              sum1(x,y) = sum1 (x,y) + f(x,y)
*exp(-2*pi*1i*(n-1)*x/r) *exp(-2*pi*1i*(m-1)*y/c);
           end
          end
          ft(x,y)=abs(sum1(x,y));
       end
end
% n and m are indices that run over the rows and columns,
respectively. x
% and y are the coordinates (referred to as u and v
in chapter 3.
t1=clock;
dt=t1-t0;
% dt gives the time that has elapsed since the beginning
of the program;
```

In the above program we have used the built-in 'clock' function to calculate the time required for the computation. The clock function can also be used as a 'seed' for a random number generator (refer to section 9.6 for a discussion about the generation of random numbers). The time required for running a program can also be calculated by pressing the 'Run and time' button, which is next to the 'Run' button in the MATLAB® Editor window.

MATLAB® took 1 min and 39 s to compute the DFT of an image that had 128 × 128 pixels.

The built-in FFT algorithm took 0.281 s to compute the DFT of the same image! Hence, in most situations it is advisable to use the FFT algorithm rather than the straightforward DFT algorithm.

The command 'FFT2(A)' calculates the FFT of a 2-D image stored in the array A.

You may recall from chapter 3 that we need to center the Fourier transform before we can apply low-pass or high-pass filters. Centering is accomplished using the command fftshift2. After filtering, we need to shift the origin of the frequency domain to the top-left corner (as per the usual convention), and then we can calculate the inverse Fourier transform.

10.4 Calculation of entropy

We have discussed a lot of algorithms that pertain to image compression in chapter 4. Many of these algorithms require sophisticated programming techniques. Hence, we discuss in detail the implementation of these algorithms using MATLAB® programs.

As discussed in chapter 4, the entropy of a source gives an upper limit on the amount of lossless compression that can be achieved. Hence, it is important to calculate the entropy of a source (which may be a text or an image file).

The entropy of a source is defined in terms of its probabilities. The histogram of an image is required to calculate the probabilities. You can use the program given in section 10.2 to compute the histogram. Once the histogram is computed, you can easily arrive at the probabilities of source symbols and hence calculate the entropy.

We give below a section of the program to calculate the entropy. Assume that the histogram of the image is already available and is stored in the array histr. The probabilities are easily calculated as follows (this is a continuation of the program given in section 10.2).

```
1.  P=histr/sum(histr);
2.  H=0;
3.  For i=1:256
4.  If P(i)>0
5.  H=H-P(i)*log2(P(i));
6.  End
7.  End
8.  disp(H)
```

What is the role of line no. 21 (the If condition)? This condition is required because the probability of a certain gray level may be zero (this gray level is not present in the input image). In such a situation, trying to calculate the logarithm of the corresponding probability will result in an error. MATLAB® will display the entropy as 'NaN' (not a number).

The above program may not have appeared very complicated to you. But suppose you were asked to calculate the second-order entropy. How would you modify the above program?

One of the ways of accomplishing this may be as follows:
1. We scan the entire image, row-wise and column-wise, and store the intensity values of the image in a 1-D array.
2. We will use a 2-D histogram (call it histr2) to store the number of occurrences of a particular combination of gray levels, i.e., the element histr2(i,j) will contain the number of occasions when a pixel of intensity i is followed by a pixel with intensity j.
3. We start from the first element of the array and also read the intensity value of its immediate neighbor. The appropriate bin of histr2 is updated.
4. The probability of the combination of gray levels and the second-order entropy are calculated as before.

We show below the MATLAB® script for calculating the second-order entropy of an image.

```
'program to calculate the second-order entropy of an
image';
a=imread('goodcontrast.jpg');
a=rgb2gray(a);
a=double(a);
k=1;
for i=1:size(a,1)
    for j=1:size(a,2)
        b(k)=a(i,j);
        k=k+1;
    end
end
% The elements of the 2-D array "a" are read into a 1-D
array b;
for i=1:256
    for j=1:256
    histr2(i,j)=0;
    end
end

% This initializes an array to store the second-order
histogram of the image;
for i=1:size(b,2)-1
    histr2(b(i)+1,b(i+1)+1)=histr2(b(i)+1,b(i+1)+1)+1;
end
p2=histr2/sum(sum(histr2));

h2=0;
%initializing the second-order entropy;
for i=1:256
    for j=1:256
%          if p2(i,j)>0
    h2=h2-p2(i,j)*log2(p2(i,j));
%          end
    end
end
h2
```

The above program calculates the entropy of an image. How do we calculate the entropy of a text file? Trying to directly count the number of occurrences of each character is not a very convenient way of doing that. MATLAB® has a provision for converting a string of characters into an array of numbers.

Assume that we have read the contents of a text file and stored it in an array named A. The command $u = double(A)$ converts each character stored in A into its ASCII value and stores it in the array u. Once we have the contents of the file available as an array of numbers (integers), we can follow the procedure employed for calculating the entropy of an image file. A MATLAB® script (program) for calculating the entropy of a text file is reproduced below.

```
clear all;
% As mentioned earlier, it is good practice to clear the
% memory at the beginning of a program;


FID=fopen('entropy.txt','r'); % This opens a text file
for reading

[A,COUNT] = fscanf(FID,'%s'); %This reads the contents
of the file and puts the contents into a character array
A. Count stores the number of characters

fclose(FID);
u=double(A); % Converts the characters in A to the
equivalent ASCII value

'Now we initialize the histogram';
for i=1:max(u)-min(u)+1
histr(i)=0;
end

' Counting the number of occurrences of each character. We
want the minimum ASCII value to go into the first element
in the array histr. Therefore, we subtract min(u) and then
add 1 because the array index should not be zero';

h=0;

for i=1:size(u,2)
histr(u(i)-min(u)+1)=histr(u(i)-min(u)+1)+1;
end
prob=histr/size(u,2);
for i=1:size(histr,2)
    if prob(i)>0
    h=h-prob(i)*log2(prob(i));
end
end
```

10.5 Huffman code

You will recall from the discussion in section 4.7 that the procedure for generating the Huffman code for a given source involves source reduction. We will now describe a MATLAB® script (program) that will implement source reduction.

'MATLAB® program to implement source reduction';

```
clear;
m=input('enter number of source symbols');
n=m;
for i=1:m,
    for j=1:m-1,
        palph1(i,j)=0;
    end
end
k=1;
for i=1:m,
    palph1(i,k)=input('enter the probabilities');
end

% the user should enter the probabilities in descending
%order';
while m>2,

symp=palph1(m,k)+palph1(m-1,k);
% adding the probabilities of the two symbols that have %
the least probability';
for i=1:m-1,
    if symp <= palph1(i,k)
        palph1(i,k+1)=palph1(i,k);
% If the sum of the probabilities is less than an element
% of palph1 (which contains all the probabilities), then
the % probability in a certain row of the kth column is
simply % copied to the (k+1)th column. If the sum is
greater, we have % to insert the sum in that location
else
    break;
end
end

        fl(i,k+1)=1;
'fl is a flag that indicates which probabilities have
been combined';
```

```
'The flag will be useful when generating the codewords';
        palph1(i,k+1)=symp;
        for j=i+1:m-1,
            palph1(j,k+1)=palph1(j-1,k);
        end

'After the sum of the probabilities is inserted, the
remaining probabilities will slide down by one posi-
tion';
m=m-1;
k=k+1;

end
```

The script shown above is only for implementing the source reduction. This program has to be extended to include the part where codewords are generated.

A sample output from this program for four source symbols is shown below.

```
>> huff
number of source symbols4
enter the probabilities0.4
enter the probabilities0.2
enter the probabilities0.2
enter the probabilities0.2
>> palph1
palph1 =
0.4000 0.4000 0.6000
0.2000 0.4000 0.4000
0.2000 0.2000 0
0.2000 0 0
```

The first column of palph1 (above) contains the probabilities of the source symbols that have been entered in descending order. The subsequent columns contain the probabilities after source reduction. It is seen that the order of the probabilities is preserved by this program.

The above program assumes that the probabilities have already been sorted and placed in descending order. In many cases, it may be convenient to have a function/script (program) to sort the probabilities and place them in descending order.

MATLAB® has a built-in function 'sort' for sorting the probabilities. The syntax for this function (for sorting in descending order) is given here. If the probabilities are stored in a 1-D array P, then the following command will sort them in descending order.

```
>> p=sort(p,'descend')
```

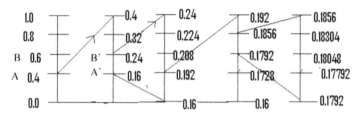

Figure 10.1. Probabilities of source symbols during successive iterations of arithmetic code.

It may also be of interest to you to learn the different methods for sorting an array of numbers. Computer scientists have devoted a lot of time to come up with very efficient sorting schemes[1].

10.6 Arithmetic code

The implementation of the arithmetic code is easier than the implementation of the Huffman code. Just to refresh your memory and to set the stage for you to write a script to implement the algorithm, we reproduce the figure for generating an arithmetic code.

Figure 10.1 should suggest the following approach to you:

1. Firstly, we are required to calculate the probabilities of the source symbols.
2. The cumulative probabilities of the source symbols (which are of course calculated from the probabilities) are also required.
3. The symbols present in the source are read one by one in the proper order.
4. The algorithm uses iteration. The interval assigned to the source symbol under consideration is scaled to 'occupy' the entire interval in every iteration.
5. The cumulative probabilities are recalculated in every iteration.
6. It may not be necessary to store the cumulative probabilities at all stages from beginning to end, but we may need to store the cumulative probabilities of two successive iterations.
7. In addition to the cumulative probabilities, we need to determine the beginning and end of the interval at each iteration.
8. Notice from the above figure that the ratio of the interval corresponding to a certain source symbol at the ith iteration is equal to the corresponding ratio in the $(i + 1)$th iteration.

In other words, referring to the above figure, we see that the interval marked AB is (1/5) of the entire range, which is equal to 1. The corresponding interval A′B′ in the next iteration is equal to 0.08, which is also (1/5) of the entire range (which is now equal to 0.4).

We now elaborate on step 8 given above. Let cumprob1 (short for cumulative probability) be an array that has the cumulative probabilities at the ith iteration, and let cumprob2 be the array that has the cumulative probabilities at the $(i + 1)$th iteration.

---

[1] *How to Solve it by Computer* by R G Dromey has an entire chapter devoted to various sorting algorithms.

We can equate the ratios mentioned in step 8 to compute the jth element of the array cumprob2. Let 'intervalstart' and 'intervalend' be the cumulative probabilities corresponding to the starting and ending of the interval allotted to the source symbol $u(I + 1)$.

We note that cumprob2(1) = intervalstart.

The remaining elements of the array cumprob2 can be generated by equating the ratios, i.e.,

$$\frac{\text{cumprod2}(j) - \text{cumprod2}(j - 1)}{\text{intervalend}(i + 1) = \text{intervalstart}(i + 1)} = \frac{\text{cumprod1}(j) - \text{cumprob1}(j - 1)}{\text{intervalend}(i + 1) - \text{intervalstart}(i + 1)}. \tag{10.1}$$

This can be rewritten as

$$\text{cumprob2}(j) = \text{cumprob2}(j - 1)$$
$$+ \frac{(\text{cumprob1}(j) - \text{cumprob1}(j - 1))*\text{intervalend}(i + 1) - \text{intervalstart}(i + 1)}{\text{intervalend}(i) - \text{intervalstart}(i)}. \tag{10.2}$$

In the sample program that will be discussed below, the difference between the starting and ending of the interval at the ith iteration is stored and used as a variable named 'interval'.

Keeping the above points in mind, we now develop a program to generate the arithmetic code for a particular source. To keep matters simple, we have included an array u at the beginning of the program; this array contains the source symbols. In this sample program the source symbols are integers. In a real-life situation, you may consider reading a text file (for example) and converting the source symbols (alphanumeric or special characters) into their equivalent ASCII values. If it is an image file, then the gray levels of the pixels are the source symbols.

The sample program for generating arithmetic code is as follows.

```
u=[2 1 3 3 4];
'u is the source. For an image, you might want to read
the pixel values into a 1-D array before using this
program';

maxu=max(u);
minu=min(u);

'Now we initialize the histogram';
for i=1:max(u)-min(u)+1
histr(i)=0;
```

```
end

'Counting the number of occurrences of each character.
The minimum ASCII value goes into the first element in
the array histr. Therefore, we subtract min(u) and then
add 1 since the array index cannot be zero';
h=0;

for i=1:size(u,2)
histr(u(i)-min(u)+1)=histr(u(i)-min(u)+1)+1;
end

prob=histr/size(u,2);

'Obtaining the probabilities of source symbols from the
histogram and storing them in the array prob';

for i=1:size(histr,2)
cumprob(i)=0;
end

'Initializing an array cumprob to store the cumulative
probabilities';

for i=1:size(histr,2),
    sump=0;
    for j=1:i
        sump=sump+prob(j);
    end
    cumprob(i)=sump;
end

'The first element of cumprob will be nonzero (it will
have the probability of the first element). Therefore,
we generate another array cumprob1 whose first element
is zero and the remaining elements are the elements of
cumprob';

cumprob1(1)=0;
for i=2:size(cumprob,2)+1
    cumprob1(i)=cumprob(i-1);
end
```

```
intervalstart=0;
intervalend=1;
interval=1;

'The number of iterations will be equal to the number of
elements in the array u';


for i=1:size(u,2)

interval=intervalend-intervalstart;

'This stores the range of the interval at the ith
iteration';

intervalstart=cumprob1(u(i)-min(u)+1);

intervalend=cumprob1(u(i)-min(u)+2);
cumprob2(1)=intervalstart;
for j=2:size(cumprob1,2)
cumprob2(j)=cumprob2(j-1)+(cumprob1(j)-cumprob1(j-1))
*(intervalend-intervalstart)/interval;

'This is the implementation of equation (10.2). (See
step 8 of the algorithm discussed earlier.)';

end

cumprob1=cumprob2;

end

codeword=(intervalstart+intervalend)/2
```

As per the algorithm for the arithmetic code, the final
number generated (codeword) can be any number within the
interval at the final stage of the iteration. We take it
to be the average of the starting and ending of the
interval.

10.7 Segmentation

Object recognition is a very vast field and it is not possible to discuss all the algorithms for object/pattern and their implementation using MATLAB®. We will discuss only a few preliminary steps that are used on many occasions.

As was discussed in chapter 5, to recognize an object we have to first segment an image into its constituent parts. The first step in this process is to threshold the given image so that the foreground pixels are separated (i.e., adequately distinguished) from the background pixels.

The thresholding may be accomplished by the method of iterative thresholding discussed in chapter 5. Once the process of thresholding has been completed, the next step is to label all the objects that are present in the image. The process of labeling is equivalent to numbering all the pixels belonging to one object by a number (say '1') and all the pixels belonging to the next object by '2', etc. This is done so that in the later steps of the recognition each object can be distinguished by the number assigned to it. This process of labeling can also be thought of as segmentation within the foreground pixels.

While you may desire to write your own program to accomplish the labeling using the algorithm discussed in section 6.5, it is also appropriate to mention at this point that a built-in MATLAB® function, 'bwlabel', which labels the different objects in an image, is also available. Upon being given an input image, the function returns a matrix that has the same size as the image. The background pixels are labeled '0' while all the pixels belonging to one object are assigned the same number. The function has an option to specify whether 4-connectivity or 8-connectivity is to be used to decide whether two pixels are connected. Two pixels that are connected to each other are said to 'belong' to the same object.

10.8 Hough transform

The Hough transform is a useful tool for detecting straight lines as well as other regular curves and shapes. Hence, a detailed discussion about its implementation is called for.

We start by giving a simple program to compute the Hough transform of a binary input image.

```
clear;
a=imread('lines.bmp','bmp');
sz1=size(a,1);

% sz1 is the number of rows in the input image;

sz2=size(a,2);

% sz2 is the number of columns in the input image;
```

```
dmax=(sz1^2+sz2^2)^0.5;
dmax=round(dmax);
```

% Consider the input image to be a rectangle, and dmax is the length of the diagonal of the rectangle. Dmax is the maximum possible value of ρ.

```
theta=-pi/2:0.01:pi/2;
d=-dmax:1:dmax;
 % The above commands create 1-D arrays for storing ρ and θ.
 % The commands given below initialize the accumulator
 'accu'
```

```
for i=1:size(d,2)+2,
    for j=1:size(theta,2)+2,
        accu(i,j)=0;
    end
end
```

```
m=0;
for i=1:size(a,1),
    for j=1:size(a,2),
        if a(i,j)<1,
```

% Here all pixels that are black are considered as the foreground and white pixels are considered as part of the background. In other words, we are looking for dark lines on a white background.

```
        m=m+1;
        for k=1:size(theta,2),
            rho(m,k)=i*cos(theta(k))+j*sin(theta(k));
```

% For every foreground point we calculate the ρ (rho) corresponding to all possible values of θ. The command below increments the corresponding accumulator cell. The value of rho calculated above may not be an integer, and hence it has to be rounded to the nearest integer before incrementing the corresponding accumulator cell;

```
accu(round(rho(m,k))+dmax+2,k)=accu(round(rho(m,k))
+dmax+2,k)+1;
            end
        end
    end
end


% As discussed in chapter 5, the Hough transform will
detect a lot of spurious lines. Any two points can always
be considered to be joined by a straight line, and thick
lines will appear as being composed of short lines in the
perpendicular direction. Hence, we set a threshold. All
accumulator cells that exceed the threshold value are
displayed below. Here the threshold value is set as
equal to 20. The threshold value is quite arbitrary and
you may need to choose it carefully.



for i=1:size(accu,1),
    for j=1:size(accu,2),
        if accu(i,j)>20,
            accu(i,j)
            inclination=(j/size(theta,2)-0.5)*pi
        end
    end
end
```

It was mentioned before (chapter 5) that the Hough transform considers all points that lie along the same straight line to be connected. Another problem is that in many cases an image may contain a single straight line figure 10.2.

A human observer would interpret that the image given in figure 10.2 consists of a single straight line (the individual pixels are shown as separate squares for clarity). However, the Hough transform will detect many straight lines. As per the Hough transform, there are four vertical lines in the above figure, each having a length of 8 pixels. It will also detect eight horizontal lines of 4 pixels each as well as lines at other angles. Hence, where we would have expected that only one of the accumulator cells would have a nonzero entry, we would find instead that many accumulator cells are nonzero. Once way of avoiding the problem of finding multiple, 'spurious' lines in the figure is to threshold the accumulator cells. In the example under discussion, we can use a threshold value of 5, which would detect only the vertical lines.

MATLAB® has certain built-in functions that not only compute the Hough transform, but also take care of the problems mentioned above.

The function

[H, THETA, RHO] = hough(BW)

computes the standard Hough transform of the binary image BW and stores it in the 2-D array H.

The built-in MATLAB® function 'houghpeaks' identifies peaks in the Hough transform.

One of the parameters in the 'houghpeaks' function is 'threshold', which can be used to remove from consideration spurious straight lines as discussed above.

The function 'houghlines' extracts line segments based on the Hough transform. One of the parameters in this function is 'fillgap', which merges line segments that have a separation less than the 'fillgap'. This feature is important to reduce the number of spurious straight lines detected by the function 'hough'. While 'houghpeaks' would help us to threshold and discard accumulator cells that are less than the threshold, it would still tell us that there are four vertical lines in figure 10.2. 'Houghlines' would get around this problem since we can merge these four lines (which are very close to each other) using the 'fillgap' parameter.

10.9 Some common error messages in MATLAB®

MATLAB® has many facilities for easy debugging of programs. We can save lot of time and debug programs easily if we are able to understand the error messages given out by MATLAB®.

Note that MATLAB® indicates some of the errors even as the programs (scripts or functions) are being typed.

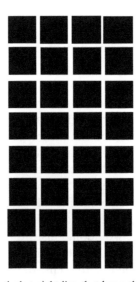

Figure 10.2. A vertical straight line that has a thickness of 4 pixels.

Unmatched brackets are indicated when the cursor is positioned near one (figure 10.3)

A pair of matching brackets are also indicated by an underscore below each of the brackets (figure 10.4).

Sometimes errors are indicated only during run time (i.e., when you click the 'run' button in the editor), as shown in figure 10.5. In figure 10.5, an arithmetic expression was typed in which the symbol for multiplication (*) was left out after the number 3. Note that the error message says only that the expression is 'unbalanced' or the bracket is unexpected. It does not say directly that you have missed the symbol for multiplication. In such cases we have to interpret the error messages carefully.

If the same expression (i.e., the expression in figure 10.4) is typed in the MATLAB® program editor, the erroneous part is indicated by a red line below it and the following error message (figure 10.6) is displayed when the mouse arrow is placed above that point.

Sometimes MATLAB® also produces warning messages even as programs are being typed in the editor.

A very common error occurs when the index of an array is negative or beyond the specified bounds (figure 10.7).

Another MATLAB® error that occurs in many image processing applications is when we do not convert the pixel intensities to double format but try to apply

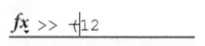

Figure 10.3. Unmatched bracket being indicated by a '–' on top of the bracket.

$$fx \gg (1+2*3\,\underline{(x+y)})\,;$$

Figure 10.4. Underscore below a pair of matching brackets.

```
>> (1+2*3(x+y));
   (1+2*3(x+y));
         |
Error: Unbalanced or unexpected parenthesis or bracket.
fx >>
```

Figure 10.5. Error indicated during run time.

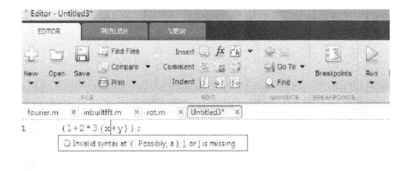

Figure 10.6. Invalid syntax is indicated when the mouse arrow is placed above the erroneous part.

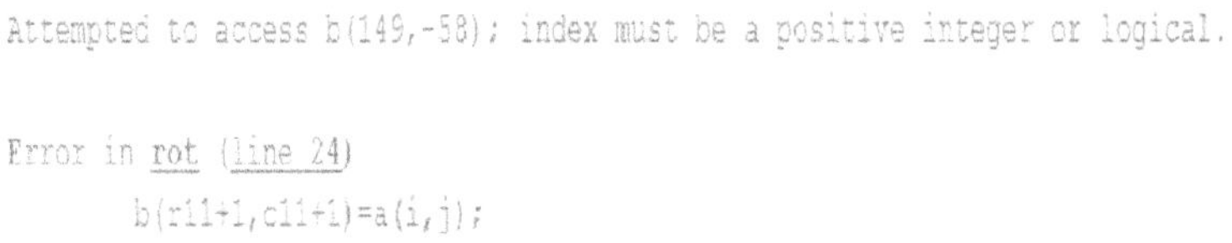

```
Attempted to access b(149,-58); index must be a positive integer or logical.

Error in rot (line 24)
        b(r11+1,c11+1)=a(i,j);
```

Figure 10.7. An error message indicating when the index of an array is outside permitted limits.

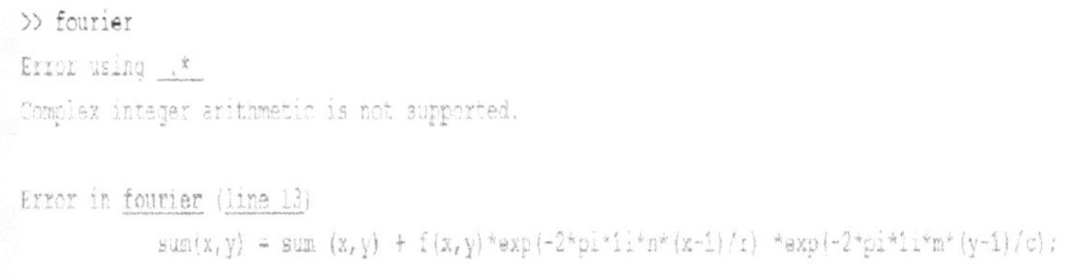

```
>> fourier
Error using  .*
Complex integer arithmetic is not supported.

Error in fourier (line 13)
        sum(x,y) = sum (x,y) + f(x,y)*exp(-2*pi*11*n*(x-1)/r) *exp(-2*pi*11*m*(y-1)/c);
```

Figure 10.8. Error message displayed when the pixel values were not converted to the double format.

various arithmetical operations on it. For example, in a program to calculate the DFT of an image (section 10.3), the pixel values were read using the 'imread' command, but were not converted into double format before the DFT was computed (figure 10.8). The error message displayed is shown in figure 10.8.

Exercises

1. The concepts that we have learned in image processing can be useful in many other fields. For example, we can use these concepts to generate images of fractals. Fractals are selfsimilar structures, i.e., they have the same appearance at many different length scales. One of the visually appealing fractals is the Sierpinski carpet. The Sierpinski carpet is generated using the following steps (figure 10.9):

Figure 10.9. The Sierpinski carpet. The boxes that are deleted are shown in white while the boxes that are retained are shown in black. The result after the first iteration is shown at the top-left corner. The result of the second iteration is at the top right, while the results of the next two iterations are at the bottom left and bottom right, respectively.

(i) Consider a square of side a (which corresponds to a pixels). This square is then divided into nine equal boxes, and the central box is deleted.

(ii) This process is repeated for each of the remaining boxes (i.e., each box is divided into nine sub-boxes and the central sub-box is deleted).

(iii) This process (step (ii)) is repeated until the size of the sub-box becomes 1 pixel.

To implement this in MATLAB® and display the output as an image you can use the algorithm given below.

(i) Initialize all elements of an array (let us call it A) of size a x a as 0. Choose a as a power of 3 for better results (this way when we sub-divide the square into boxes, the side of the box remains an integer).

(ii) The elements of the array that are part of the box that is to be 'deleted' are set equal to 1.

(iii) Once the box has been deleted, display array A using the 'imshow' command. 'imshow' displays the elements of an array in the MATLAB®

figure window. Once the array is displayed, pause the program using the 'pause' command. *Pause(x)* will pause the program for x seconds, where x is an integer. The pause command is to be used because otherwise the image of the carpet will change very fast and we will not be able to perceive the different stages of the carpet.

If you have implemented the above algorithm correctly, the successive images that you will see will be similar to those given in figure 10.9.

IOP Publishing

A Course on Digital Image Processing with MATLAB®

P K Thiruvikraman

Chapter 11

Video processing

11.1 Introduction

Up to now, we have concentrated on processing images (still photographs). Video processing is also a very important field since video cameras are used extensively for surveillance and millions of videos are transferred over the internet on a daily basis for education and entertainment.

Many of the techniques we have studied in the context of single images can also be applied for videos if we are able to extract the individual frames from the video. MATLAB® has built-in functions for extracting frames from a video. We now study this function, which will be the basis for all further discussions.

11.2 Extracting frames from a video

A small MATLAB® program that extracts frames from a video is given below.

```
readerobj = VideoReader('testvideo.wmv');
 vidFrames = read(readerobj);
 numFrames = get(readerobj, 'NumberOfFrames');
 for k = 1 : numFrames
 image(vidFrames(:,:,:,k));
 pause(1);
 clf;
 'clears the figure window before displaying the next
frame'
end;
```

Here, the MATLAB® function 'VideoReader' extracts the individual frames from a color video and stores them in a four-dimensional array 'vidFrames'. The first three dimensions are for color (RGB values) and the 4th dimension specifies the frame.

Extracting frames from a video is only the first step. Further processing can be done to either compress the video or to detect motion/moving objects in the video.

11.3 Video compression

In chapter 4, we saw that compression can be achieved by removing redundancy. A single image can be compressed by reducing interpixel redundancy. A video can be compressed by reducing interframe redundancy. This is because corresponding pixels (i.e., pixels that have the same coordinates) in a sequence of frames will usually have the same gray level (assuming that the camera does not move). Changes in gray level of corresponding pixels can occur only if objects that are present in a frame move with respect to the camera.

We can detect changes between corresponding pixels by taking the difference between corresponding pixels in successive frames. This is illustrated in figures 11.1–11.3. Three successive frames in a video are shown in these figures.

The difference between figure 11.2 and figure 11.2 is shown in figure 11.4.

In the sequence of images only the hand was in motion. Therefore, the difference image is nonzero only near the location of the hand. It is to be expected that the entropy of the difference images should be much lower than the entropy of the original images.

The entropies of figure 11.1, figure 11.2, and figure 11.3 are 7.62, 7.67, and 7.69 bits/pixel, respectively. The entropies of figure 11.4 and figure 11.5 are 2.13 and 2.22 bits/pixel, respectively. The lower entropies of the difference images indicate that compression can be achieved by using the concept of the difference image. Hence, to compress a video, we can send the first frame of the video as it is and then we can perform (for example) Huffman encoding of successive frames. Since the difference image of frames contains a lot of interpixel redundancy we can achieve further compression by doing run-length encoding and then implementing Huffman

Figure 11.1. The first frame extracted from a video.

Figure 11.2. The second frame of the same video.

Figure 11.3. The third frame of the video.

Figure 11.4. Difference between figure 11.2 and figure 11.1.

encoding of the run lengths. It has to be kept in mind that compression algorithms like Huffman coding involve enormous amounts of computation. Hence, in practice, it may be necessary to strike a balance between the amount of compression and the time required to achieve compression.

Figure 11.5. Difference between figure 11.3 and figure 11.2.

11.4 Detection and analysis of motion: optical flows

The difference between corresponding pixels in two successive frames may also be used to detect and analyze the motion of objects. By analyzing the difference image it was hoped that one could arrive at a vector field that specifies the direction and magnitude of 'flow' (i.e., motion) of pixels in an image. However, it turns out that extracting the optical flow from successive images is not very straightforward.

Assume that the intensity of pixels within a frame is specified by a function $I(x,y,t)$, where t is the time at which the frame under consideration was taken. If the image is shifted by an amount (dx,dy) in the time dt between successive frames, then we have

$$I(x + dx, y + dy, t + dt) = I(x, y, t). \tag{11.1}$$

Furthermore, $I(x + dx, y + dy, t + dt)$ can be expanded in a Taylor series:

$$I(x + dx, y + dy, t + dt) = I(x, y, t) + \frac{\partial I}{\partial x}dx + \frac{\partial I}{\partial y}dy + \frac{\partial I}{\partial t}dt + \dots. \tag{11.2}$$

Ignoring second- and higher-order derivatives in equation (11.2), and using equation (11.1), we have

$$\frac{\partial I}{\partial t} = -\left(\dot{x}\frac{\partial I}{\partial x} + \dot{y}\frac{\partial I}{\partial y} \right). \tag{11.3}$$

This equation can also be written as

$$\frac{\partial I}{\partial t} = -\nabla I. \, \bar{v}. \tag{11.4}$$

The LHS of equation (11.4) can be calculated by subtracting pairs of images (i.e., the difference image mentioned in section 11.3), while the gradient of $I(x,y)$ can be calculated using the gradient operators. If we succeed in calculating both these quantities, then the velocity vector at a point can be calculated. Calculation of the velocity vector at all points in the frame helps us to determine the velocity vector field or optical flow for the sequence of frames in the video.

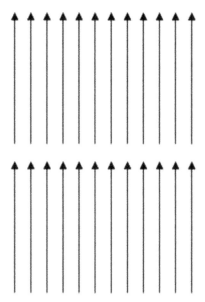

Figure 11.6. Such an optical flow indicates uniform motion of all objects in the field of view.

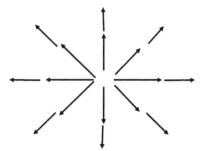

Figure 11.7. All objects diverging from a point. The camera is probably moving toward that point.

However, equation (11.4) is a single equation with two unknowns, i.e., v_x and v_y, the two components of the velocity vector. Another problem arises since the calculation of the velocity vector involves derivatives of the intensity distribution in the frames and derivatives are very much susceptible to noise.

Equation (11.4) can be solved iteratively. This essentially means a solution by trial and error.

Once the velocity vector field or optical flow has been computed, we can try to interpret the optical flow. A few examples of optical flows are shown below (figures 11.6–11.8).

In general, motion of an object toward or away from the camera will result in a vector field with divergence. Similarly, motion of the camera will also result in a vector field (optical flow) with divergence.

Rotation of an object will result in a vector field that curls.

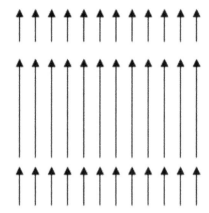

Figure 11.8. Optical flow that can result from rotation of an object about an axis perpendicular to the line of sight. The parts of the object toward the center of image are moving perpendicular to the line of sight while the other parts appear to have a smaller motion as they are moving toward or away from the camera.

The divergence of a vector field (in the present context it is the velocity field or optical flow) can be calculated using the following expression:

$$\vec{\nabla} \cdot \vec{v} = \frac{\partial v_x}{\partial x} + \frac{\partial v_y}{\partial y} \tag{11.5}$$

The curl of a vector field[1] can be calculated using the following expression:

$$(\nabla \times v)_z = \left(\frac{\partial v_y}{\partial x} - \frac{\partial v_x}{\partial y} \right). \tag{11.6}$$

Example 11.1 Can you think of a nonconstant vector field whose divergence and curl are both zero?

One such field is

$\vec{v} = y\hat{i} + x\hat{j}$.

This field is plotted in the figure below.

---

[1] You may refer to any standard book on vector calculus for more details about these concepts. For example, *Vector Analysis* by Murray R Spiegel (Schaum's outline series) is a good source.

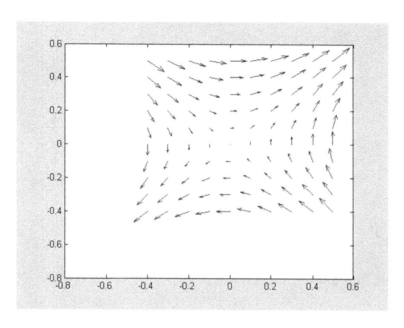

Exercises:

1. Calculate the divergence of the vector field $\bar{v} = \dfrac{\hat{j}}{y}$ and plot the result.
2. Use equations (11.5) and (11.6) to show that the field mentioned in example 11.1 has zero curl and zero divergence.
3. Does the field given in the figure below have a nonzero curl?

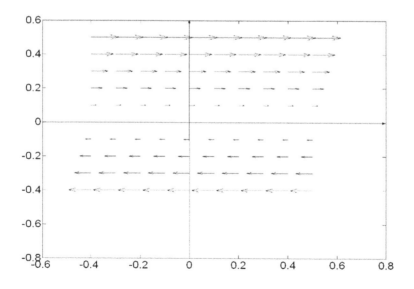

Chapter 12

Solutions to selected exercises

Solutions to Chapter 1 exercises

1. For storing a 1024 × 1024, 12 bit grayscale image, you would require 12 582 912 bits.
2. Conversion of a continuous image to a digital image is not reversible since it is a many-to-one mapping. When converting an analog image to digital form, we sample the image at certain points, and hence we lose information about the intermediate points. If we want to get back an image that is very close to the original continuous image, we can use interpolation to obtain the intensity values for the intermediate points where we had not sampled.
3. The black squares at the corners of a QR code and also at the corners of OMR sheets are to get the orientation of the image. The OMR sheet is scanned and digitized. A program then searches for the circles that have been darkened. The coordinates of the darkened circles are then calculated with respect to the black squares at the corners. One of the black squares is taken as the origin and the other squares are used to get the orientation of the coordinate axes.

Solutions to Chapter 2 exercises

1. a) A is found from the condition that the probability distribution function should be normalized, i.e., $\int_0^1 p(r)dr = \int_0^1 A \sin(\pi r)dr = 1$.

   By performing the integration and substituting the limits, we get $A = \dfrac{\pi}{2}$.

   b) The transformation required to obtain a uniform histogram is

   $$s = \int_0^r p(r)dr = \frac{\pi}{2}\int_0^r \sin(\pi r)dr = \frac{1}{2}[1 - \cos(\pi r)].$$

c) The transformation function obtained above is plotted in the figure given below.

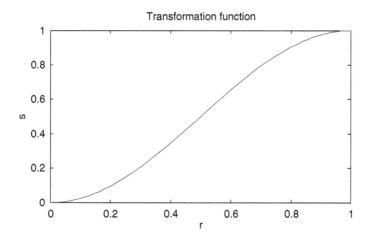

2. a) It will be a uniform histogram, i.e., $n(r) = 1$ for $r = 0$ to 255.

   If the most significant bit is set to zero, then all pixels will have a value less than 128. 128 is mapped to 0, 129 is mapped to 1, ... 255 is mapped to 127.

   Therefore, $n(r') = 2$ for $r' = 0$ to 127 and $n(r') = 0$ for $r' = 128$ to 255.

   b) The average of $f(x) = (1 + 2 + 3 + ...\ 255)/256 = (255 * 256)/(2 * 256) = 127.5$.

   c) If all odd-numbered pixels are set to zero, $n(s = 0) = 128$ and $n(s) = 1$ for $s = 1, 3, ... 255$.

   d) The average gray level of the modified image is given by $(1 + 3 + 5 + ...\ 255)/256 = 256 * 64/256 = 64$.

3. a) Since s represents the gray level of the negative of the image:

$$s = 1 - r$$
$$\bar{s} = \int_0^1 sp(s)ds = \int_0^1 (1 - r)p(r)dr = 1 - \bar{r}$$

   b) $\sigma_s = \int_0^1 (s - \bar{s})^2 p(s)ds = \int_0^1 (\bar{r} - r)^2 p(r)dr = \sigma_r.$

4. a) Average gray level of original image = 3.03, and standard deviation = 1.982.

b) Implementation of histogram equalization is shown in the table given below.

r	$n(r)$	$\sum\limits_{j=0}^{r} n(j)$	$S = 7* \sum\limits_{j=0}^{r} n(j)Z$	S rounded to the nearest integer
0	5	0.05	0.35	0
1	10	0.15	1.05	1
2	50	0.65	4.55	5
3	2	0.67	4.69	5
4	3	0.70	4.9	5
5	10	0.80	5.6	6
6	15	0.95	6.65	7
7	5	1	7	7

c) The output histogram is given below.

S	$n(s)$	$(s - \bar{s})^2 p(s)$
0	5	1.761 25
1	10	1.482 25
2	0	0
3	0	0
4	0	0
5	55	0.012 375
6	10	0.132 25
7	20	0.9245
Sum	100	3.7275

Average value of $s = 4.85$.
Standard deviation $= 1.93$.
Therefore, we conclude that while the brightness of the image has increased, the contrast has actually reduced.

5. The histogram does not uniquely specify an image. This is because it does not have information about the position (location) of the pixels with a certain gray level. It only has information about how many pixels have a certain gray level.
Number of binary images with the same histogram $= \dfrac{n^2!}{\dfrac{n^2}{2}! \dfrac{n^2}{2}!}$.

6. a) $n(s) = 1$ for $s = 0$ to127
   $n(s) = 1$ for $s = 192$ to 254
   $n(s) = 0$ for $s = 128$ to 191
   $n(255) = 65$

b) There are 65 pixels with the a gray level of 255.

c) Average gray level of output image = 151.375; average gray level of original image = 127.5.

7. a) The mean value of $r = \int_0^1 rp(r)dr = \int_0^1 6r^2(1-r)dr = 1/2$; and the variance of

$$r = \int_0^1 \left(r - \frac{1}{2}\right)^2 p(r)dr = \int_0^1 \left(r - \frac{1}{2}\right)^2 6r(1-r)dr$$

$$= 6\int_0^1 r(r^2 + 0.25 - r)(1-r)dr$$

$$= 6\left[\int_0^1 -r^4 dr + \int_0^1 r^3 dr + \int_0^1 0.25r dr - \int_0^1 0.25r^2 dr - \int_0^1 r^2 dr + \int_0^1 r^3 dr\right] = 0.05.$$

Standard deviation = 0.223.

b) If both s and r range from 0 to 1, then $c = 1$.

c) $p(s)ds = p(r)dr$.

Therefore,

$$p(s) = p(r)\frac{dr}{ds} = 6r(1-r)2r^{1/2} = 6s^2(1-s^2)2s = 12s^3(1-s^2).$$

d) The mean value of $s = \int_0^1 sp(s)ds = \int_0^1 12s^4(1-s^2)ds = 24/35.$

Variance $= \int_0^1 (s - \bar{s})p(s)ds = \int_0^1 \left(s - \frac{24}{35}\right)^2 12s^3(1-s^2)ds = 0.0297972.$

Standard deviation = ~0.1725.

The standard deviation has reduced marginally.

8. a) It is given that $s = cr^\gamma$.

If $L - 1$ maps to $L - 1$, we have

$$L - 1 = c(L - 1)^\gamma.$$

Therefore, $c = (L - 1)^{1-\gamma}$.

b) The slope of the transformation function is given by

$$m = \frac{ds}{dr} = \gamma\left(\frac{r_{max}}{L - 1}\right)^{\gamma - 1}.$$

The slope is a maximum when $\dfrac{dm}{d\gamma} = \left(\dfrac{r_{max}}{L - 1}\right)^{\gamma - 1} + \gamma\left(\dfrac{r_{max}}{L - 1}\right)^{\gamma - 1}$

$\ln\left(\dfrac{r_{max}}{L - 1}\right) = 0.$

Therefore, $\gamma = -\dfrac{1}{\ln\left(\dfrac{r_{max}}{L - 1}\right)}.$

9. The black square is indistinguishable from the background if the value (after averaging) for the center of the square is 250.

   This happens when

   $$\frac{(n^2 - 25) * 255}{n^2} = 250.$$

   From the above equation, we get $n = \sim 37$ (rounded up to the next higher odd integer).

10.

$$\frac{1}{16} \times \begin{array}{|c|c|c|} \hline 1 & 2 & 1 \\ \hline 2 & 4 & 2 \\ \hline 1 & 2 & 1 \\ \hline \end{array}$$

Observe that the weights of the cells in column 2 are twice that of the corresponding cells in column 1.

To calculate the weighted average, we multiply the gray levels of the pixels by the weights and do the addition columnwise and store the result in the variables C_1, C_2, and C_3.

When the mask is moved to the next pixel, a new column (C_4) has to be included and the column C_1 has to be deleted (as it has moved out of the mask).

Therefore, we have

$$\text{average} = \frac{1}{16}\left[\frac{C_2}{2} + 2C_3 + C_4\right].$$

As opposed to nine multiplications, one division, and eight additions, we have four additions (two are explicitly shown in the expression for the average and two more are involved in the calculation of C_4).

We also need to perform four multiplications. The algorithm will be roughly twice as fast as the brute force method.

11. When an image is reduced to ¼ of its original size, the number of rows and columns are reduced by half. This is done by retaining only the alternate rows and columns. Therefore, some information (fine detail) about the original image is lost. When the image is restored to its original size, we do not get back the lost information. The restoration process will introduce additional rows and columns, whose values are obtained by interpolation, but this does not bring back the lost information or fine detail in the image.

12. There are three assignment operations for sorting each pair of numbers. Therefore, for computing the median there is a maximum of 90 operations required for computing the median value corresponding to one pixel.

In the histogram method, there are 9 assignment operations for computing the histogram and at most 9 more addition operations to get the median value. Nine more assignment operations are required to initialize the histogram when we move to the next pixel. Therefore, there is a total of 27 assignment operations required in the histogram method; this is less than the number of operations required in the simple sorting approach. Of course, we need N^2 (number of pixels) assignment operations to compute the histogram for the first time, but this has to be done only once.

Solutions to Chapter 3 exercises

1. a) The Fourier transform of the given function is

$$F(u) = \int_{-\infty}^{\infty} e^{-\frac{|x|}{x_o}} e^{-2\pi jux} dx = \int_{-\infty}^{0} e^{\frac{x}{x_o}} e^{-2\pi jux} dx + \int_{0}^{\infty} e^{\frac{-x}{x_o}} e^{-2\pi jux} dx$$

$$= \int_{-\infty}^{0} e^{x\left(\frac{1}{x_o} - 2\pi jux\right)} dx + \int_{0}^{\infty} e^{-x\left(\frac{1}{x_o} + 2\pi jux\right)} dx$$

$$\times \frac{1}{\left(\frac{1}{x_o} - 2\pi ju\right)} + \frac{1}{\left(\frac{1}{x_o} + 2\pi ju\right)} = \frac{2/x_o}{\left(\frac{1}{x_o}\right)^2 + 4\pi^2 u^2}$$

$$= \frac{2x_o}{1 + 4\pi^2 u^2 x_o^2}.$$

b) The given function $f(x)$ is an exponentially decaying function. Hence, the attenuation it provides (at a given frequency) will be much more than the corresponding Butterworth filter of the first order.

2. a)

$$F(u) = \frac{1}{M} \sum_{x=0}^{M-1} f(x) e^{-\frac{2\pi jux}{M}} = \frac{1}{M} \sum_{x=0}^{M/2-1} e^{-\frac{2\pi jux}{M}}$$

$$= \frac{1}{M}\left[1 + e^{-\frac{2\pi jux}{M}} + e^{-\frac{4\pi jux}{M}} + \ldots e^{-\frac{2\pi ju}{M}\left(\frac{M}{2}-1\right)}\right]$$

This is a geometric series whose sum is given by

$$F(u) = \frac{1 - e^{-\pi ju}}{1 - e^{-\frac{2\pi ju}{M}}}.$$

For $u = 0$, $F(u)$; hence, we use L'Hospital's rule to evaluate $F(u)$ and obtain $F(u) = \frac{1}{2}$.

$F(u)$ will be zero for even values of u. It will be nonzero for odd values of u.

b) The expression for $F(u)$ can be written as

$$F(u) = \frac{e^{-\frac{\pi j u}{2}} \sin\left(\frac{\pi u}{2}\right)}{e^{-\frac{\pi j u}{M}} \sin\left(\frac{\pi u}{M}\right)}.$$

Therefore, the magnitude of the Fourier transform is $|F(u)| = \frac{\sin\left(\frac{\pi u}{2}\right)}{\sin\left(\frac{\pi u}{M}\right)}$.

c) $F(0) = \frac{1}{2}$

3. Let (x', y') be the coordinates of the pixels with respect to the center of the image and (x, y) be their coordinates with respect to the origin (at the top-left corner).

Then, $x' = x - M/2$ and $y' = y - N/2$.

Rotation by 180° is equivalent to an inversion about the origin.

Therefore, $g(x', y') = f(-x', -y')$.

$g(x,y) = f(M/2 - x, N/2 - y)$

The DFT of $g(x,y)$ is given by

$$G(u, v) = \frac{1}{MN} \sum_{x=0}^{M-1}\sum_{y=0}^{N-1} g(x, y) e^{-\frac{2\pi jux}{M}} e^{-\frac{2\pi jvy}{N}}$$

$$= \frac{1}{MN} \sum_{x=0}^{M-1}\sum_{y=0}^{N-1} f\left(\frac{M}{2} - x, \frac{N}{2} - y\right) e^{-\frac{2\pi jux}{M}} e^{-\frac{2\pi jvy}{N}}$$

$$= \frac{1}{MN} \sum_{x=0}^{M-1}\sum_{y=0}^{N-1} f(-x', -y') e^{-\frac{2\pi ju}{M}\left(x' + \frac{M}{2}\right)} e^{-\frac{2\pi jv}{N}\left(y' + \frac{N}{2}\right)}$$

$$= (-1)^{u+v} F(-u, -v).$$

4. The continuous Fourier transform of the given cosine function is

$$F(u) = \int_{-\infty}^{\infty} \cos(2\pi u_o x) e^{-2\pi jux} dx$$

$$= \int_{-\infty}^{\infty} \left(\frac{e^{2\pi ju_o x} + e^{-2\pi ju_o x}}{2}\right) e^{-2\pi jux} dx$$

$$= \int_{-\infty}^{\infty} \frac{e^{2\pi jx(u_o - u)}}{2} dx + \int_{-\infty}^{\infty} \frac{e^{-2\pi jx(u_o + u)}}{2} dx$$

$$= \frac{e^{2\pi jx(u_o - u)}}{4\pi j(u_o - u)} \bigg|_{-L}^{L} + \frac{e^{-2\pi jx(u_o + u)}}{-4\pi j(u_o + u)} \bigg|_{-L}^{L}.$$

We are using $\pm L$ for the limits of the integral instead of $\pm\infty$ because substituting ∞ leads to an indeterminate quantity. We will later take the limit $L \to \infty$. By substituting the limits, we obtain

$$\frac{\sin\left(2\pi L(u_o - u)\right)}{2\pi(u_o - u)} + \frac{\sin\left(2\pi L(u_o + u)\right)}{2\pi(u_o + u)}.$$

In the limit $L \to \infty$, both these sinc functions will become δ functions: one at $u = u_o$ and the other at $u = -u_o$.

5. a) The Fourier transform of the given function is

$$= \int_{-a}^{0}\left(1 + \frac{x}{a}\right)e^{-2\pi jux}dx + \int_{0}^{a}\left(1 - \frac{x}{a}\right)e^{-2\pi jux}dx$$

$$= \int_{-a}^{a}e^{-2\pi jux}dx + \int_{-a}^{0}\frac{xe^{-2\pi jux}}{a}dx - \int_{0}^{a}\frac{x}{a}e^{-2\pi jux}dx$$

$$= \frac{e^{-2\pi jux}}{-2\pi ju}\bigg|_{-a}^{a} + \int_{-a}^{0}\frac{e^{-2\pi jux}}{a(2\pi ju)}dx + \frac{xe^{-2\pi jux}}{-2\pi jua}\bigg|_{-a}^{0} + \frac{xe^{-2\pi jux}}{2\pi jua}\bigg|_{0}^{a} - \int_{0}^{a}\frac{e^{-2\pi jux}}{a(2\pi ju)}dx$$

$$= \frac{1}{2\pi^2 u^2 a}[1 - \cos(2\pi ua)] = a\frac{\sin^2(\pi ua)}{(\pi ua)^2}.$$

b) The given function can be thought of as a convolution of the 'hat' function given in part (a) and two impulse functions at $x = +a$ and $x = -a$.

Therefore, by following the convolution theorem, the Fourier transform of the given function is the product of the Fourier transforms.

$$= \Im[\delta(x - a) + \delta(x + a)]a\frac{\sin^2(\pi ua)}{(\pi ua)^2} = 2a\cos(2\pi ua)\frac{\sin^2(\pi ua)}{(\pi ua)^2}$$

6. a) $f(x, y) = \frac{1 + (-1)^{x+y}}{2}$

b)

$$F(u, v) = \frac{1}{64}\sum_{x=0}^{7}\sum_{y=0}^{7}\left[\frac{1 + (-1)^{x+y}}{2}\right]e^{-\frac{2\pi jux}{8}}e^{-\frac{2\pi jvy}{8}}$$

$$= \frac{1}{128}\sum_{x=0}^{7}\sum_{y=0}^{7}e^{-\frac{2\pi jux}{8}}e^{-\frac{2\pi jvy}{8}} + \frac{1}{128}\sum_{x=0}^{7}\sum_{y=0}^{7}e^{-\frac{2\pi jux}{8}}e^{-\frac{2\pi jvy}{8}}$$

The first term is zero except for when $u = 0$, $v = 0$. When $u = v = 0$, the first term is equal to ½.

The second term can be rewritten as

$$= \frac{1}{128} \sum_{x=0}^{7} \sum_{y=0}^{7} e^{j\pi x \left(1 - \frac{u}{4}\right)} e^{j\pi y \left(1 - \frac{v}{4}\right)}.$$

This is nonzero only when $u = v = 4$.

Therefore, the DFT is nonzero at only two frequencies: (0, 0) and (4, 4).

$$F(0, 0) = \tfrac{1}{2} \quad F(4, 4) = \tfrac{1}{2}$$

7. a) This is actually a 1-D version of the previous problem.

$$F(u) = \frac{1}{N} \sum_{x=0}^{N-1} f(x) e^{-\frac{2\pi j u x}{N}}$$

From the given values of $f(x)$,

$$F(u) = \frac{1}{N}\left[1 + e^{-\frac{4\pi j u}{N}} + e^{-\frac{8\pi j u}{N}} + \ldots e^{-\frac{2\pi j u (N-2)}{N}}\right] = \frac{1 - e^{-2\pi j u}}{1 - e^{-\frac{4\pi j u}{N}}}.$$

Since u is an integer, the numerator is zero for all values of u. $F(u)$ is nonzero only when the denominator is also zero. This happens for $u = 0$ and $u = N/2$.

Using L'Hospital's rule, we see that the value of $F(u)$ at these frequencies is equal to $\tfrac{1}{2}$.

8. a) $g(x) = 255 - f(x)$

$$G(u) = \frac{1}{N} \sum_{x=0}^{N-1} [255 - f(x)] e^{-\frac{2\pi j u x}{N}}$$

$$= \frac{1}{N} \sum_{x=0}^{N-1} 255 e^{-\frac{2\pi j u x}{N}} - \frac{1}{N} \sum_{x=0}^{N-1} f(x)^{-\frac{2\pi j u x}{N}}$$

The first summation is equal to zero except when $u = 0$. When $u = 0$, $G(u) = 255 - F(u)$.

Otherwise, $F(u) = -G(u)$.

9.
$$h(x) = \frac{1 + (-1)^x}{2}$$

The representation of this filter in the Fourier domain is given by

$$H(u) = \frac{1}{N} \sum_{x=0}^{N-1} \left(\frac{1 + (-1)^x}{2} \right) e^{-\frac{2\pi j u x}{N}}$$

$$= \frac{1}{2N} \sum_{x=0}^{N-1} e^{-\frac{2\pi j u x}{N}} + \frac{1}{2N} \sum_{x=0}^{N-1} e^{j\pi x \left(1 - \frac{2u}{N} \right)}.$$

The first term is nonzero only for $u = 0$ and the second term is nonzero only for $u = N/2$. Hence, the filter allows only these two frequencies. It cannot be classified either as a high-pass or a low-pass filter since it allows one high frequency and one low frequency.

10. Two images having identical histograms need not have identical Fourier transforms. This is so because the histogram does not contain any positional information about the image while the Fourier transform uses positional information. However, the zero-frequency component, which is the average gray level, will be equal for both images. Identical histograms imply that both images have the same average gray level.

11. The Fourier transform of the given image is

$$F(u, v) = \frac{1}{30} \sum_{x=0}^{4} \sum_{y=0}^{5} f(x, y) e^{-\frac{2\pi j u x}{5}} e^{-\frac{2\pi j v y}{5}}$$

$$= \frac{1}{30} \sum_{x=0}^{4} \left[6e^{-\frac{2\pi j u x}{5}} e^{-\frac{4\pi j v}{6}} + 6e^{-\frac{2\pi j u x}{5}} e^{-\frac{6\pi j v}{6}} \right]$$

$$= \frac{1}{5} \left[e^{-\frac{4\pi j v}{6}} + e^{-\frac{6\pi j v}{6}} \right] \sum_{x=0}^{4} e^{-\frac{2\pi j u x}{5}}.$$

The summation over x is nonzero only for $u = 0$.
Therefore, $F(0, v) = e^{-\frac{2\pi j v}{3}} + e^{-\pi j v}$.

Solutions to Chapter 4 exercises

1. If a code satisfies Kraft's inequality, it only means that there is an IDC with the same length of codewords. The given code may or may not be instantaneously decodable. For example, the code given below satisfies Kraft's inequality, but is not an IDC.

Symbol	Codeword
A	0
B	01
C	011
D	010

The given code satisfies Kraft's inequality, but violates the no-prefix condition. Hence, it is not an IDC.

2. The image of a chessboard has coding redundancy, interpixel redundancy, and psycho-visual redundancy.

3. Since the first codeword should have only 1 bit (refer to table 4.3), it can be 0 or 1. If we choose 0 as the first codeword, then all the subsequent codewords should begin with 1 (to satisfy the no-prefix condition). We have two choices for the second codeword (i.e., the codeword for the second symbol): 10 or 11. Choosing either one of them rules it out as prefix for the other codewords. The different possibilities for the codewords can be shown via a tree diagram.

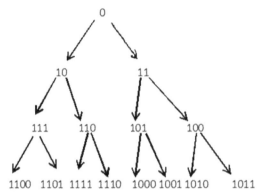

   By following each branch of the tree we find a different set of codewords. There are a total of eight branches, i.e., eight different codes. If we had started with a 1 instead of a 0, we would have obtained eight other codes. Therefore, there are a total of 16 codes with the lengths 1, 2, 3, and 4.

4. The 12th of June of the next year may be Tuesday (if the next year is not a leap year) or Wednesday (if the next year is a leap year).
   A leap year has a probability of ¼ (approximately). Hence, the probability of the 12th of June being Tuesday = ¾.
   The probability of the 12th of June being Wednesday = ¼.
   Average amount of extra information $= -\sum_i p_i \log_2 p_i = -\frac{1}{4}\log_2\frac{1}{4} - \frac{3}{4}\log_2\frac{3}{4} = 0.8113$ bits

5. The 2×2 binary matrices that have an inverse are

$$\begin{bmatrix} 1 & 0 \\ 0 & 1 \end{bmatrix}, \begin{bmatrix} 1 & 0 \\ 1 & 1 \end{bmatrix}, \begin{bmatrix} 1 & 1 \\ 0 & 1 \end{bmatrix}, \begin{bmatrix} 1 & 1 \\ 1 & 0 \end{bmatrix}, \begin{bmatrix} 0 & 1 \\ 1 & 1 \end{bmatrix}, \begin{bmatrix} 0 & 1 \\ 1 & 0 \end{bmatrix}.$$

There is a total of 16 binary matrices. Therefore, the probability of a 2×2 matrix having an inverse = 6/16.

Information content $= -\log_2 (6/16) = 1.415$ bits

6. a) Yes. It is definitely advantageous if the candidate changes their choice. To see this, consider that you have chosen cubicle 1. The probability that it is not in cubicle $1 = 2/3$. Therefore, it makes sense to switch.
   b) The probability that the car is not in cubicle $2 = 2/3$.
      Therefore, the information content $= -\log(2/3) = 0.585$ bits.

7. The equality $\log_2(x) = x - 1$ is satisfied for two different values of x, i.e., $x = 2$ and $x = 1$. Therefore, in between these two values the inequality is not satisfied.

8. The words of the English language do not form an IDC, as some words are prefixes of other words. For example, 'the' is a prefix of 'then'.

9. The correct order of the given operations is as follows:
      bit-plane slicing, gray coding, run-length coding, and Huffman coding.

10. a) $n(r) = 1$ for $r = 0$ to 255
    b) If the MSB is set to zero, then

    $$n(r) = 2 \quad \text{for } r = 0 \text{ to } 127$$
    $$n(r) = 0 \quad \text{for } r = 128 \text{ to } 255.$$

    c) The entropy of the original image is 8 bits/pixel, whereas the entropy of the modified image is 7 bits/pixel.

11. a) The power law transformation is a one-to-one mapping, and hence, even though the range of gray levels may increase, the entropy does not change.
    b) Similarly, the histogram equalization is a one-to-one mapping, and hence the entropy should not change. However, due to rounding-off effects, many gray levels may get mapped to the same level. In such cases the entropy actually reduces.

12. Website A is using an IDC, whereas website B is using transform coding. Website B initially transmits the lower frequencies and thus the image is not very sharp. It gets progressively sharper as we receive the higher frequencies.

13. a) The probability that the object is to the left of O is ½. Therefore, the information content of this statement is 1 bit.
    b) The probability that it is between O and C is proportional to the time spent by the particle between O and C. The probability that the object is between O and C $= (\pi/3)/2\pi = 1/6$.

Therefore, the associated information $= -\log_2(1/6) = 2.585$ bits.

One bit has already been conveyed. Therefore, the additional information $= 1.585$ bits.

c) The information conveyed $= 2.585$ bits. The total information is actually infinite since x is a continuous variable and the object can be at an infinite number of points.

14. The entropy of the random number generator $= \log_{10} 10 = 1$ digit.

15. The term $-p\log p$ can be written as $\dfrac{\log\left(\frac{1}{p}\right)}{\left(\frac{1}{p}\right)}$.

Using L'Hospital's rule, we differentiate both the numerator and the denominator.

Therefore, $\dfrac{-p \times \frac{1}{p^2}}{\left(\frac{-1}{p^2}\right)} = p$. In the limit, p tends to zero, and the ratio tends to zero.

16. a) The entropy of an m-bit image that has a completely uniform histogram is m bits/pixel.
   b) Since the average length of a variable length code cannot be less than the entropy, variable length coding cannot compress such an image.
   c) We have to use a coding scheme that reduces interpixel redundancy to achieve compression in such a case.

17. If the codeword is chosen to be 0, then the next codeword can be 1 or 2. If we choose 1 for the second word, the third word can be 20 or 21 or 22. Therefore, we get the following codes.

0	0	0	0	0	0
1	1	1	1	1	1
20	21	22	22	20	21
21	20	21	20	22	22

By interchanging 0 and 1 in the above codes we can generate six more codes.

If we make the cyclic shift $0 \rightarrow 1$, $1 \rightarrow 2$, and $2 \rightarrow 0$, we will get 12 more codes.

By using 0 and 2 instead of 0 and 1, we will get 12 more codes. Therefore, we have a total of 36 codes.

18. For a three-symbol source, one possible Huffman code is 0, 10, and 11. By interchanging 10 and 11, we get another code. Upon replacing 0 with 1 and 1 with 0, we get two more codes. Hence, a total of four binary Huffman codes are possible for a three-symbol source.

19. a) The given code is not instantaneous because the codeword for the source symbol 2 has the codeword for source symbol 1 as a prefix.
    b) To check whether an instantaneous code is possible with the same length of codewords, we have to see whether the given code satisfies Kraft's inequality. By substituting
    the given lengths into Kraft's inequality, we have

    $$\frac{1}{4} + \frac{1}{8} + \frac{1}{4} + \frac{1}{16} + \frac{1}{16} + \frac{1}{16} = \frac{13}{16} < 1.$$

    Hence, it should be possible to construct an instantaneous code for the given length of codewords.

20. a) A Huffman code will include a codeword of length 1 if the symbol with the highest probability occupies the first position during the source reduction until the penultimate round of source reduction (when there are three source symbols). Therefore, the probability of this symbol should be greater than that of the other two. Since the total probability is 1, the most probable symbol should have a probability of at least 1/3 so that it is allotted a codeword that is 1 bit.
    b) The average length of codewords becomes equal to the entropy when the probabilities of the source symbols are inverse powers of 2 (refer to equations (4.8) and (4.9)).

21. The ternary Huffman code can be constructed by performing source reduction in a manner similar to the construction of the binary Huffman code.

A	0.4	0.4	0.6
B	0.2	0.3	0.4
C	0.1	0.2	
D	0.1	0.1	
E	0.1		
F	0.1		

In the source reduction performed above, we have added the probabilities of the last three symbols. The source reduction is performed repeatedly until the number of source symbols is three or less.

In the last stage we can allot 0 to the compound symbol with the probability of 0.6, and allot 1 to the symbol with the probability of 0.4. Note that this assignment is not unique. We can choose any two of the three symbols 0, 1, and 2.

Working backward, we 'split' the compound symbol just as we had done for the binary Huffman code.

A	1	1	0
B	01	00	1
C	02	01	
D	000	02	
E	001		
F	002		

Average word length $= 1 \times 0.4 + 2 \times 0.2 + 2 \times 0.1 + 3 \times 3 \times 0.1 = 1.9$

If we had used a fixed ternary length, the average word length would have been 2.

22. Performing run-length encoding on the given bit stream, 11101100110001000101, yields run lengths of 3, 1, 2, 2, 2, 3, 1, 3, 1, 1, 1.

Consider the probabilities of the run lengths. Run length 1 has a probability of 5/11. Run length 2 has a probability of 3/11. Run length 3 has a probability of 3/11.

Therefore, the entropy of the run lengths $= H_2 = 1.54$ bits.

The entropy of the original binary source is of course less than 1 bit. However, it may make more sense to compare the total information content rather than average information content as the total length of the source is different in the two cases. The total information carried by the run lengths is entropy × number of run lengths $= 16.93$.

There were a total of 20 bits in the original binary source. Hence, it makes sense to do run-length encoding. The average information content or H_2 will in general be greater than H_1.

23. Histogram equalization is a one-to-one mapping; hence, the entropy should not change. However due to rounding-off effects, many gray levels may get mapped to the same level. In such cases, the entropy actually reduces.

24. If we have a large number of source symbols with almost comparable probabilities, then it makes sense to go for a B_3 code rather than a B_2 code. This is because by using a B_2 we can accommodate at most four symbols with 3 bits (1 continuation bit and 2 information bits). By using B_3, we can accommodate nine symbols with 4 bits (1 continuation bit and 3 information bits). However, if the most probable symbol has a very high probability compared to the other symbols, then it is more efficient to use a B_2 code rather than a B_3 code.

26. From the definition of the DCT (equation (4.25)), we have

$$Y(k + 4N) = \sum_{i=0}^{N-1} 2y(i)\cos\left(\frac{\pi(4N + k)}{2N}(2i + 1)\right)$$

$$= \sum_{i=0}^{N-1} 2y(i)\cos\left(2\pi(2i + 1) + \frac{\pi k}{2N}(2i + 1)\right)$$

$$\times \sum_{i=0}^{N-1} 2y(i)\cos\left(\frac{\pi k}{2N}(2i + 1)\right) = Y(k).$$

Solutions to Chapter 5 exercises

1. a) Since the coordinates of B are (3, 0), the coordinates of the centroid are (1, 0).

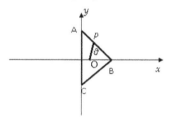

Use the sine rule in triangle ABC:

$$\frac{r}{\sin 30°} = \frac{OB}{\sin OPB} = \frac{2}{\sin(180° - (30° + \theta))} = \frac{2}{\left(\dfrac{1}{2}\cos\theta + \dfrac{\sqrt{3}}{2}\sin\theta\right)}.$$

By rearranging the above equation, we get

$$r = \frac{2}{\cos\theta + \sqrt{3}\,\sin\theta}.$$

This is the equation for the signature of the triangle, valid for $\theta = 0°$ to $120°$.

b) To obtain the equation for the signature valid for $\theta = 120°$ to $240°$, we note that the equilateral triangle has a three-fold symmetry. Therefore, r $(\theta - 120°) = r(\theta)$, and thus the equation of the signature for $\theta = 120°$ to $240°$ is

$$r = \frac{2}{\cos(\theta - 120°) + \sqrt{3}\,\sin(\theta - 120°)} = \frac{-1}{\cos\theta}.$$

2. a) The trajectory of the stone will be a parabola of the form

$$y = x\tan\theta - \frac{gx^2}{2u^2\cos^2\theta}.$$

Here, u is the velocity with which the stone is projected and θ is the angle at which it is projected to the horizontal.

b) It is seen from the equation of the parabola that the parameter space will be 2-D (the two variables are the velocity and the angle).

3. The Hotelling transform is defined as $y = A(x - m_x)$. Here, x and m_x are vectors in 3-D (RGB) space and A is a 3×3 matrix. Therefore, for each vector x, we need to perform three additions (or subtractions) to calculate $x - m_x$. Additionally, while multiplying with the matrix A, we need to perform six additions. Thus we need to perform $9N^2$ additions (for the N^2) pixels in the image. For evaluating the product with A, we need to perform nine multiplications for each pixel, and therefore we need to perform a total of $9N^2$ multiplications.

5. Since the signature has three-fold symmetry, it is an equilateral triangle. Since r is a minimum for $\theta = 60°$, we conclude that one of the medians is along the x-axis.

The orientation of the triangle must be as shown below.

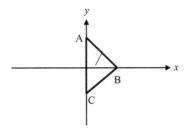

From the given figure, it is seen that the minimum distance is 32 (pixels). This must be the perpendicular distance from the centroid to one of the sides of the triangle. The farthest distance (which must be the distance from the centroid to one of the vertices of the triangle) is approximately 69. Therefore, consider the right triangle enclosed within the triangle ABC. Using Pythagoras theorem on this triangle, we obtain $\sqrt{68^2 - 32^2} = 60$. This must be half the side of the triangle. Therefore, the signature corresponds to an equilateral triangle 120 pixels in size.

6. In a 2-D image a sphere will also appear as a disk, but there will be variation in the intensity of such an image. The gradient of such an image can be used to distinguish it from a disk. We expect the gradient to be almost zero for the image of a disk.

7. The equation of an ellipse with a center at (c, d) is
$$\left(\frac{x - c}{a}\right)^2 + \left(\frac{y - d}{b}\right)^2 = 1.$$

This assumes that the major and minor axis of the ellipses are along the x- and y-axes. If this is not true, we need one more parameter to specify the orientation of the major and minor axis. Therefore, in general, the parameter space will be five-dimensional.

Assuming that the ellipse is completely within the image, a and b will range from 1 to 72, c and d from 2 to 99, and the orientation angle from 0° to 180°. Therefore, the number of accumulator cells is $72 \times 72 \times 98 \times 98 \times 180 = 8.9617 \times 10^9$.

8. We can determine the eigenaxes of the characters. This will help us to determine the inclination of the characters.

9. The dark squares at the corners of the OMR sheet help us to fix the origin of the coordinate system of the image and the orientation of the axes. The OMR sheet could get rotated or translated in the process of scanning. Hence, determining the location and orientation of the sheet is important for detecting the circles/ellipses on the OMR sheet.

10. The average is calculated by integrating this expression over the domain of the function and showing that it is zero.

$$\int_{-\infty}^{\infty} \int_{-\infty}^{\infty} \left[\frac{x^2 + y^2 - 2\sigma^2}{\sigma^4} \right] e^{\frac{-(x^2+y^2)}{2\sigma^2}} dx dy$$

This integral can be evaluated easily by converting to plane polar coordinates.

$$\int_{0}^{\infty} \int_{0}^{2\pi} \left[\frac{r^2 - 2\sigma^2}{\sigma^4} \right] e^{-\frac{r^2}{2\sigma^2}} d\theta dr = \frac{2\pi}{\sigma^4} \int_{0}^{\infty} e^{-\frac{r^2}{2\sigma^2}} r^3 dr - \frac{4\pi}{\sigma^2} \int_{0}^{\infty} e^{-\frac{r^2}{2\sigma^2}} r dr$$

Substitute $(r^2/2\sigma^2) = t$ to evaluate this integral and apply integration by parts on the first integral:

$$2\pi \int_{0}^{\infty} 2e^{-t} t \, dt - 4\pi \int_{0}^{\infty} e^{-t} dt = 4\pi \int_{0}^{\infty} e^{-t} dt - 4\pi \int_{0}^{\infty} e^{-t} dt = 0.$$

11. The correct order of operations is given below:
    a) thresholding, edge detection, determination of centroid, calculation of signature;
    b) thresholding, edge detection, determination of eigenvalues, determination of eigenvectors;
    c) edge detection, thresholding, Moore's boundary tracking algorithm, chain code.

Note that the order of edge detection and thresholding can be interchanged without affecting the result.

12. To detect chess pieces, the image processing system can proceed as follows. The first step would be to detect the individual squares within the chessboard. This can be accomplished by looking for vertical and horizontal lines that separate the black and white squares. Once the individual squares are detected, then we can calculate the variance in gray levels within each square. Unfilled squares will have zero variance while filled squares will have a nonzero variance.

Solutions to Chapter 6 exercises

1. a) Suppose we have a random number generator at our disposal that generates random numbers in the range of 0 to 1.

$$p(r)dr = p(z)dz$$

Since $p(r) = 1$ for the entire range,

$$r = \int_0^z 2az \exp(-az)dz = -2z \exp(-az) + 2\int_0^z \exp(-az)dz$$

$$= -2z \exp(-az) - \frac{2}{a}[1 - \exp(-az)].$$

This equation has to be solved iteratively to determine the value of z corresponding to each value of r.

b) Following a similar procedure, we obtain the equation

$$r = \int_a^z \frac{2}{b}(z - a)\exp\left(-\frac{(z - a)^2}{b}\right)dz.$$

By substituting $(z - a)^2/b = t$, we obtain

$$r = \int_a^z \exp(-t)dt = \exp(-z) - \exp(-a).$$

This equation can be easily inverted to obtain

$$z = \ln\left(\frac{1}{r + \exp(-a)}\right).$$

2. a) The value of A is obtained by normalization (i.e., the total probability = 1).

$$\int_0^1 \frac{A}{1 + z^2}dz = \tan^{-1}(z)\Big|_0^1 = \frac{\pi}{4}$$

b) We can generate 100 values of z that have the required distribution by using the following relation:

$$r = \int_0^z \frac{A}{1+z^2}dz = \frac{\pi}{4}\tan^{-1}z\Big|_0^z = \frac{\pi}{4}\tan^{-1}z.$$

This relation can be inverted to obtain $z = \tan\left(\frac{4r}{\pi}\right)$. This gives the mapping between r and z

3. The degraded image $g(x)$ will have a part where the intensity will increase linearly from 0 to 255 over a length of a pixels. For a distance $L - 2a$ the intensity will remain at 255 and then the intensity will decrease from 255 to 0 over a length a.

4. We observe white spots at periodic intervals; therefore, statistically it is salt noise. Since there are periodic impulses, the Fourier spectrum will also have a train of impulses. The median filter can be used to remove this noise.

5. a) We know that magnification $= \frac{\text{size of image}}{\text{size of object}} = \frac{v}{u} = \frac{R'}{R}$.

   Moreover, we have from the lens formula (for the camera) $\frac{1}{v} + \frac{1}{u} = \frac{1}{f}$.

   Rearranging the lens formula yields

   $$v = \frac{fu}{u-f}.$$

   By substituting this expression for v in the expression for magnification,

   $$R' = \frac{Rf}{u-f}.$$

   u, the object distance, is given by $u = D_o - vt$.

   b) By substituting for u in the expression for R' and assuming that $D_o - f \gg vt$, we obtain an expression for R'.

   $$R' = \frac{fR}{D_o - f}\left[1 + \frac{vt}{D_o - f}\right].$$

   Therefore, the radius of the image increases linearly with time.

   c) The intensity would be constant for the distance R' from the center and would then decrease linearly with radial distance.

6.
$$g(x) = \frac{1}{5}\sum_{i=0}^{4} f(x - i)$$

Since $g(x)$ is an averaged version of $f(x)$, $\langle g(x)\rangle$ and $\langle f(x)\rangle$ will be almost equal.

Solutions to Chapter 7 exercises

1.

$$H_8 = \frac{1}{\sqrt{8}} \begin{bmatrix} 1 & 1 & 1 & 1 & 1 & 1 & 1 & 1 \\ 1 & 1 & 1 & 1 & -1 & -1 & -1 & -1 \\ \sqrt{2} & \sqrt{2} & -\sqrt{2} & -\sqrt{2} & 0 & 0 & 0 & 0 \\ 0 & 0 & 0 & 0 & \sqrt{2} & \sqrt{2} & -\sqrt{2} & -\sqrt{2} \\ \sqrt{4} & -\sqrt{4} & 0 & 0 & 0 & 0 & 0 & 0 \\ 0 & 0 & \sqrt{4} & -\sqrt{4} & 0 & 0 & 0 & 0 \\ 0 & 0 & 0 & 0 & \sqrt{4} & -\sqrt{4} & 0 & 0 \\ 0 & 0 & 0 & 0 & 0 & 0 & \sqrt{4} & -\sqrt{4} \end{bmatrix}$$

2.

$$\begin{bmatrix} \frac{1}{2} & \frac{1}{2} & 0 & 0 \\ 0 & 0 & \frac{1}{2} & \frac{1}{2} \\ \frac{1}{2} & -\frac{1}{2} & 0 & 0 \\ 0 & 0 & \frac{1}{2} & -\frac{1}{2} \end{bmatrix}$$

3. We can pad the column vector with additional elements (usually taken to be 0) so that we have the number of elements as a power of 2.

4.

$$\begin{bmatrix} \frac{3}{2} \\ \frac{7}{2} \\ \frac{11}{2} \\ \frac{15}{2} \\ -\frac{1}{2} \\ -\frac{1}{2} \\ -\frac{1}{2} \\ -\frac{1}{2} \end{bmatrix}$$

www.ingramcontent.com/pod-product-compliance
Lightning Source LLC
Chambersburg PA
CBHW080359060326
40689CB00019B/4070